Mumfor

Date Due

BRODART   Cat. No. 23 233   Printed in U.S.A

FROM GERSON TO GROTIUS

AMS PRESS
NEW YORK

STUDIES OF POLITICAL THOUGHT

FROM GERSON TO GROTIUS
1414—1625

by

JOHN NEVILLE FIGGIS, M.A., *1866 - 1919,*
Rector of Marnhull; sometime Lecturer in
S. Catharine's College, Cambridge

The Birkbeck Lectures delivered in Trinity College,
Cambridge, 1900

CAMBRIDGE:
at the University Press
1907

Library of Congress Cataloging in Publication Data

Figgis, John Neville, 1866-1919.
   Studies of political thought from Gerson to
Grotius, 1414-1625.

   Reprint of the 1907 ed. published at the Univer-
sity Press, Cambridge, Eng., as the 1900 Birkbeck
lectures.
   Includes bibliographical references and index.
   1. Political science—History. I. Title.
II. Series: The Birkbeck lectures; 1900.
[JA82.F5   1978]   320.5'09   75-41092
ISBN 0-404-14540-X

First AMS edition published in 1978.

Reprinted from the edition of 1907, Cambridge, England,
from an original in the collections of the University of
Chicago Libraries. [Trim size and text area have been
slightly altered in this edition. Original trim size:
11 x 17.4 cm; text area: 6 x 15.2 cm.]

MANUFACTURED
IN THE UNITED STATES OF AMERICA

PREFACE.

IT is now nearly seven years since these lectures were delivered. At the time I delayed publication in order to secure completeness. Since then, many causes have increased the delay, and made perfection farther off than ever. Still, I have read a good deal more in the six literatures, all so vast, with which the lectures deal, and the conclusions are based on a wider induction than when first set forth. The volume, however, is but a course of lectures, intended merely to convey suggestions, and not a comprehensive treatise. Some day, perhaps, Mr Carlyle will give us that.

So far as the notes go I have made them as little numerous as possible. Those familiar with the literature will be aware that adequately to illustrate by quotation topics in the text would swell this little volume into a Cyclopaedia. I have reduced the errors, both in text and notes, so far as was practicable for one with many other occupations, to whom the use of a great library has been the fleeting boon of an occasional holiday. In so vast a range of topics I cannot hope to have avoided mistakes. They will not, it is hoped, militate against such interest as the book may possess.

Increasing reading in this subject has had one main result. It has confirmed the writer in his opinion of the unity of the subject, of the absolute solidarity of the controversies of our own day with those forgotten conflicts which form the argument of these lectures. The debt of the modern world to the medieval grows greater as one contemplates it, and the wisdom of the later ages less conspicuous. Some phrases, especially in the first lecture, would be different if they were to be written again. A glance at Lord Acton's essays on "The Protestant Theory of Persecution," or "Political Thoughts on the Church," or his lectures on Liberty will show what I mean. The mention of his name leads me to say that the obligations of this book to great Cambridge teachers are too obvious to need more elaborate expression. I feel, however, bound to set down here my gratitude to the Rev. T. A. Lacey for a suggestion respecting the Church as a *societas perfecta*, which more than anything else has helped to illuminate the subject, and is the main ground of any improvement there may be in the present form of the lectures on that in which they were delivered. The introductory lecture then, as now, is the least satisfactory; and would have been omitted were not some such preface a necessity. Besides, it has for the writer a personal interest. The late Professor Maitland, whose kindness was even greater than his genius, was good enough to come and listen to it. Since then, while the book was being rewritten, nearly three years back, I asked his permission to dedicate the lectures to one who had taught me so much. At the very time when he accepted this suggestion with his accustomed graciousness, I felt that the end might come before my task was accomplished.

It has come. And now I can only say how unworthy of his memory is this bungling treatment of a subject some aspects of which he had himself illuminated. Maitland, as a student and a writer and a friend, touched nothing that he did not adorn; and his grave needs fairer wreaths than most of us can offer. Yet the humblest of his pupils may be allowed to say that he wishes his work had been more worthy of his teacher.

J. N. F.

May, 1907.

CONTENTS.

LECTURE I.

EMERSON did not say whether it was a student of political theories who made the remark that "there is nothing new and nothing true, and nothing matters"; yet this must assuredly be the first, though not the better thought of such a student. Rarely indeed can he declare of any political idea, that it is quite new. Even though it seems to him to appear for the first time, probably his feeling is due to ignorance and someone better informed could tell him differently. In regard to truth, the more one reads of man's notions about the meaning and method of civil society, the more often is one inclined in despair to say that truth has as little to do with politics as it has with most politicians.

Whether, again, these ideas have much practical effect may well seem doubtful, when we see how circumstances conquer principle, and necessity is the mother of invention. Political thought is very "pragmatist."

Yet we must not leave the other side out of our reckoning. If ideas in politics more than elsewhere are the children of practical needs, none the less is it true, that the actual world is the result of men's thoughts The existing arrangement of political forces is dependent at least as much upon ideas, as it is upon men's perception of their interests. If we allow little to the theorist in momentary influence we must admit, that his is the power which shapes the "long result of time." The normal value, in fact, of political theories is a "long period value." The immediate significance of an Algernon Sidney or an Althusius is small and less than nothing as compared with a practical politician, like Maurice or Jeffreys. But his enduring power is vast. Hildebrand, Calvin, Rousseau, were doctrinaires, if ever there were such. Yet neither Bismarck, nor even Napoleon has had a more terrific strength to shape the destinies of men. In literature as in life, the thinker may be dull ; but it is with a significant dullness.

In these Lectures we shall be regarding a Literature without charm or brilliancy or overmuch eloquence, voluminous, arid, scholastic, for the most part; dead it seems beyond any language ever spoken. Dust and ashes seem arguments, illustrations, standpoints, and even personalities. Its objects are forgotten, and even the echo of its catchwords rings faintly. Yet it was living once and effectual. And it is worth studying if we would understand the common facts of to-day. For these men whose very names are only an inquiry for the curious, are bone of our bone, and their thought like the architecture of the Middle Ages, is so much our common heritage that its originators remain unknown. It is because of this common heritage that the study seems to be worth making. Owing to the nature of the subject much that is said here will be dry. But I desire to confess that I have made no conscious effort to be dull. Such a confession will not be regarded by all as creditable.

No subject illustrates more luminously the unity of history than the record of political ideas. Although there is no value in erudition as such, it is not purpose-less erudition to dive into Gerson or Cusanus. They are, though we do not know it, a part of our own world ; and even from those forgotten controversies we may perhaps find something more than mere explanation of the world we live in. The study, remote and recondite though it appears, may give us an added sense of the dignity of our heritage and a surer grasp of principles amid the complexities of the modern world.

It is not to revive the corpse of past erudition that I have any desire, but rather to make more vivid the life of to-day, and to help us to envisage its problems with a more accurate perspective. Otherwise my task would be as ungrateful as it is difficult. To raise once more the dust of controversies, which time has laid, seems both useless and disagreeable. There is no adventitious attraction to allure us. No one who has the descriptive faculty would seek for its material in the dignified decorum of John Torquemada, the inartistic invective of Boucher or Reynolds, or the exhaustive and exhausting lucubrations of Peninsular divines. The taste for the picturesque is often misleading. These lectures may be misleading but nobody shall call them picturesque. If they guide only into a blind alley, it will not be through an excess of " atmosphere."

There is indeed as little of philosophical depth as there is of literary charm in this wilderness of books. With the exception of Hooker and Machiavelli none of these writers has the charm that conquers time. Mariana is indeed pleasant reading, and a few pamphleteers like Louis D'Orleans are amusing. But nobody travels

through a desert merely for the sake of the oasis; it
is to get somewhere else, that men ride over the Sahara.
And so here. We seek to see our own day as from a
watch-tower; and we are trying to know more closely
the road we have been travelling. Our subject is those
changes in men's thoughts about politics which bridge
the gulf between the medieval world and the modern.
We cannot, indeed, cover all the time of transition,
or even attempt to treat of every aspect of the revolution. For there was a revolution. No theory of the
unity of history, no rhetoric about continuous evolution
and orderly change must blind us to the fact. The most
significant illustration of this is the recent judgment of
the House of Lords in the Free Church of Scotland
Appeals. This judgment in its implication marks the
final stage in that transposition of the spheres of Church
and State which is, roughly speaking, the net result of
the Reformation. In the middle ages the Church was
not a State, it was the State; the State or rather the civil
authority (for a separate society was not recognised)
was merely the police department of the Church. The
latter took over from the Roman Empire its theory of
the absolute and universal jurisdiction of the supreme
authority, and developed it into the doctrine of the
plenitudo potestatis of the Pope, who was the supreme
dispenser of law, the fountain of honour, including regal
honour, and the sole legitimate earthly source of power,
the legal if not the actual founder of religious orders, university degrees, the supreme "judge and divider" among
nations, the guardian of international right, the avenger
of Christian blood. All these functions have passed elsewhere, and the theory of omnipotence, which the Popes
held on the plea that any action might come under their

cognizance so far as it concerned morality[1], has now been assumed by the State on the analogous theory that any action, religious or otherwise, so far as it becomes a matter of money, or contract, must be matter for the courts[2].

The change which substituted the civil for the ecclesiastical authority is a part of our subject; for though we can trace the later claims of the civil power in the controversies of the eleventh and the twelfth centuries, yet the main stages of the transition took place in the period before us, and its chief promoters were Martin Luther and Henry VIII and Philip II, who really worked together in spite of their apparent antagonism.

But if we study this aspect of things, we must also study the other; the steps by which some limits were imposed to the new autocracy of the State; and the growth of the principles on which the distribution of power was justified. The task is no easy one. Yet something, even in six lectures, may be said which may suggest a little, even if it does not instruct much. We may see something of the way in which certain new-old ideas found expression more potent, though little more perfect than before; how they allied themselves with political needs, and so were no mere dreams, but active forces; how out of conflicts and controversies, in essence religious, modern politics have developed themselves.

The difficulty of understanding the history of the Reformation is not lessened by the fact that in a very real sense the age of the Reformation is still proceeding. As Newman said, "the Reformation set in motion that process of which the issue is still in the future." What I hope to do is to bring into a little clearer light the figures of modern politics, as seen upon this background. Whether the motive was opportunism or conviction, the fact remains that to religious bodies the most potent expressions of political principles has been due. Political liberty, as a fact in the modern world, is the result of the struggle of religious organisms to live. Of political principles, whether they be those of order or those of freedom, we must seek in religious and quasi-theological writings for the highest and most notable expressions. Treumann justly remarks that the democratic politics of the Scotch reformers were the result of their determination to prevent the whole of the monastic endowments from falling into the hands of the nobles[3].

Religious forces, and religious forces alone, have had sufficient influence to ensure practical realisation for political ideas. Reluctantly, and in spite of themselves, religious societies were led by practical necessities to employ upon their own behalf doctrines which are now the common heritage of the Western world. In fact that world, as we live in it and think it, was really forged in the clash of warring sects and opinions, in the secular feuds between the clergy and laity, Catholic and Protestant, Lutheran and Calvinist.

In the great contest between Popes and Emperors the Middle Ages witnessed one more attempt of the Titans to scale the height of heaven. But they were hurled back, and the last of the Hohenstauffen perished in ignominy. In the period however with which we shall be concerned the old gods were displaced by new, save for the heroic and partly successful attempt, known as the Counter-Reformation, to bring back the Saturnian reign of the Papacy ruling a united West.

We may trace back for ages that sovereign conception

of the original contract, which may be unhistorical and
unphilosophical, but is the bulwark of sixteenth and
seventeenth century Liberalism, which only withdraws
from English thought with Burke, and has its most
renowned exponent in Rousseau. Manegold of Lauten-
bach during the Investiture controversy makes use of the
notion[4]. Later on Augustinus Triumphus of Ancona
employs it in a form afterwards found serviceable by
the Jesuits : the Baptismal vow in this view comprised
a series of conditions which cannot be fulfilled by
heretics or excommunicate persons and therefore they
may be deposed[5]. Augustine also includes the Pope
as a person who, in case of heresy, is *ipso jure* deprived
of his jurisdiction. We may indeed find the source of
the Counter-Reformation view of the inadmissibility of
heretic royalty in this doctrine propounded by one
who treats the Pope as head of the world-state. Even
Augustinus Triumphus will not allow infidel monarchs to
be disturbed, unless they molest the Church. The Pope
has power even then, *i.e.*, of an international order but
not of the same kind as that which he wields over heresy,
which is essentially rebellion[6]. Perhaps S. Thomas Aquinas may be taken as the beginning of the later medieval
rationalising political thought, which either blends with
or substitutes for the old mainly theocratic and Scriptural
arguments, general considerations derived from the
nature of political societies and founded on the "Politics"
of Aristotle[7]. Anyhow it is to S. Thomas that many
of the writers we shall discuss avowedly go back, and
he is made the basis of the various systems of the
Jesuits, and of their defence of resistance and even
tyrannicide[8].

It was Lord Acton who said that "not the devil but

S. Thomas Aquinas was the first Whig." With the
revived study of Roman Law there had come an
increasing reverence for the Law Natural with which
even a Pope cannot dispense[9]. This notion was to be
of great service to all theorists, who desired to subject to
some limits the all-embracing activity of the modern
state, whether these limits were internal and concerned
the interests of individuals or external and imposed on
the ground of international equity.

It is not an accident that men like Machiavelli,
and Hobbes, whose aim is to remove all restraints
from the action of rulers except those of expediency,
should be agreed in denying all meaning to the idea
of natural law. On the other hand for Grotius with
his theory of inter-state morality, for Du Plessis Mornay
with his claim that the governor must have regard
to the good of the governed, the notion of natural
law which makes promises binding anterior to positive
rules, is essential and obligatory. The basis of both
the original contract and international law is the same.
Both ideas have their necessary roots in the belief in the
law of nature; for so only in these days could the idea
of right be justified against reason of state.

To the same source there was due the idea of the
fundamental equality of men[10]. In addition to this the
study of civil law, while leading to the hardening of
all theories of lordship whether public or private, tended
on the one hand to individualism in regard to private
property, and on the other naturally raised a controversy
as to the import of the *Lex Regia* by which all power
was surrendered to the Emperor.

If this law be taken not as a mere historical fact in
the history of a single people, but as a universal truth,

expressing the origin of civil authority, it may be used
to assert either the omnipotence of the ruler, as being
endowed with all authority, or the fundamental sovereignty of the people, as the original of that authority.
Why should the people make the absolute surrender
contemplated by Hobbes? Why should they not say
in the words of the oath of Aragon that the people has
as much right and more power than the king[11]?

The tendency to argue thus was increased by the
fact that there is no text of the *Lex Regia* in the
Corpus but only an account of it. Salamonius in his
very interesting dialogue *De Principatu* makes great
play with this, and takes a text he does find to prove
that the royal power is not irresponsible[12]. It is also
one of the most effective weapons of Papalist advocates.
When they desired to shew the essential differences
between Papal and regal authority and to rebut the
assertion that royal power came "immediately from
God alone" all they had to do was to quote this statement about the *Lex Regia*. For in so far as it was
generally admitted as a good account of the popular
origin of political authority, it made against the theory
of the Divine right of Kings. It might almost be said
that the foundation of the anti-autocratic theory of
government in the sixteenth century lay in the use
of the *Lex Regia*, to describe the origin of regal
power[13], and in that of the *Digna Vox* to indicate its
limits[14]. It is in the atmosphere created by this
text, together with the absolutist maxims, that since
the prince was *legibus solutus*[15] *quod principi placuit
legis habet vigorem*[16], that all political discussion
takes place. Even the maxim *salus populi suprema
lex* comes into general consciousness through a great

advocate[17], and we cannot over-estimate the influence of this legal atmosphere on the development of political thought, even on into modern times. Nor must we forget that the code as developed by Justinian, with the few additional extravagants which became authoritative, is at least as much a medieval as an ancient monument. Its conception of the duty of the government in regard to heresy and of the nature of the Christian Commonwealth is definitely medieval. Even if it has not that exaggerated notion of the clerical authority which became a Western characteristic, its ideas are by no means those of the world of antiquity. Its fundamental idea is that of a uniform single state existing on a Christian basis, with a place for bishops no less than counts, and orthodoxy a condition of citizenship—a *Civitas Dei* in fact. Add to these the maxim which our own Edward took from the code—*quod omnes tangit ab omnibus approbetur*[18] —and made a basis for his theory of representation, and we see how large a part was played by Roman Law in the development of political thought.

On the other hand we must not ignore the influence of feudalism in the same development. It tended more than anything else towards the growth of the doctrine of hereditary right, and the notion that the king's claims were unassailable, in fact towards the treating of the State as an estate. When feudalism decayed and property became pure *dominium* under the influence of the Roman Law, the king's estate underwent the same change. The Commonwealth under feudal notions is a pure *Herrschafts-verband*, not a *Genossenschaft*; and the king's rights are those of a landed proprietor.

Again, it is in the feudal system that the contractual theory of government took its rise; for it is of its essence. It was feudalism which led to that comparison between private and public rights which makes "the case of the king" a precedent in private law[19]. In fact, as Professor Maitland pointed out, under feudalism there is no public law; all rights are private, including those of the king[20]. It is this absence of a theory of the State as such which characterises especially medieval history, except for the great Church as a whole. In the strict sense of the term, there is no sovereign in the Middle Ages; only as we find even a little later in France, there is an *état* which belongs to the king; but there is also an *État de la République*, while even a lawyer in the Paris Parlement has his *état*. Only very gradually does State come to mean the organisation of the nation and nothing else. The change is probably due to the influence of Italian life and Machiavelli its exponent. For the contractual theory of government an atmosphere was needed, in which politics were argued on legal principles, in which public powers were assimilated to private rights, and in which some general system of law was assumed, and government was a matter of bargain. That atmosphere was afforded by feudalism and by the titles *De Feudis* in the completed editions of the Corpus.

Of the original compact theory feudalism was an obvious basis; not merely did the *droit de défiance* all but suggest, and the final clause of such documents as Magna Charta inevitably imply it, but the actual legal atmosphere of feudalism is that in which the theory was likely to arise. The two elements, the assimilation of public to private right, and the mutual nature of the tie between governed and governor, existed in the feudal system far more obviously than in any other;

and these two elements were necessary to the contract theory.

It could not have arisen except in an age when public rights were conceived inductively, inferred that is from particular rights of ruling lords, and in an age dominated by the idea of private law; for the contract theory assumes the existence of private rights and private legal obligations as anterior to all public rights and indeed to the existence of the State. · That is, the contract theory really has reference to the medieval world, when all public law except that of the Pope was inductive; not to the modern world created by Bodin and Hobbes working hand in hand with political conditions in which the theory of the powers of the State is abstract and deductive, and is reasoned down from general ideas of necessary authority.

In the Middle Ages we see public right shaping itself out of private rights. The powers of the sovereign are the special attributes of a peculiarly placed person, whether prerogative of Crowns or privileges of Parliament. They are not the necessary attributes of public authority conceived as something quite other than any other rights. The *casus regis* (John's succession to the Crown, instead of that of his nephew) is to Bracton merely a case like any other case. The contractual theory is in fact the last phase of that juristic conception ·of politics which is largely medieval, but remained an influence till the eighteenth century.

It is, if not medieval, an important part of the legacy of the Middle Ages to the modern world; the juristic framework for schemes of popular rights and international duty was the product of conditions that were past or passing. With the full recognition of the State, these juristic ideals passed away, although even now we sometimes see a moral justification for disobedience to the law masquerading as a legal right.

The attitude of the common lawyers in the seventeenth century was largely due to their failure to perceive, or their refusal to admit, the modern doctrine of sovereignty. Yet even the claims of the sovereign State were no new discovery. Taken over and developed by the Papacy from the ancient Empire, the *plenitudo potestatis* asserted nothing less than this, and the Imperialist party grasped (at least in theory) at similar principles for themselves. The writer of the *Tractatus Eboracensis* under Henry II developed a theory of royal omnipotence by Divine right, as complete if not as systematic, as that which we shall have to consider later[21]. His theory of excommunication might have given hints to Erastus. His arguments on the superiority of royal to priestly authority might have arrested Wyclif.

Yet when all is said (and in studying this subject one is at times inclined to deny that political doctrines ever began at all) there remains a great gulf fixed between medieval and modern thought. We in the twentieth century think of the State as essentially one, irresistible in theory and practice, with a uniform system of law and a certain government. Rights of personal liberty, of the security of property, of general protection, of legal equality, and religious liberty, are so generally recognised that however difficult it may be to agree upon an abstract basis we take them for granted and they have become a part of the furniture of our minds. In our view the world of politics is composed of certain communities entirely independent, territorially omnipotent, and to some extent morally responsible. A set of rules founded upon an insecure basis of custom, convenience, humanity, or natural reason admittedly exists, to which under the name of international law they pay a nominal, reluctant, and none too regular obedience—which is however more regular and less reluctant than was the obedience six centuries ago paid to the common law by any decently placed medieval feudatory.

Again, the theocratic and still more the jural conception of political right has gone from the educated world. Providence, doubtless, has to do with politics as with other human affairs, and all Theists must allow that political associations have some divine sanction. But most are now agreed to relegate the part of Providence to that of final cause ; indeed there has been a revolution in political thought, not dissimilar to the substitution of efficient for final causes as an account of natural phenomena. I do not of course mean that all hold the same ethical theory, but that institutions and all alleged rights must be able to show some practical utility if their existence is to be maintained. All arguments but those of public policy are to a great extent laughed out of court. Now in the Middle Ages political argument went on the basis of alleged private rights, whether divine or purely human in origin. Of course arguments from convenience are found ; and at no time can institutions maintain themselves for which some form of utility cannot be argued. We have passed from the defence of rights to the realisation of right and it is not at all clear that we have gained. Perhaps it would be most accurate to say, that in the Middle Ages human welfare and even religion was conceived under the form of legality, and in the modern world this has given place to utility.

Again, in the Middle Ages the omnipotent territorial

State, treated as a person and the coëqual of other states, was non-existent. It might be a dream, or even a prophecy, it was nowhere a fact. What we call the State was a loosely compacted union with "rights of property and sovereignty everywhere shading into one another[22]" and the central power struggling for existence. Neither Normandy nor Burgundy, neither the dominions of Henry the Lion nor those of a Duke of Aquitaine, formed a State in the modern sense, yet how far can their rulers be regarded as in any real sense subjects? At last indeed, with the growth of federalism in idea and fact and in our own possessions beyond the seas, we are going back to a state of things in some ways analogous to the medieval. But the modern post-Reformation State *par excellence* is unitary, omnipotent, and irresistible, and is found in perfection not in England, but in France or the German States of the *ancien régime*. Joseph II dotted the i's of Luther's handwriting.

Yet even granting that the King of France or Germany was a true sovereign in his temporal dominions, the power of the Church and the orders was a vast inroad on governmental authority. It is to be noted that Suarez and others developed a doctrine of extra-territoriality out of rights preserved by the universities and the monastic orders of the Church. There was one really universal order in Western Christendom and its right name was the Church. It was true the Canonists never got quite all that they wanted, yet as has been said "no one dreams that the King can alter the Common Law of the Catholic Church," and that Common Law included a great deal of what is really civil law[23]. Nowadays it is to be decided on grounds of public policy how far the State shall permit the freedom of religious bodies, although our own views of policy may be, that interference is inexpedient because it is wrong. But at that time it was the State which existed on sufferance, or rather the secular authority, for the very term State is an anachronism. It would be an interesting point to determine accurately the causes which have led to the substitution in general use of the term State for Commonwealth or republic. I think that Italy and Machiavelli are important factors. The object of the civil power, the wielder of the temporal sword, *within* the Church-State was not attack, but defence against a claim to universal dominion. The Holy Roman Empire, the most characteristic of all medieval institutions, did indeed attempt to realise the idea of an all powerful State, but that State was the Church. The ideal was realised only very partially and then as a rule only by the undue predominance of the ecclesiastical element. Innocent III was a more truly universal power than most of the successors of Charles the Great. The conflict with the Popes which prevented the Emperors realising this idea was also an assistance to the gradual growth of national States, and the break-up of Christendom. That word is now merely a geographical expression. It was a fact in the Middle Ages. The real State of the Middle Ages in the modern sense —if the words are not a paradox—is the Church. The priest in the *Somnium Viridarii* (a fourteenth century book) declares that all civil laws are at bottom canon laws[24], in other words that there can be no true polity or real law which has not the sanction of the Pope's authority. Another illustration of the purely political theory of ecclesiastical office is to be found in the argument of that most uncompromising of Papalists, Augustinus

Triumphus about Papal jurisdiction.   After arguing
that the lordship of the whole world belongs to the
Pope, he declares that so far as jurisdiction is concerned
a layman might well be Pope : and election would give
him all rights except those of order[25].

It has been said that there is no Austinian sovereign
in the medieval State.   This is true of the individual
kingdoms.   It is not true of the Church.   For nothing
could be more Austinian in spirit than the Bull *Sacrosanctae Ecclesiae* which promulgated the Sext in 1298[26].
There was no doubt that the canonists meant by the
plenitudo potestatis everything that the modern means
by sovereignty.   Indeed one later writer says plainly
that *plena potestas* means *absoluta potestas.*   The second
title of the Sext contains the statement, that law
exists in the bosom of the Pope, and goes on to assert
the principle that whatever the sovereign permits he
commands[27].   There is another point.   The medieval
state had one basis of unity denied to the modern—
religion.   Baptism was a necessary element in true
citizenship in the Middle Ages and excommunication
was its antithesis.   No heretic, no schismatic, no excommunicate has the rights of citizenship.   This principle,
admitted as it was by Catholic princes, and founded on
the Code of Justinian, was the ground of the Pope's
claim to depose sovereigns, and of all the conflicts that
ensued.   Few really denied it till the Reformation.
Philip of Spain's famous remark, that he would rather
not reign at all than reign over heretics, was merely an
assertion of medieval principles by a man who really
believed in them.

In regard to infidels there is a slightly different

theory. The priest in the *Somnium Viridarii* does
indeed declare that the dominion of no infidel can ever
be really just, and hence war with the Turks is always
permissible[28]. And this is the real principle of the
Crusades. It is the view of thorough-going medievalism.
Yet all the influences which later on were to develop into
the theory of the indirect Papal power went towards
admitting a limited right even among infidels. This is
the view of Augustinus Triumphus[29]. This more
moderate view is that infidel sovereigns do not hold
their titles from the Pope and therefore may not be
molested without cause. We may regard this as
marking the end of the Crusading era and the beginning of modern views. This principle may be used
so as to become a basis for agreement with heretic
sovereigns, after they have become established, *e.g.*, it
might be right to depose Elizabeth, but not Victoria
unless she began to persecute. We cannot over-
estimate the change in men's minds required to produce the ideal of heterogeneity in religion within one
State.

In these lectures we shall only see the beginning of
it. When the change had been completed, it carried
with it the entire destruction of theological politics and
for a time undoubtedly assisted to spread the purely
Machiavellian theory. In the Middle Ages politics
was a branch of Theology, with whatever admixture
derived from Aristotle and the Civil Law. Its basis
was theocratic. Machiavelli represents the antithesis
of this view, discarding ethical and jural as well as
theological *Criteria* of State action.

The Reformation on some sides of it retarded the

secularising tendency, and made politics more, not less theological. Finally, owing to the clash of competing religions a theory of the State purely secular was developed. That however was in the future.

Yet the change to the heterogeneous family of States, from a uniform Christendom with some shadow of deference to the Emperor and a real pre-eminence for the Pope, heralded and assisted that transition still incomplete from a state of a single religion to one of several. The notion that uniformity in religion is necessary to political stability was disproved by facts, and then became discredited in theory. This one change is significant of much else. The imaginative vision of the Middle Ages could see but one state worthy of the name upon earth, the *Civitas Dei*. Everything else, including the rights of kings, is mere detail and has but a utilitarian basis. The very contempt for the secular power paved the way to make it more secular, more non-moral, and to discredit the notion of right in politics.

Further, before the modern world of politics could arise, it was needful not merely to deprive the Emperor of any shadowy claim to supremacy, but the Pope must be driven from his international position. The rise of Protestantism was the condition for the founding of International Law, as a body of doctrine governing the relations of States supposed to be free, equal, and in a state of nature. This was not true of the medieval princes, and their wars were, as Stubbs says, "wars for rights." With the (international) state of nature arrived the period of "wars of interest."

Of course all these statements are merely approximate, we can say no more than that certain tendencies were dominant at one time rather than another. The theocratic ideal is still discoverable; and there was very little theocracy about the Venetian Constitution in the Middle Ages. In the same way there was some real equality and independence among nations long before Dante wrote the *De Monarchia,* and if the State is not to be called such because it is loosely knit, what are we to say of the British Empire to-day? That, however, looks to the future. With all reservations there remains a broad difference between the self-sufficing unit of International Law, and the spoke in the wheel of medieval Christendom. The closer we look the more we see that it is the resemblance which is superficial, and the differences that are profound, between medieval and modern notions.

It would require an intellectual revolution—quite inconceivable in magnitude—to induce us to regard it as an argument for the Papal power, that the sun is superior to the moon, or that S. Peter gave two swords to Christ; that the Pope is like Sinai, the source of the oracles of God, and is superior to all kings and princes, because Mount Sinai is higher than all other hills (which it is not); that when Daniel speaks of beasts, the writer meant that tyranny is the origin of earthly power; that the command to feed my sheep, and the committal of the Keys to S. Peter gave to the Papacy the absolute political sovereignty of the world; or on the other side that Adam was the first king, and Cain the first priest, that the text forbidding murder proves immediately the Divine origin of secular lordship, that unction is not indelible save in France, but there it is so because the oil is provided by an angel.

The endless discussions over the exact significance

of irrelevant texts and the sophistry lavished upon those
few that are relevant are barely intelligible to our eyes.
To take an instance, it is argued that the words "My
Kingdom is not of this world" so far from being an
objection to the political claims of the Papacy are a
support to them, as they prove that Christ's kingdom
is of Divine and not of human origin.   The same inference is drawn from His refusal to allow the multitude
to make him King.   Had he consented, his title would
have been popular like that of an earthly monarch.   The
whole method rests on the belief that the most perfect
polity can be discovered within the pages of the Old and
New Testaments, and that the actions of Samuel, or
Uzziah, or Jehoiada, or Ehud could be made into a system
whereby all future political methods could be judged.
All such arguments (and they go into endless detail) not
merely illustrate the gulf between our own age, and those
in which such considerations seemed serious and serviceable, but very often deprive us of all sympathy for the
men who lived in them, and are a hindrance to our dis-
cerning the kernel beneath the thick husk of inconclusive
ingenuity and illegitimate metaphor.

The best illustration of the changed mental standpoint can be afforded by comparing the *Unam Sanctam*
or the decree *Solitae* of Innocent III, or even the *De
Monarchia*, with the following passage dealing with
religious bodies from Professor Sidgwick's *Elements of
Politics*.

"A stronger means of control without anything like
establishment may be exercised in the form of a super-
vision of the wealth of Churches derived from private
sources.   If indeed, the expenses of religious teaching

and worship are defrayed by contributions from the in-
comes of its members, it will be difficult for Government
to interfere in the employment of such contributions,
without measures of violent and invidious repression :
but if they are paid from funds bequeathed to form
a permanent endowment for the association, the case is
different.   Here, in the first place, Government may refuse
to admit any religious society to the position of a cor-
poration capable of holding and administering property,
unless its organisation fulfils certain conditions, framed
with the view of preventing its 'quasi-government' from
being oppressive to individual members of the association
or dangerous to the State.   Secondly Government may
take advantage of a collision to bring the funds of any
such society permanently under its control, in pursuance
of its general duty of supervising the management of
wealth bequeathed to public objects, and revising the
rules under which it is administered, in the interest
of the community at large.   But further, the bequest
of funds to be permanently employed in payment of
persons teaching particular doctrines, is liable to supply
a dangerously strong inducement to the conscious or
semi-conscious perpetuation of exploded errors, which,
without this support, would gradually disappear : hence
it should be the duty of Government to watch such
bequests with special care, and to intervene when necessary, to obviate the danger just indicated, by modifying
the rules under which ancient bequests are administered."

It will at once be seen that we are in a different
world.   Still further illustration might be the (unconscious) coupling of kings and bishops, as the highest
earthly authorities, in the *Imitation,* or the decretal

in the Sext[30] forbidding the secular Courts to make the clergy pay their debts. The very title of Professor Sidgwick's chapter, "The State and Voluntary Societies," is a proof of the distance the world has travelled since Boniface VIII promulgated the *Unam Sanctam.*

Yet we must bear in mind that in political theory many of the medieval arguments and methods subsisted until the eighteenth century. In some form or other the discussion of theories of Divine Right lasted a thousand years ; while, as we have seen, many of the notions we regard as modern can be traced back to the medieval world, or even earlier.

Mr Carlyle has recently demonstrated the continuity of political thought from Cicero to Rousseau[31]. Indeed it seems true that the root idea of equality on the one hand and absolute dominion on the other came from the ancient world through the Stoics, the Roman Law and the Fathers ; while the ideas of liberty and association in government are Teutonic, or in other words Whiggism is German, and Radicalism Latin. Yet if S. Thomas was the first Whig why was Whiggism as we know it so long in making an effective appearance? The answer to this is largely to be found in the unity of the medieval Church. So long as the Holy Roman Empire remained even an ideal, a really modern theory of politics could not be generally effective. Even after it had well developed into the theory of the Holy Roman Church with universal supremacy, no truly modern system of politics was possible, until that theory was shattered. Christendom, the union of the various flocks under one shepherd with divine claims, divine origin, and divine sovereignty, had to be transformed into Europe, the habitat of competing sects and compact nations, before the conditions of modern politics arose.

This process was of long duration. In Italy it was accomplished earlier, or rather the independence of the cities, and the secularisation of the Papacy in practice made possible a work like Machiavelli's long before trans-Alpine Europe could have produced it. Professor Sidgwick did well to call attention to the fact that the modern world in England, so far as politics are concerned, began at the Restoration[32]. From one point of view we might assert that the Middle Ages ended with the visit of Nogaret to Anagni, and from another it might be said to end only when the troops of Victor Emmanuel entered Rome and the Lord of the world became the prisoner of the Vatican, and of course it ended at different times in different places. Hence arises the extreme difficulty of disentangling the conflicting tendencies and complex political combinations of our period.

So far as the Reformation helped to produce the compact, omni-competent, territorial, bureaucratic State, so far as directly or indirectly it tended to individual liberty, it must be regarded as modern in its results. But so far as it tended to revive theocratic ideals, theological politics, and appeals to Scripture in regard to the form of Government, it was a reversion to the ideals of the earlier Middle Ages, which were largely disappearing under the combined influence of Aristotle and the Renaissance.

All that can be attempted in these lectures is to show how both one and the other tendency came to influence the thoughts and the lives of men ; how for instance the doctrine of natural law became the residuary legatee of the theory of Divine Right and assisted in the formation of international rules, popular sovereignty and later on individual rights; how on the other hand the theory *cujus regio ejus religio* was a stage in the process from " indefinite, incoherent homogeneity to definite, coherent heterogeneity," which marks the evolution of political and religious organisms, no less than of natural.

Before, however, we directly approach the subject, it may be well to trace some of the earliest steps of the movements, which prepared for the coming catastrophe. With the death of Frederick II in 1250 and the destruction of the Hohenstauffen, the Papacy had to all appearance won a final victory in the secular contest; and its supporters might and indeed did think, that little remained but to make more stringent the bonds that chained temporal rulers to their ecclesiastical superiors. It would bind kings in chains, and nobles in fetters of iron. The praises of God should be in the mouth of the Pope, and a two-edged sword in the hand of his vassals. But the Popes had reckoned without their guest. Owing to a variety of causes, of which not the least important was the success of the Popes in undermining the Imperial authority, the national States had been left to develop in their own way, and though the most significant example was France, it was an English king who called himself *entier empereur dans son royaume.*

The limitation on this regality involved in a recognition, however grudging, of the Papal supremacy is very real; clerical immunities, and appeals to Rome and the authority of the Canon Law made the power of even Edward I or Philip the Fair far less universal than that of even a weak modern State. It was true that the king could get out of the theoretic difficulty by saying that the Pope only exercised so much power as he allowed him ; and the Courts Christian were circumscribed by the royal writs. Practically, however, within certain limits the king could not exercise jurisdiction. But at any rate he was strong enough to repudiate the claims of the Pope, on any point which touched the national honour. And this was seen when Boniface VIII strained the medieval theory of Papal dominion to breaking point in the *Unam Sanctam*. As has been well said, "The drama of Anagni must be set against the drama of Canossa[33]." France repudiated the Papal claims by the help of that body, assembled for the first time, which was after centuries of neglect to repudiate the claims of absolute monarchy, to cleanse the Augean stable of feudal corruptions and conflicting legal systems and to launch modern France on her career as a central-ised uniform democracy.

Concurrently with this, Edward I united England more than it ever had been united in the past by the summoning of a parliament which should supersede or absorb feudal " Liberties," municipal privilege, pro-vincial home rule, and ecclesiastical immunity. The *praemunientes* clause was the herald of the Reformation, the death-knell, though it sounded two centuries before-hand, of the Church, as a non-national universal State. Popular liberty and national independence for a time went hand in hand.

From the death of Boniface VIII to the rise of Luther we mark the upgrowth of ideas which were only to find their full fruition as the result of the Reformation. The French king put the Pope in his pocket and took him to Avignon. The Papal pretensions, while against the Imperial claims they grew more extravagant than ever, were no longer allowed to disturb the practice of the Gallican Liberties[34]. William of Ockham in his great anti-papal dialogue uses the admitted independence of the French king as an argument in favour of German freedom[35].

In this period we note the rise or rather the development of that notion of the secular power which was to conquer at the Reformation; and at the same time the most notable medieval expressions of anti-autocratic theory. Pierre Dubois' little pamphlet *De Recuperatione Terrae Sanctae* is a mine of reforming ideas. Disendowment of the Church, and of monasteries, absolute authority for the secular State, women's enfranchisement, mixed education, are all advanced in the one object of increasing the power of the French king, who is to be made Emperor and rule at Constantinople. International Arbitration was to decrease the horrors of war, and educated women were to be sent to the Holy Land in order to marry and convert both the Saracens and the priests of the orthodox Church, and also to become trained nurses and teachers. Studies are to be modernized, the law simplified. For the influence of the old theological and papal universities the writer had no respect. The whole spirit of the book is secular and modern. Bishop Stubbs was wont to declare that everything was in it including the new woman[36].

Dante in the great Ghibelline pamphlet the *De Monarchia* set up once more the authority of the Emperor. He saw in Henry of Luxemburg the chance of realising his dream of a Christian world-monarchy.

Mr Bryce says this book is "not a prophecy but an epilogue." Perhaps it is fairer to say that it is both. In its ideal of a universal Empire realising the notion of the *Civitas Dei*, in its scholastic argumentation, in its reverence for Rome, the *De Monarchia* is certainly an epilogue, the last and the noblest expression of that conception of the Kingdom of God upon earth, the heir at once of the ancient world and the depositary of Christian tradition, which ever and anon gave to the struggles of the Middle Ages a touch of Romance, and redeemed its squalid brutality from contempt by its sense of the inherent dignity of human affairs. Both the form and the grandeur of this ideal were passing away when Dante wrote. But in so far as Dante sets the temporal above the spiritual Lord. and asserts the right of the State to be, uncontrolled by ecclesiastical expediency, his work is a prophecy—a prophecy of the modern State, and of that doctrine of the Divine Right of kings, which formed for long its theoretical justification against clerical pretensions.

It was in the struggle between John XXII and Louis of Bavaria, the culmination of the long medieval conflict between *sacerdotium* and *imperium*, that the ideas of each side received their most complete expression. In this struggle Augustinus Triumphus wrote the book we have already discussed, and thus produced the most complete and uncompromising expression of the Papal claim to be sovereign of the world, which existed before the Reformation sharpened the pen of Bozius[37].

On the other side we have in the *Defensor Pacis* of Marsilius of Padua one of the most remarkable books in the history of politics. The contents are too well known to need a lengthy description. Here it will suffice to note that the author asserts (1) the complete authority of the civil power, and the purely voluntary nature of religious organisation, thus entirely repudiating every kind of political claim put forward for the ecclesiastical organisation: (2) the consequent iniquity of persecution: (3) the original sovereignty of the people, implying the need of a system of representative government, whereby the action of the State may have the full force of the community at its back and the " general will " be no longer confused with particular interests or individual caprice.

The importance of Marsiglio is illustrated by the fact that from that time forward there is hardly a Papalist pamphleteer who does not take him as the *fons et origo* of the anti-clerical theory of the State. Wyclif, for instance, is condemned for sharing his errors, in the day when Wyclif was a political not a theological heretic[38].

Another work, less interesting, less modern, more scholastic, and perhaps therefore more immediately effective, is the great dialogue of the English nominalist, William of Ockham. In this work the author sets the authority of the civil power very high, denounces the political claims of ecclesiasticism, asserts the supremacy of natural law, and the need of limitations to monarchical authority.

If we pass to England we find in Wyclif something of the tone and the principles of a French anti-clerical. Scholastic in form, Wyclif's writings are modern in spirit. His *De Officio Regis* is the absolute assertion of the Divine Right of the king to disendow the Church. Indeed his stated theory is more Erastian than that of Erastus. His writings are a long-

continued polemic against the political idea of the
Church or rather the political claims of the clergy; for
his State is really a Church. How far his communism
was more than theoretical is very doubtful. In practice,
and now and then in theory, he was the supporter of
aristocratic privilege[39]. Yet he asserts the duty of
treating all authority as a trust, and there can be little
doubt that he recognised the dignity of every individual
as a member of the community in a way which we are
apt to regard as exclusively modern. Wyclif indeed
was in many respects more modern than Luther, as he
was a deeper thinker—except in his entire lack of sentiment. His world of thought is the exact antithesis of
medieval ideals, in regard to politics, ecclesiastical
organization, ritual and external religion.

These then are some illustrations of the fact that the
old landmarks were disappearing and a new world was
coming into being, at the close of the fourteenth century.
It is impossible to do more than sketch them.

What I have tried to do is to indicate that we must
not study political theories apart from political conditions. We must never lose sight of the connection
between theory and practice. In actual facts we shall
find if not always the cause of new doctrines appearing
at least the condition of their prevalence and efficacy.
The reactions of practice upon theory, and theory
upon practice, are abundantly illustrated in the centuries
before us.

The conditions for the growth of our modern politics
were not afforded until the Reformation, or to be more
accurate the intellectual revolution and practical catastrophe which destroyed the system of the Middle Ages,

both in the external framework of society and in the inward life of its members.

It is this which makes it so hard at once to enter into the mind as distinct from learning the outward facts of the medieval world, and still harder to understand a period of transition like that before us. We are always in danger of reading our thoughts into their words ; of drawing modern deductions from non-modern premises. On the other hand the mere use of obsolete phrases and worn-out methods of discussion is apt to repel our sympathy. We are too often blinded by our dislike of the form to our agreement with the substance of writers of a long past age. Against all these dangers we must guard ourselves. Perhaps the most valuable of all the lessons which the study of this subject affords is that of the permanence of fundamental notions amid the most varying forms of expression and argument.

Yet when all reservations have been made, there can be little doubt that it is right to treat the growth of political ideas, during the fifteenth and sixteenth centuries, as a branch of ecclesiastical history. With a few exceptions religion or the interests of some religious body gave the motive of the political thought of the period; to protect the faith, or to defend the Church, or to secure the Reform, or to punish idolatry, or to stop the rebellion against the ancient order of Christendom, or to win at least the right of a religious society to exist ; this was the ground which justified resistance to tyrants and the murder of kings ; or on the other hand exalted the Divinely given authority of the civil rulers.

Except at the beginning with Machiavelli, and at

the end among the Politiques and in the Netherlands, the religious motive is always in the foreground. Montaigne in an *obiter dictum* regards it as the supreme question of his day, "Whether religion justified resistance," and does not hint at other grounds, though the League put forward a good many political grievances, in addition to the toleration of heresy.

On the whole, however, the religious motive was at the bottom of political thinking not only during the age of the Reformation, but for a century or more after it, and juristic methods determined its form. In the world of the Italian renaissance this was not the case. There politics were argued on a modern basis much earlier than in the North. In general, however, it was only in the clash of competing religions and the struggle for their existence that political liberty and secular politics as we know them were born.

In connection with the movement for a reformation of the Church in head and members we shall find the medieval theory of limited monarchy raised to its highest power by the Conciliar party, and stated in a form which politicians in other ages found serviceable; while the triumphant Papacy framed for itself a theory of monarchy by Divine right, which was afterwards to be at the service of secular princes. This will form the subject of the next lecture.

In the third we shall see how Luther's whole system rested on ideas of the relation of laymen to clerics, which led him naturally to exalt the State, and assert the Divine and uncontrollable authority of the Prince.

Machiavelli explicitly represents that anti-clerical ideal of civil autocracy which has not yet reached its final development ; while his conception of the relation of the individual conscience to the development of the community owes much to the greatest of all communities, the Church, and found its fullest political outcome in the practice of ecclesiastical organisations.

In the fourth Lecture I shall deal with the writers, Huguenots, Presbyterians, Ligueurs, who, in order to protect their own communion, formulated theories of natural rights, and derived from feudalism the idea of the original compact. We shall then see how the Jesuits took from the Protestants their theory of government, made it more universal, less aristocratic ; how political convenience led to a doctrine of tyrannicide; how, when their political opportunism turned them for the nonce into revolutionaries, the universal ideas of law which were their peculiar heritage led them to lay the foundations of international jurisprudence. Lastly, in the sixth Lecture we shall see all or nearly all these ideas making themselves practically effective in the resistance to Philip of Spain, and producing in the Netherlands, its thinkers, and its Universities a centre of light whence the political education of the seventeenth century largely proceeded.

We may guess, if we cannot discern, at something of the strength of the chain that at once unites and separates medieval views, grotesque, visionary and ineffectual as they seem to us, from the modern world and the dignified assurance of the Declaration of Independence or the flaming rhetoric of the Marseillaise.

The change from medieval to modern, though in some respects greater than that from ancient to modern, thought is gradual, unceasing and even yet unended. Our politics are largely due to ecclesiastical differences which we are apt to despise, or to theological animosities which we ignore. To the fact that political thought after the end of the seventeenth century was so largely theological is due our inability to understand its methods, and to discern the kernel beneath the husk. To the fact that ecclesiastical bodies were in their necessity the nursing mothers of our modern political ideas is due their prevalence and indeed their existence. Only because these bodies were able to make good their right not to be exterminated (and after they had done so) could their doctrine shed its swaddling clothes and take shape to influence the modern world. To understand Rousseau you must read Rossaeus, and to appreciate the latter you must go back to Aquinas, to Hildebrand and to Augustine. The sonorous phrases of the Declaration of Independence or the Rights of Man are not an original discovery, they are the heirs of all the ages, the depositary of the emotions and the thoughts of seventy generations of culture. "Forty centuries look down upon you," was a truer picture of the mind of the Revolution than the military rhetorician knew or cared to know.

In this attempt to trace a very small part of the embryology of modern politics we shall at least be able to discern on the one hand how near the present is to the past, and how slow is the growth from seed to harvest; and on the other how different is the world of our ideas from that of which it is the child. Mariana planted, Althusius watered, and Robespierre reaped the increase.

LECTURE II.

THE CONCILIAR MOVEMENT AND THE PAPALIST REACTION.

PROBABLY the most revolutionary official document in the history of the world is the decree of the Council of Constance asserting its superiority to the Pope, and striving to turn into a tepid constitutionalism the Divine authority of a thousand years[1]. The movement is the culmination of medieval constitutionalism. It forms the watershed between the medieval and the modern world. We see in the history of the movement the herald of that struggle between constitutional principles, and the claims of autocracy in the State which was, save in this country and the Netherlands, to conclude by the triumph of the latter and the riveting of despotism upon the peoples until the upheaval of the French Revolution.

Eugenius IV is the forerunner of Louis XIV. For the most remarkable of all the facts about this movement is its failure. In this failure and in its causes are to be discerned at once the grounds of the religious revolution, the excuse for ultramontane ideals, and the general tendency to autocracy in all States.

The failure of the Conciliar movement, either to

restrain the Pope permanently, or to further the growth
of federalism in the Church, forms the justification at
once of the Reformation and of ultramontanism—of
ultramontanism on one side, for there must apparently
have been some grounds for absolute monarchy, either
in the nature of political society, or in the condition of
the Christian Church, for the Papal monarchy to
triumph in so overwhelming a fashion, over a movement
so reasonable, and so respectable, supported by men
of such learning and zeal as Gerson and Zabarella,
secure as they were from all suspicion of heterodoxy by
that *auto-da-fé* which made the reputation of John Hus
—of the Reformation, for the fate of the efforts of the
Councils of Pisa and Constance and Basel and the
triumph of vested interests over principle would seem to
show, that all hope of constitutional reform of the
Church was vain, and that Luther was justified in
appealing to the laity to wield, in her spiritual welfare,
that temporal sword with which traditional theory en-
trusted kings and princes, for her material defence.

As Cesarini told the Pope, unless the clergy of
Germany were reformed, there would infallibly arise
a worse schism, even though the present one should be
concluded[2]. If the methods of 1688 produce no result,
corruption of the body politic demands a 1789. Where
the conservative liberalism of Gerson or Halifax had
proved useless, recourse must be had to the revolutionary idealism of Calvin or Rousseau. We may condemn
as we will the violence of the Reformation, but it was
a catastrophe rendered inevitable by the failure of
milder methods. Cautery succeeded to physic. True
indeed, internal reform eventually took place under the
pressure of the new attack. The Counter-Reformation,

or whatever it be called, did attempt to save the Church
from the scandals of the past, and to a certain extent
succeeded.

But it did so by increased centralisation, and a
hardening of temper, alien from earlier movements of
reform. The Jesuits made the Papacy efficient, not by
developing the variety of national differences, but by
concentrating every power at the centre, and compen-
sating for the loss of their Church in extension by its
rigidity of discipline intensively. This process which
had its last result at the Council of the Vatican began
before the Reformation. The victory of Eugenius IV
over the Council of Basel had its logical issue in the
doctrine of Papal infallibility, its political expression
in the theory of a community created *serva*[3]. The
triumph of the Pope over the Council is the beginning
of the triumph of centralised bureaucracy throughout
the civilised world[4]; a triumph which was apparent
everywhere but in England, up till 1789, and in many
countries has only changed its form even as the issue
of that Revolution. Even in England it was only the
fortunate accident of religious differences, that saved
the country from an efficient administrative despotism,
inspired by men such as Bacon, Strafford, or Cromwell.

All this was heralded by the Conciliar movement
or rather by its failure[5]. Aeneas Sylvius Piccolomini
was more than the historian of the Council ; he was the
prophet of the Papacy. Pupil of circumstances as he
was he discerned which way the tendencies of the future
were developing. Deserting the fathers of Basel in the
knowledge that fortune, his real deity, had turned against
them, he spent his whole life in making the Papacy
a real power. Pius II, cultivated, literary, modern,

prepared the way for Pius IX, narrow, credulous, and reactionary. Never have two such different men worked for the same ends, for they agreed in nothing but their humour—and even there the later Pope had the distinction of decency.

The principles of Constance are the last effort of medieval Constitutionalism.

Their failure marks the beginning of the modern world. It paved the way for Luther and Machiavelli in the State, for Ignatius Loyola and Manning in the Church. It was not unnatural, however, that the Conciliar movement should fail. It was an attempt to borrow from the rising States of Western Europe, and from the schemes of Imperialists like Marsilius and Ockham a theory of limited monarchy, and a plan for some form of representative government in the Church. The circumstances which made it possible to make the attempt were the scandal of the great schism, and the spectacle of a divided Church.

But the moment the Council had put an end to the schism its real hold on public opinion was lost. The men who manœuvred it were perhaps in their theories as much in advance of their time as the Whig leaders in 1688. Just as the work of the latter would certainly have collapsed, had the one condition of its success— the continued bigotry of the Stuarts—disappeared, so when the only source of the Council's power, pontifical competition, was removed the Council ceased to have any but an academic importance.

As I said at the beginning, the most revolutionary official document in the history of the world is the decree which asserts its powers. The theory of the ultimate sovereignty of the community had, it must be remembered, been already proclaimed in regard to the civil State by Marsilius. It remained only for the fathers of Constance to apply the idea to the ecclesiastical sphere. This is a crude way of putting it. Marsilius and Wyclif saw in imagination a single society in which all executive power was secular; a State but also a Church; the conciliar party saw also a single society of which kings and peoples were members; but it was primarily a clerical hierarchy which had the power. It was not so much a taking over of principles from the State to the Church; it was the application of those principles by men who held the traditional views (combated by Marsilius and Wyclif) in regard to the authority of the clergy.

This decree is at once the expression of medieval Constitutionalism and its development. That the ideas which it expresses could ever have been applied to the Church without there being already in existence assemblies of estates, exercising the powers of a whole people, is unlikely. Yet the decree asserts the principles which underlay acts like the deposing of Richard II in a far more definite and conscious form than had yet been done; and lays down a theory of the sovereignty of the community which was to pave the way for future controversy[6]. For a long time discussions had been proceeding as to whether Popes or kings held immediately of God. In this decree we find the question definitely put which was eventually to supersede (though not for a long while) that conflict. Is the sovereignty of a community inherently in the ruler or in the representative organ of the people? True there is no reference to politics but only to the special conditions of the Church. But the atmosphere of the day did not allow of questions of polity being raised in the Church, without their affecting theories of the civil power. It is easy to connect this decree with documents like Magna Charta, easy also to see how much more self-conscious are the politics of the age which produced it.

In the same way the decree *Frequens*[7] which directs the summoning of the Council at stated intervals, helped to prepare the way for the claims of the League, and the Parliament to a regular assembling of the Estates of the Realm. Yet here an earlier law directing annual Parliaments formed the precedent.

The theorists and pamphleteers, Conrad of Gelnhausen[8], Henry of Langenstein[9], Gerson and D'Ailly, who prepared the way for the Council, did not invent new principles, nor dig them up from a long forgotten past. They were not, like some of the Renaissance writers, driven back into the early history of Rome and Greece, for precedents, and theories. Theirs was no academic republicanism, like that of Étienne de la Boeotie[10].

They rest on a historical development of realised fact. They appear to have discerned more clearly than their predecessors the meaning of the constitutional experiments, which the last two centuries had seen in considerable profusion, to have thought out the principles that underlay them, and based them upon reasoning that applied to all political societies ; to have discerned that arguments applicable to government in general could not be inapplicable to the Church. In a word they raised the constitutionalism of the past three centuries to a higher power ; expressed it in a more universal form, and justified it on grounds of reason, policy and Scripture. This is why it seems truer to regard the movement as medieval rather than modern in spirit.

Yet it helped forward modern constitutional tendencies, because it expressed them in a form in which they could readily be applied to politics, especially by all those whose sympathies were at all ecclesiastical. It was the lament of an English royalist in the seventeenth century that the dangerous theories of the rights of the people first became prevalent with the Conciliar movement. And even Huguenot writers like Du Plessis Mornay were not ashamed of using the doctrine of the Council's superiority over the Pope to prove their own doctrine of the supremacy of the estates, over the king. Owen calls them *par excellence* political divines. The principles of Constance are in fact almost as frequently cited in general politics as the law of Edward the Confessor or Magna Charta in English. In the writings of Barclay the name of Gerson occurs more than once as a bugbear.

The movement was an audacious one. Nothing but the actual facts of inter-Papal rivalries could have given it any hope of success. The origin of the Papal power, and its relation to Councils need not be here discussed. For centuries however it had been extending its theoretical claims. From being the equal and sometimes the second power in the Empire, the Popes had claimed to be the first and had largely made good their claim. They had set up and pulled down kings. From a claim to freedom to pursue their objects they had advanced to an assertion of supremacy over all kings and princes.

Although indeed this claim was never admitted in full by the leaders of the laity, the clergy rarely denied it. However they might grumble, nations did not care to set up for themselves in religious matters, although the notion was distinctly put forward. The idea that Christendom was one was still predominant. With a visible unity felt as essential, the doctrines of the Divine right of civil power and the duty of submission as taught by S. Paul had been easily wrested from the service of kings to that of Popes. The claim of the Popes to exercise illimitable authority had been worked out logically by generations of canonists. Even in regard to such very independent monarchs as Edward I or Philip the Fair it was only after a struggle that it became necessary to permit concessions in practice, yet the claims in theory remained unaltered or even heightened. The principles of *Clericis Laicos* were never formally withdrawn. The *Unam Sanctam* was put into the Clementine Extravagants by an Avignonese Pope.

As we saw last time the Papal theory was developed a little further by the contest between John XXII and Louis of Bavaria, while the practice of reservation and provisions continued to assert his power, any acts of the State to the contrary notwithstanding.

Quod principi placuit legis habet vigorem was at least as true of the Popes as of Justinian. Louis of Bavaria had been afraid of these claims, and yielded the real point at the critical moment. Claims so ancient, so intertwined with vested interests all over Europe, were not likely for any length of time to be resisted by a parcel

> "Of Dons and of Doctors, of Provosts and Proctors,
>   Who were paid to monopolise knowledge."

For that is what the Conciliar party really was. It had the weakness of a purely academic movement except in so far as it expressed the general desire to close the schism.

By doing this the party decreed its own extinction.

Any chance of really popular support was removed by its attitude to the Bohemians.

The European public, just beginning to awaken to the futility of medieval constitutionalism, was not going to make sacrifices, only to introduce the same thing into the government of the Church.   There might be roseate dreams of representative government, of ruling by consent, of cabinet control, of a cardinalate formed to express the federal and nationalist principles inside the Imperial Church, of a mixed or limited monarchy in the Church, with the dangerous power of dispensation curbed, and the Pope obeying his own laws.   But they remained dreams.   Even the dreamers in some cases, like Nicolas of Cues, went over to the other side.   The fathers of Constance separated with their work but half done.

The Council of Ferrara, which was afterwards transferred to Basel, proved nearly as impotent as the Barebones' Parliament, and served to give point to a later saying of Bellarmin, that it might be all very well to base an aristocratic constitution, or a limited monarchy, on the *Politics* of a Greek City, but that Aristotle had not in view the problems of a country, still less those of an Empire State (the Church).   By the end of the Council of Basel in 1449 it was abundantly clear, that whenever reform, more needed than ever, was to come it could not come from constitutionally summoned Councils—even though they admitted the laity to vote[11].

You know the facts of the movement.   Catharine of Sienna had preached at Avignon and elsewhere the duty of the Pope once more to make the eternal city his home. When however Gregory XII died in 1378 the French Cardinals, who did not wish to lose their influence, refused to recognise the election of Urban VI as valid, and chose an anti-Pope (Clement VI). For forty years the schism went on, the successor on each side refusing to surrender his pretensions. The scandal of such a situation was manifest. Greater than ever was the need of reform, demands for which had been growing in strength for a long time.

At Pisa a Council at last assembled with the object of ending the schism. Instead of this it succeeded merely in setting up a third competitor in the person of Alexander V, who was followed by Baldassare Cossa (John XXIII) in 1410. Since the other Popes refused to resign in his favour, and his reputation did not make the refusal strange, something had to be done.

Just as the existence of States with different religions forced upon men the thought, that there must be a different bond of union of civil society than religious uniformity, so the spectacle of competing Popes drove men to consider seriously the claims of conciliar authority and to discuss in whom the power of the Christian community was ultimately inherent. The need of help from the secular power, and the hopes entertained of Sigismund led to a not unnatural development of the claims of the laity—though most of the writers are very cautious in this respect.

In 1414 the Council of Constance met. It had three objects: (1) to end the Schism, (2) to arrest the Hussite movement in Bohemia, (3) to reform the Church "in head and members."

The second seemed easiest, but it did not prove so. Nationalism which in some ways the Council fostered,

was in this case too strong for them. There ensued
a series of sanguinary wars, ending indeed in a victory
over heresy, but not without a terrific struggle and the
offer of important concessions. As to the third point
little was done at all; there were some reforming decrees ;
Martin V made concordats with the different nations ;
annates, unreasonable Provisions and other abuses were
condemned. A decree ordering the regular assembling
of the Council was promulgated. The net result was
however very small, except in regard to the Gallican
liberties. We cannot disassociate the Pragmatic Sanction
of Bourges in 1438 from the extremely independent and
nationalist attitude taken up by Gerson and other
members of the University of Paris, which was the real
source of the Conciliar movement and its main support,
certainly in its best days. The true trend of things however was exhibited in the concordat of Bologna, in which
the rising authority of the king in that State combined
with the increasing power of the Pope to destroy for
ever the rights of the laity and clergy in France.

In regard to the schism the Council achieved its end.
John XXIII refused to do as he had promised and
abdicate. Eventually he fled from Constance, and after
wandering about, and submitting to many humiliations,
was deposed by the Council. Afterwards he was forced
to sanction this deposition, and make confession of his
crimes in a document far more humiliating than that
imposed upon Richard II.

Gregory XII, the representative of the Italian line
of Anti-Popes, also resigned. Eventually Clement VIII,
the successor of what had been the French and had
become the Castilian line, did the same.

But this was not all. The Council of Constance in the decree *Frequens* had decreed, that it should meet at regular intervals. In 1423 one was summoned at Sienna, but prorogued almost at once. The seven years interval allowed by the decree having elapsed, the need of reform still being pressed, the Hussite struggle by no means ended, the Pope (Martin V) reluctantly summoned a Council (at which he was not present) at Basel. Almost at once he strove to transfer it to Ferrara and so bring it to an end ; but on this point he had to give way. Gradually the numbers of the Council grew smaller and smaller until it dwindled into a mere band of irreconcilables. The real strength of the movement was gone by with the departure of Cardinal Cesarini in 1438. The Pope made ingenious use of the request for assistance from Byzantium, and outwitted the Council in negotiations with the Greeks for the union of Eastern and Western Churches. He held a Council at Ferrara in 1438 which was afterwards transferred to Florence.

The Basel fathers were summoned thither, but remained away. Eugenius IV, by apparently bringing to an end the schism with the East, restored the Papal prestige, although it was, as Aeneas Sylvius remarked, a strange fact that unity with the East was proclaimed at the very moment when the West was bitterly divided.

The new Emperor, Albert II, accepted the reforming decrees of Basel, and Germany for the nonce remained neutral in the struggle.

After affording a precedent to the Long Parliament by declaring that it was not to be dissolved without its own consent, the Council deposed Eugenius IV and elected Amadeus of Savoy Pope by the name of Felix V.

It is significant that since his time Europe has never known an anti-Pope. Aeneas Sylvius, who had seen that time was against the fathers, left them to their impotent eloquence, and after pretending to weigh the arguments made his peace with the Pope, and succeeded in restoring the obedience of Germany. The Council of Basel ended in 1449, the anti-Pope retired from business, which he had found less lucrative than he expected. From time to time the threat of a Council was used as a means of diplomatic pressure ; Alexander VI was worried, as well he might be, by the thought of one, and in 1501 a hostile assembly actually met at Pisa. This was rendered impotent by the astuteness of Leo X, who himself summoned a Council at the Lateran where, of course, it was not dangerous.

Thus the movement went on, or its relics lingered on until the Reformation. This fact is noteworthy. But for practical purposes it may be considered as closed in 1449.

So much by way of introduction.

Let us now seek to examine a little further into the governing ideas of the movement[7].

The writings I wish to treat of begin with Conrad of Gelnhausen[8], and include many works by Jean Charlier Gerson, Chancellor of the University of Paris—a man who enjoyed the reputation for sometime of being the author of the *De Imitatione*. The other chief French writer is Cardinal Pierre Ailly. We have from Germany Dietrich of Niem, Henry of Hesse or Langenstein, Gregory of Heimburg, and Cardinal Nicolas of Cues[9].

There was an Italian Cardinal Francesco Zabarella, who wrote the *De Schismate* ; and a Spaniard Andrea of Randulf. Aeneas Sylvius Piccolomini (Pius II) is also a prime authority for the ideas of the period.

One point is clear. Speculation on the possible power of the Council, as the true depositary of sovereignty within the Church, drove the thinkers to treat the Church definitely as one of a class, political societies. If it cannot be said that the thought was new, that the Church was a political society, it was certainly developed by a situation which compelled men to consider its constitution. Moreover since the constitution of the Church, whatever it may be, is undeniably Divine, universal principles of politics could be discovered by a mere generalisation from ecclesiastical government. The claim made that since the Church was a perfect society, it must have within itself all necessary means of action, and could not suffer its independence to be thwarted by the State, is one associated with later, and (in a different form) with earlier conflicts ; at this period however the notion is used to justify the deposing power of the Council as against the Pope. The Church being a perfect society cannot, it is urged, be without the means of purging itself, and may consequently remove even a Pope, if his administration is merely *in destructionem* instead of *in aedificationem* and thus opposed to the end of the Church, the salvation of souls.

The habit of arguing about the Church as a political society and drawing inferences from the powers of other political societies and the constitution of the civil States prepared the way for the new form in which all questions between the spiritual and lay authority could be discussed; the form of a transaction between two societies distinct in origin and aim.

The medieval struggles between Popes and Emperors are wrongly regarded as a conflict between Church and State, if by that is meant the relations between two societies. The medieval mind, whether clerical or anti-clerical, envisaged the struggle as one between different officers of the same society, never between two separate bodies; this is as true of Dante and Marsilius as it is of Boniface and Augustinus. It is this, and only this, that explains the ease with which the transition was made from the Papal, to the princely or municipal system of Church Government, alike by Luther and Musculus or Whitgift and Hooker. It is quite clear from the tone both of Whitgift and Hooker that the notion of Church and Commonwealth as two transacting bodies was novel. This could not have been the case, if the medieval controversies were not regarded as struggles for precedence between different officers of a single society, or at most the ambitions of rival departments in one body. The claim made by Simanca[12] and Bellarmin for the indirect power of the Popes is based partly on a right of international law; they say that the Pope like any other sovereign may intervene to secure the interests of his subjects; in this way they perhaps unconsciously placed the Church on an equality with other bodies politic, and prepared the way for the language of the Encyclical *Immortale Dei*[13], which demands for the Church rights of independence as a *societas genere et jure perfecta*.

The way for this was partly prepared by the constitutional problem set to the world by the great schism; while we have evidence of the fact that the old ideas were still at work in the intermingling by writers like Nicolas of Cues of schemes for the constitution of the Empire with his plans of ecclesiastical reformation.

A second point of interest in the Conciliar movement is that, arguing from the precedent of constitutional States, it decides upon the best form of government in general, and lays down the lines which controversy took until Whiggism succumbed to the influence of Rousseau.

It could not be denied that the most perfect possible constitution was that which Christ had left to his Church; nor was it denied by the Papalist antagonists of the Council. The question with them was one of fact.

Now the belief of the Conciliar writers, which was derived really from the facts of the political world of their day but based in argument on appeals partly to Aristotle and partly to the Mosaic system, was that this constitution was a πολιτεία, a mixed, or as later times have called it a limited monarchy, in which while the monarchical principle is preserved the danger of tyranny should be removed by the power of a small body of permanent advisers, a continual council, and ultimately checked by a large representative assembly. The speculations on the nature of government were of more avail owing to the fact that they were not concerned, like most of the political theorising of the Middle Ages, with the controversy between the two great powers, spiritual and temporal, within the Church-State. At the same time there were discussions as to the rights of the laity in the Council, and the need of Imperial support drove men like Zabarella to a strong assertion of the claims of the successor of Constantine and Theodosius. This was carried farther at Basel.

The union of political principles with utilitarian notions, heightened by their religious significance, considered with reference to a body which might be a model for all smaller States, and decided upon universal grounds, was the work of the Conciliar party and their opponents. That that discussion ultimately redounded to the benefit of monarchy in the Church was ominous for the cause of liberty for three centuries and a half; that such liberty as existed took the form and acquired the influence it did was partly at least due to the fact that Gerson, D'Ailly, and Nicolas placed the constitutional monarchy in such high light that it could not be altogether obscured even in later and more subservient ages. Further than this, the victory of the Papalist reaction meant the victory of the unitary and Roman over the federalist and Teutonic conception of society. Had the Conciliar movement secured lasting success, the principles which were symbolised by the division of the Council into nations and in the Concordats with which it closed might have become fruitful in the future. As it was, alike in England and abroad, the notion of a single omni-competent social union set over against a mass of individuals became the normal idea of the State. The *Communitas Communitatum* becomes a mere collection of units; and modern society is at once more individualistic and more socialistic than medieval.

Only now, as a result partly of the United States Constitution and partly of other causes, is it beginning to dawn upon men's minds that we cannot fit the facts into the unitary State, as the true source of all power and the only ground of every right except so far as it is controlled by certain claims of the individual.

That this process of education has yet to be accom-

plished is very largely the result of that failure of
Teutonic before Latin ideals of law and government,
which is the lasting result of the triumph of the Papacy
over the Council in the sixteenth century.

Probably the absorption of feudalism before an
all-encroaching governmental omnipotence was necessary
if the modern world was to enter upon its task.   That
this absorption was so generally accomplished is due
partly to the direct influence of the spectacle of Papal
monarchy, and partly to the prevalence of the ideas
which it expressed.   From 1450 onwards it seemed to
most practical statesmen, and to all sovereigns, that
"the tendency of advancing civilisation is a tendency
towards pure monarchy"; and popular movements in
every land were deemed by men like Cecil, or Strafford,
or Richelieu, or sovereigns like Elizabeth and Charles I, as
not merely wrong but stupid—inefficient clogs upon the
wheels of government, which would retard the progress
of intelligence and enlightenment.   Pure monarchy was
the only gentlemanly form of government.

Their attitude was that of Frederick the Great, and
Joseph II.   Even where pure monarchy was regarded
as an ideal, it only gave way to a notion of the unlimited
sovereignty of the State, however constituted, which
is false to the facts of human life, and creates an
unnecessary chasm between the individual and the
supreme power, instead of bridging the gulf by the
recognition of other and smaller societies, with inherent
powers of life, not the result of the fiat of governmental
authority.   The point however is this.   Constance and
Basel saw the last, the most splendid, and in the event
the most unfortunate of all the many medieval attempts
to limit the sovereign power.   Since the Church must

clearly be Divinely governed, the answers to the questions it put must be final as to the ideal of human society politically organised.

These questions were old ones. Had the sovereign illimitable authority from the first, or did the Church confer his power, and if so on what condition ? Was he really *solutus legibus* ? Is it true that in the Church *Quod principi placuit legis habet vigorem* ? or was the opposing maxim the real one *Quod omnes tangit ab omnibus approbatur* ? Was the prince (the Pope) lord or minister of the Church ? What in fact is the nature of dominion ? Might he be removed if his tyranny was patent and ruinous to the souls of men ? Or is it to be allowed to reverse the very end of the Church's being ? If not, was every private man a judge of his insufficiency, or must we await a public and formal pronouncement ?

Is not a mixed government the principle of Moses, and the Jewish Church, the theory of Aristotle, the practice of every nation which is not being ruined ? Have we not an obvious mixture, our sovereign lord the Pope, our lords the Cardinals his continual council, and the prelates in council "virtually" representing the visible Church ? Are commands such without sanction ? Are those laws which "public approbation hath not made such"? Is not consent and user the essence of valid law ? How far are unjust laws to be obeyed ? Need they be considered laws at all, if we understand St Thomas aright? Can any government exist or claim rights apart from the consent of the governed ? Is there vested in any governor secular or ecclesiastical the dominion over the property and lives of individuals ? Can any power, however appointed, dispense with the precepts of natural law? These and such like questions were actually asked; they form the basis of political disunion until the days of Locke. Whatever we may think now, there is no doubt that such words as king, republic, aristocracy, and the maxims of the civil law, were then regarded as perfectly applicable to the concerns and the constitution of the Church. They did not anxiously argue from the State to the Church or *vice versâ*, but from the idea of a society to its consequences.

A very slight acquaintance with Locke or Algernon Sidney, to say nothing of the *Vindiciae contra tyrannos*, will enable the reader of Gerson, and the *Concordantia Catholica* to see how great is the debt of the politicians to the ecclesiastics. The crisis in the Church was thus, I think, responsible for bringing these questions before men in a more universal form than they had hitherto assumed; the arguments for constitutional government were stripped of all elements of that provincialism, which might have clung to them for long, had they been concerned with only the internal arrangements of the national States; and the theory of a mixed or limited monarchy was set forth in a way which enabled it to become classical. Certainly it was actually so used in later controversies. Whatever be the case with Basel, to the Council of Constance the eyes of Christendom were turned; it was not for nothing that the greatest University in the world, which was far more influential than any such seminary now, was the main factory of its principles. Emperors might be the fathers of the Council, and kings its nursing mothers, but the child they nurtured was Constitutionalism, and its far off legacy to our own day was "the glorious revolution." The superiority of the interests of the Community over those of its officers, asserted in 1414 and rendered nugatory in the Church, received a tardy justification at the hands of history in the State. On the other hand the Papacy took an enduring vengeance on those of its subjects who temporarily abased it ; and rising on the ruins of the medieval system more imposing and autocratic than before asserted in oracular tones the Divine irresponsibility of the Papal monarchy, and succeeded in making the ideals of autocratic rule the intellectual fashion of an age, which imitated the Pope even when it most opposed him.

The discussions of Constance were, as we saw, far more purely political than those of the Middle Ages, because they were not concerned with the conflicts between ecclesiastical and spiritual authority, but with the depositary, the functions, and the limits, of sovereign power, in a perfect society.

Still we must not forget that it was the politics of a Divine Society that were under discussion. The end of the Church is the salvation of souls; so the doctrine of utility is sanctified, and expediency loses the touch of vulgarity which far more than his immorality repels men from Machiavelli. In one aspect the thought of Gerson and D'Ailly is very utilitarian and the main defence of their attitude towards the Popes was *salus populi suprema lex.* All this because they were idealists and cared little for utility in the narrower sense. For, whatever be thought of the doctrine of either side, it was not as in most topics of ordinary political controversy a question as to the balance of comfort and material well-being, but one between the ruin and the salvation of human nature. If the power of the Pope was really irresponsible, there was nothing to save men from eternal misery, should his policy drive that way. If the command "Feed My sheep" may be interpreted as the gift of an authority to starve them, it was not poverty, or disease, that would result, but the eternal destruction of the soul. For if the Pope transformed into its opposite the duty of promoting the edification of the Church, and pulled down instead of building up, there was on Papalist principles no surety for the souls of men.

You remember how just before our own day, what was intended as a purely scientific course of Lectures on "Jurisprudence" was prefaced by John Austin with some lengthy chapters about the paramountcy of the Law of God and its revelation in the principle of utility. They are generally omitted now, even by the few students who read the living book instead of an abstract, from which the impress of the strong personality of the author is removed. They ought not to be forgotten, however, for they serve to show the highly practical character of such theorising, even when it is professedly purely scientific.

But to the fathers of Constance, standing as they felt in the middle of the road of the Church, and with no mind to traverse Dante's terrific spiral, this principle, quoted by them often in its ancient form *salus populi suprema lex*, was the necessary bulwark against the Canonist theory of sovereignty (substantially the same as Austin's); that whatever legal and prescriptive rights could be alleged for the Papal Autocracy, the supreme need of the Church must override them. It was a case of right before rights. There is a point of view from which expediency is the same thing as right, and to men who were seeking for eternal life the short period valuation, which gives to political expediency its ill fame, was impossible.

For these men righteousness was pitted against rights, and they were willing to overthrow the latter, in their desire for the former. Hence we find their governing thought, reiterated in writer after writer, that the Church's necessity knows no law; that Papal claims can plead no prescriptive title, when the Church needs that they should be disregarded; that when the legal authority will not perform its functions, we are driven back to the *pristinum jus* inherent in the nature of human society; that we must not forget the end in the means; and that the Pope's power itself and even his existence is the creature of the Church and may not abrogate its *raison d'être*. For no Pope can dispense with natural law; and natural law teaches the original equality of man, and the necessity of consent to the rightfulness of any government. Thus to Nicolas and Zabarella it is certain that the Christian community cannot be the mere slave of the Pope (for this was the theory of their opponents); he cannot be Lord, but must be the minister of all, as Christ said; besides, the Christian Law is a law of liberty, and so the Christian cannot be the mere chattel of an autocrat. A king in the last resort may be assailed not as a king but as a public enemy; the like is true of the Pope. Originally the whole power of the Church must have been in the community. S. Peter was only given the primacy by the consent of the other Apostles; neither in the Church nor out of it does government exist without consent, and the end for which such consent was first given cannot be ignored. If the Church chose it could make the Archbishop of Trier universal head, and take away from Rome a

prerogative founded on custom, consent and forgery
(Nicolas of Cues denied the genuineness of the Donation
of Constantine). In brief *orbis major urbe.* The Pope
is a member of the body politic of the Church, of which
Christ is the head ; and a diseased limb may be am-
putated. The Church is indefectible; the right of the
majority of the Council is secured by an appeal to the
word of Christ :—" Lo I am with you always." All
the world can be saved without the Pope, but not
without the Church. The Church, not the Pope, is
the spotless bride of Christ. In the last resort, as a
Council may continue, so it may meet without Papal or
even imperial authority. If it be asked under whose
authority in such a case the Council is summoned, it is
to be answered, by authority of its head Jesus Christ.
The Pope is the Vicar of the Church rather than of
Christ.

The destructive criticism of the autocracy of the
Pope, the appeal from purely legal, to general considerations of utility and natural law, is one side of the
movement. Its other aspect is constructive. The party
aimed definitely at establishing a constitution for the
Church. Treated as a whole it was nationalist, representative, and aristocratic. Election is to make the
officers of the Church really represent their subjects.
The Cardinals are no longer to be the Italian entourage
of the Pope, but national leaders. As a matter of fact
the custom of making national resident cardinals did
not begin till after the Council.

A brief account of the *De Concordantia Catholica* of
Nicolas of Cues will give the best exposition of the
ideals of the movement. Like the rest in being a *Livre
de circonstance*, it is distinguished from them by its

elevation and breadth. As closing the Middle Ages
we might compare it with that other *Concordantia*
of Gratian, which expressed their spirit in its prime,
and was the most influential political pamphlet ever
published.

Like the *De Monarchia* of Dante the work of Nicolas
is at once a prophecy and an epilogue—an epilogue in
respect of its ideal of a rejuvenated *Civitas Dei* with
Pope and Emperor again shining forth as twin though
limited rulers; a prophecy in its conception of society
as organic, in its proclamation of the right to consent,
in its universality. It is almost the last book which
treats Christendom as a single organic system, in which
a complete theory of politics, whole and parts, is set
forth.

Its key-note is harmony. The author strives to
find the harmony which unites earthly government to
heavenly; secular to spiritual; he takes the various
members of the body politic. The unity of the whole,
not in spite of but manifested in and through difference,
is the constant thought of the author, and the (indirect)
Divine origin of all government, but he strives to harmonise the two notions of the Divine and human origin
of authority. For if power is in the ultimate resort from
God; immediately, and apparently it comes from man.
The consent and agreement of the Christian community
is the origin of Papal authority, which is a delegation
from the people, and may be removed at their will.
The civil power is to be free from ecclesiastical
interference, and unhampered by clericalism. Yet it
needs reforming. The Emperor is to be surrounded by
a continual Council and to do nothing apart from them.
There is also to be an annual representative assembly at

Frankfort. Electors are to give up their evil habits of corruption and the securing of concessions beforehand. Taxation must be reformed. Customs and laws, so far as possible, are to be unified. The book was written nearly seventy years before the "reception" of Roman law in Germany.

Like Zabarella, Nicolas would grant to the Emperor large powers in regard to the Church; while he sets very high the authority of the synods of single nations. Only for strictly universal legislation is a general Council necessary. Like Gregory of Heimburg, Nicolas of Cues appears to have doubted the efficacy of persecution, and had at least some leanings towards religious toleration.

Whether or no this was really the case the Catholic Concord sheds a sunset glory over the medieval world. Its sweet reasonableness of tone, its calmness and serenity of argument, its lofty eloquence, the sanctified common sense which refuses to allow the absolute claims of legal rights upon a society which needs renovation, suggest a comparison with Hooker, to whose theory of Law that of Nicolas bears a strong resemblance. Could indeed the ancient world have been reformed in the way Nicolas suggests, our debt to the Middle Ages might be even greater than it is; nor should we have been divided from them by a revolution [14].

But it was not. The Papalist reaction, both in theory and practice, drove on with speed; and helped, though indirectly, to secure the general development of absolutism in the next two centuries [15]. Reform when it came took a harder and more self-contained form than the federalist union of Nicolas's dreams.

This book however remains a magnificent expression of the ideal of a Christendom ruled by the principle of harmony, rather than that of uniformity, in which one polity shall still embrace both civil and spiritual activities, and brotherhood, the supreme principle of Christianity, shall become the inspiration of a delicately articulated society, the source of a varied and developing activity[16].

LECTURE III.

LUTHER AND MACHIAVELLI.

A CYNIC might remark that religion was merely the ἀγώνισμα ἐς τὸ παραχρῆμα of the Reformation, its κτῆμα ἐς ἀεὶ was the State. It was the function of Luther, of Zwingli, of Anglicans like Whitgift and Hooker, to transfer to the State most of the prerogatives that had belonged in the Middle Ages to the Church[1]. Or rather what happened was this; the one society, with civil and ecclesiastical authorities functioning within, was conceived as a Church in the Middle Ages, as the *Civitas Dei* of Christendom, the Holy Roman Empire, an institution which is as much, if not more, a Church than a State; by Protestantism the limits of society are narrowed to the nation or the territorial estate, while its nature is more that of a State than a Church. Or, to phrase it again differently, the medieval mind conceived of its universal Church-State, with power ultimately fixed in the Spiritual head bounded by no territorial frontier; the Protestant mind places all ecclesiastical authority below the jurisdiction and subject to the control of the " Godly prince," who is omnipotent in his own dominion. It was not until the exigencies of the situation compelled the Presbyterians to claim rights independent of the State, that the theory of two distinct kingdoms is set

forth ; though it is proved speedily to be of service by
all sides, and is adopted by Jesuits as against the civil
power, by French royalists like Barclay as against
ultramontane claims, and finds eventually in Warburton
the most complete exponent of the contractual theory of
government.   The change is a change from a world-
empire to a territorial State, and from ecclesiastical to
civil predominance.   In the first phase of the Reformation, it was the civil power that reaped all or most of
its fruits.   By the destruction of the independence of
the Church and its hold on an extra-territorial public
opinion, the last obstacle to unity within the State was
removed.   The secularisation of monastic property meant
on the one hand an increase of wealth to the prince,
on the other restored a large mass of inhabitants to
the jurisdiction of the ordinary authority.   The true
monastery is the State, said Erasmus ; by which he
meant that the communal life, supposed to be the
distinction of the monastery, ought to inspire all the
members of a civil society, which should not consist of semi-private cliques.   The violence of both
Luther and Melanchthon in regard to the monastic ideal
is at least partly political.   They felt the monastic
system to be a constant rebuke to their conception both
of a Christian family and a Christian commonwealth.
Only recently has the meaning of this denunciation been
indicated by M. Combes, some of whose speeches are
inspired by exactly the same notion, that loyalty to a
small corporate society is incompatible with loyalty to
the State, while the vow of obedience when understood
completely is opposed to the development of individual
conscience[2].   Further than this, the Reformation coin-
cided either with the destruction of feudal privilege by

the power of the State as in France, or else as in Germany with its elevation into a sovereignty. The authority of the Emperor decayed; the authority of the Prince from being merely feudal became paramount and ubiquitous, largely through the influence of Luther. We may arrange the influence in this respect of Luther under the following heads.

It was definitely an influence in favour of the lay authorities. Later on doubtless the Lutheran theologians tended to become hieratic and clerical. But so far as Luther's feelings were concerned, the whole bent of his mind was in favour of the sanctity of the lay power as against the ecclesiastical. Nor had he any means to his hand but the ruling classes of Germany. He therefore appealed to them and by so doing gave an immense increase to their power. It was true that certain phrases in the *Liberty of a Christian Man*, and his individualist tendency, might be and were interpreted in another way. So far as Luther, however, was concerned, the Anabaptist movement only had the effect of throwing him more strongly than ever on the side of authority. For the rest of the century " respectable " Protestantism was nervously apprehensive of being regarded as politically revolutionary. This is the motive of such books as Tyndale's *Obedience of a Christian Man* on the one hand, and of Cartwright's bitter resentment at Whitgift's attempt to show that his opinions were Anabaptist in tendency; and the same note can be found in some of the Huguenot apologies.

Luther's language and attitude were by no means always consistent; yet he was quite justified in claiming to have done more than anyone else to promote princely authority[3]. Even his deviations from this are explicable.

In regard to the peasants in 1525 we must bear in mind that Luther never allowed the right of overt resistance. The earlier phase of his attitude, in which he rebuked the nobles for oppression and showed some sympathy with the peasants, never amounted to more than a desire for the redress of their grievances. If his attitude at this time was not that of the violent instigator of carnage which he afterwards adopted, he never permitted the peasant to suppose that he regarded resistance to the powers that be as lawful. There was no change of theory, only a slight shifting of sympathy.

It would indeed be hard to find a more thoroughgoing expression of the doctrine of " Passive Obedience," than that of Luther's first address to the peasants. He scoffs at the idea of standing up for one's rights, " *Leiden, Leiden, Kreuz, Kreuz ist der Christenrecht, das und kein anderes*[4]." Not only God's Law (both of the old and the new dispensation) but national law is against the right of the peasants to resist. If they are bent on resistance they had better give up the name of Christians and adopt some other more suitable, for our rights are not to resist, but to pray for our enemies and do good to our persecutors.

In addition to this he asserts the necessity of inequalities of rank in the civil State, and declares that the third article would make all men equal, and reduce Christ's spiritual kingdom to a merely external earthly realm[5].

It was not in theory that Luther's attitude underwent a change. It was in the practical question, to what extent the lords were to exercise their right of oppression, and how far they were to make concessions, that he was inconsistent, and from a general assertion of the duty

F.   5

of just dealing passed to a support of indiscriminate massacre.

Luther, in fact, rated both the office and the utility of the Christian prince so high, that it was natural that he should be a main supporter of the doctrine of passive obedience in its modern form[6]. We must not forget that the Middle Ages never denied the common interpretation of such texts as those of Romans xiii. and I Peter ii., which assert the religious duty of obedience to the powers that be, and the wickedness of rebellion. What the ordinary medieval theorist did was to assert that in the last resort the " powers that be " in the Commonwealth of Christendom were the ecclesiastical authorities ; hence it is only to the Pope that Passive Resistance is a possible duty ; as against the King active resistance is allowed, when authorized from Rome. In some cases doubtless this duty was claimed for the lay power, but even then there was a large reservation in favour of the Pope's authority. Now the movement inaugurated by Luther denied all coercive authority to the ecclesiastical officer ; as Melanchthon said, the power of making laws did not belong to the spiritual sword. Consequently the limitations of the text must apply to the civil power, and obedience was claimed unreservedly for the "godly prince"; *i.e.*, the ruler of a Christian State. It is the reiterated complaint of Whitgift against Cartwright that he allows to the Christian no more authority than to a Turkish prince. We shall see later on how it is to the ecclesiastical party, whether Jesuit or Presbyterian, that the purely secular theory of the civil State is due. To Luther, however, to the Protestants in Germany, to Zwingli and to the Anglican Divines, and to

Althusius the civil power is essentially holy; it is formed for the purpose of fulfilling one great object of Christ's religion, the love of man towards his neighbour, which again is dependent on his love towards God. Hence he is far from the view that regards the civil power as a mere contrivance to secure external tranquillity and peace, and entirely external except so far as it obeys the Church. Luther, in fact, refuses to make that sharp distinction of sacred and secular so characteristic of the Latin world ; and paves the way for the exalted theory of the State entertained by Hegel and his followers. He is as much the spiritual ancestor of the high theory of the State, as the Jesuits and their allies are of the narrower, utilitarian theory.

Yet in one respect must it not be admitted, that Luther was inconsistent ? Surely no one can assert that his life and his precepts did anything to maintain the tottering authority of the Empire. Was it not on the contrary the effect of his action, if not of his theory, to destroy the last relics of any practicable unity in the Empire, and to leave of it nothing but the corpse which crumbled at the touch of Napoleon ? Exactly. The Holy Roman Empire, of which it must be borne in mind the Pope was an official, as well, as the Emperor, the *Civitas Dei* of the Middle Ages, received its death-blow from Luther. Its impotence was of long standing, and was due to the inability of Popes and Emperors to come to any working agreement. Maximilian, however, had done something to restore efficiency to the constitution. What Charles V might have done but for the religious revolution, we cannot say. But at any rate the religious revolution gave to the territorial magnates the last thing they needed to make their power into an autocracy and to rule out all effective interference from above. It is not of the secular head as universal monarch, not of a president of a federal State, that the Reformation affirmed the god-given authority. It tended to reduce the notion of any Divine superintendence of affairs from the international to the territorial sphere; and of the Divine origin of the ruler from a federal to a purely unitary power. Both inside and outside the Empire federalism was at a discount from the Reformation onwards. Either the Church became as in Protestant countries a purely national organization, helping at once to maintain and to vivify the principle of territorialism; or as among the Roman Catholics, while remaining extra-territorial and non-national, it became more unitary, more compact, more autocratic than in the Middle Ages. There was far less of the federal spirit at Trent than at Constance, and the letter of Carlo Borromeo declaring that the last thing the Pope would consent to was the voting by nations is expressive of the spirit which became dominant in the Roman Church[7]. Everywhere we see the triumph of the unitary system. The ideal of Christendom as a whole, with Pope and Emperor at its head, gave way to the notion of the godly prince; and potent in some respects as was Luther's nationalist influence, it was not so much the German people as the sovereign territorial prince that reaped the benefit. The prince officially "most religious," within a nation unitary in religion, in finance, in bureaucratic management, striving to secure morality, and to repress vice as well as crime, is the ideal alike of the Reformation and the Counter-Reformation. Outside that limit, the reign of force proceeds unchecked, and international relations are less than ever subject to the notion of any guidance beyond that of the "law of the beasts." Luther's principles for the internal, and Machiavelli's practice for the external direction of the State were to be the ideal for many generations.

This is true even of the "Catholic kings," and is of course obvious in the case of Venice and France. The sentiment of all Europe was against Paul V in his attempt to take up the position of a rigid canonist in regard to the Venetian Republic, and he had to give way. No Pope could afford, at any rate for some time, to risk a new investiture controversy. The saying of Maximilian that Luther might be useful some day proved literally true, and true for all Catholic princes until the French Revolution provoked by reaction an increase of the ultramontane spirit. It was only when, as in the case of France under Louis XIV, the King had given hostages to orthodoxy by the revival of the spirit of persecution that the Gallican spirit was beaten. On the whole, however, the supremacy of the common law of the land over everyone within its borders, including the clergy, triumphed universally with the Reformation. Luther's influence tended to give this the widest extension possible. He based the Royal authority upon Divine right with practically no reservation; and by asserting the duty of the prince to play the part of Josiah made it possible for an Elector Palatine to assert that his subjects' consciences belonged to him. The principle of *Cujus regio, ejus religio* was the seeming result of the competitive spirit in religion, coupled with the growth of territorial power. It exalted the power whose religion was dominant rather than the particular religion he might adopt. The uniformity of ecclesiastical law which had formed a common law for the West gave place to an international system of religion; only with the modern growth of toleration did religion from a public become a private matter, the concern of the individual.

Whatever practical limitation to the power of the Sovereign might be recognized by the form of the State, the gain to its pretensions, whether king or republic, and the assurance of its legal omnipotence were lasting, and only to be measured by the destruction of any common extraterritorial authority. The increase of unity within, at the expense of all forms of federalism, and the denial of any kind of unity without, except such as was maintained by the very shadowy forces of International Law, were at once the consequence and the condition of Luther's success.

We must not exaggerate, and in the remaining lectures we shall be tracing the growth of the influences that formed some check upon these tendencies. The practical abolition of benefit of clergy, the substitution of the ideal of the good householder for that of the saint and the monk, the unification of all powers within the State, the ascription of all coercive authority to the civil ruler, and the inculcation of the duty of absolute non-resistance are not, of course, Luther's sole work, even in politics; but they are the most salient features of the whole movement, of whose spirit his career is a symbol. The Church had, in fact, been the first and greatest "immunist"; as it was the first so it was the last. If Bluntschli's much canvassed statement that the State is male and the Church female be accepted, we must regard the Middle Ages as the period *par excellence* of woman's rights, except that we have no right to speak of two societies. Of divided allegiance, of authorized separation of powers in the body politic, the Pope could say as was said of another independence, " I watched by its cradle, I followed its hearse." Richelieu, no less than Cecil or Parker, was a product of the Reforming movement. Had there been no Luther there could never have been a Louis XIV. In fact, the religion of the State superseded the religion of the Church. Its first form was the Divine Right of Kings. Luther and Machiavelli were two of the most important factors in the change. But its results lasted longer. The unified democracy of Rousseau's scheme, and the realization of "the Idea " in Hegel's State-system both owe something of their nature to this movement. Both start from the assumption that the State is man's chief good upon earth, that its authority is to be all pervading and irresistible, that its rights are inalienable, and that no individual rights, not even those of religion, can stand against it. Luther's conception of the State and of duty to one's neighbour directly paved the way for that of Hegel.

The doctrine of the Divine Right of Kings is in its origin, as a rapid reference to Dante will show, an assertion of the rights of the lay as against the ecclesiastical power. Its purport is to deny all theories of ecclesiastical supremacy. Whatever power may be granted to the spiritual authority by believers in this doctrine—and it may be a good deal—this much is denied, that the temporal power exists by its favour, that the State is but a department of the Church. The Divine Right of Kings asserts the inherent right of political society to exist ; that the civil sword is God's ordinance no less

than the ecclesiastical; or in the " terms of art," the
power of the prince comes immediately from God, not
mediately through Pope or Kirk.   Hence the Prince or
the State which he represents is accountable to none but
God, and political sovereignty " is at all times so free as
to be in no earthly subjection in all things touching the
regality of the said power."

The supporters of Divine Right were thinking first
and foremost of the secular independence of foreign or
internal ecclesiastical power, only secondarily of the
Rights of the King or the State against the individual.
Carried to its completest extent and interpreted without
any reservations, the doctrine obviously might and does
in some cases lead to the absolute destruction of individual liberty and the absorption of all rights in the
power of an arbitrary monarchy, and certainly of an
uncontrollable State.   This doctrine, so far as it rests on
the notion of secular independence, was not new ; it had
been forged in the conflicts of Pope and Emperor.   In
the 16th and 17th centuries, indeed, it became hardened
and took up into it certain other elements, such as the
doctrine of indefeasible hereditary right, which afterwards overshadowed the others.   But it was the need
of a Reformation, or rather the political aspect of the
Reformation, which gave the doctrine a new vogue, and
for a couple of centuries rendered political speculation
rather more than less dependent on theology, or at least
on Scripture, than it had been becoming.   The influence
of Aristotle, and later on of the Renaissance, was all
away from the theological conception of politics ; we
see the two combined in S. Thomas, while in Étienne
de la Boeotie or in Machiavelli we see political thought
entirely non-theological.

The tendency, however, was counteracted by the Reformation in Germany. Presbyterianism, both in theory and practice, alike in Germany, Heidelberg and in Scotland, was not less but more ecclesiastical in spirit and in pretensions than the medieval Church. It was not, indeed, quite the same, for the Presbyterian theory, whether in Cartwright or Melville, developed the notion of Church and State as two distinct societies with different aims and officers; to the medieval mind there was always one society with its temporal and spiritual officers. The same change, however (as we shall see), came over the Roman hierarchical doctrine ; and the Jesuits developed the notion of the Church as a *societas perfecta* over against the other *societas perfecta*. This theory is not necessarily one of the tutelage of the lay power by the ecclesiastical, like the ordinary hierarchical doctrine of the Middle Ages. There can, however, be no doubt, that in its earlier phase the Presbyterian doctrine was fully as ecclesiastical and anti-secular, as was the Romans ; that it equally denied all real independence to the civil ruler, and demanded that ecclesiastical interests should dominate in politics.

When the Reformation is spoken of as redounding to the advantage of the civil ruler, and largely an expression of the advent of the secular power to omnipotence, it is not of the Presbyterian or Calvinist side of it that we are thinking, but rather of the Reforming movement as it developed in Germany, England, or Sweden. There the movement was at bottom a lay movement. When Luther burnt the *Corpus Juris Canonici*, he symbolised and intended to symbolise the entire abolition of all claims, not only to superiority, but even to any kind of coercive or inherent jurisdiction in the Church. He destroyed, in fact, the metaphor of the two swords; henceforth there should be but one, wielded by a rightly advised and godly prince. It is a curious fact that Luther, whose fundamental motive was a love of liberty and care for the rights of one's neighbours, should have been so powerful a supporter of absolutism.

With his exalted view of the power of the Civil Governor, and with the very low view Luther took of the value of sacerdotal gifts, it is not surprising that Luther's accession to power resulted in those principles known as Erastian. Even here we must distinguish. Luther and the Zwinglians, who in this respect were very similar, did not really intend to make truth the sport of political exigencies, and to recognize in the civil magistrate the right to define the faith. Luther, at any rate in his earlier stages, makes large reserves in regard to matters of doctrine and order. Erastus himself says distinctly he is only considering the case of a State where but one religion is permitted, and that the true one, and left Heidelberg when in 1580 the new Elector reverted to Lutheranism[8]. The position of Protestantism, even of Knox, is that the godly prince, *i.e.*, the lay power within the Church, has power to make the necessary reforms when the Pope will not: the king, in fact, is to do right, when no one else will. The administration and all coercive jurisdiction over the clergy in the last resort springs from the prince; he is completely to be master in his own house. As Melanchthon said, legislative power does not belong to the Church, for so far as it is a kingdom at all it is one not of this world. The only *Civitas Dei* in any sense of the word commonwealth which is not purely metaphorical is the State; to Luther the Anabaptist claim (which was very medieval in spirit) to find it in the Church, like the Peasants' claim that men are all equal, only produced a sharpened sense that the Kingdom of God is a purely inward, spiritual thing ; in fact he was largely instrumental in destroying, not merely the fact, but even the principle of liberty, so far as individuals were concerned, throughout Germany ; while Calvin, whose own motives were essentially those of iron authority and order, largely helped to produce those conditions which kept it alive both in practice or theory. The reason of this is that Calvin happened to influence permanently either a minority in a hostile State as in France or England, or a nation struggling to be free like the Dutch. That his principles were in themselves in no way based on any ideal of individual liberty may be illustrated from the history of Geneva, New England, Scotland, the Synod of Dort, and the Puritan Revolution. But just because as in the Netherlands and France Calvinism was in-extricably mingled with a struggle against tyranny and insurrection, which required a theoretical basis, or as in England it became the *cachet* of a persecuted minority, the determination not to be suppressed which these bodies of men displayed helped to keep alive the fire of liberty for other influences to fan into a flame. Luther, on the other hand, really believed in individual freedom, a fact which may be proved by a perusal of the *Liberty of a Christian Man* ; but while on the one hand his extreme conservatism and his literal view of the New Testament led him to a strong doctrine of non-resistance, on the other he saw in the existing condition of the Empire, that the person whose freedom at that moment it was most necessary to proclaim was not the individual but the prince. As against Pope and Emperor his life and writings equally helped to make the princes realize for themselves the liberty of a Christian man[9]. So far as Luther really assisted to promote despotism, it is due partly to his being frightened by the Peasants' revolt, and the excesses of the Anabaptists, partly to the fact that, having substituted in his own mind a lay power for an ecclesiastical, to him the State was that which, in the Middle Ages, the Church had been, "a partnership in every art, a partnership in every science, in every virtue and all perfection." That this omnipotence was at the moment in the hands of individuals, was probably only to his mind an accident; it is as a matter of fact the reforming despots of the *Aufklärung* who are the final goal of Luther's efforts[9]. Undoubtedly the real effect of his writings was revolutionary. He did more than any other man to shorten what Acton called the "reign of the dead." But in politics, the revolution was one not in favour of liberty but against it, and so far from improving the position of the poor it rendered it more abject, and added contempt to misery. Freedom from a spiritual tyranny which was at bottom also political, was the actual motive vivid and present to his mind[10]. Luther's thought was essentially practical; and he fell back upon the only power that could effect his ends. Even the Conciliar party fell back, to a large extent, upon the lay power, and that movement was not only nationalist, it was lay in its leaning. It is interesting to compare the *Letter to the German nobility* with the *De Concordantia Catholica*, and see how at this early stage Luther's views pointed on the one hand to the carrying forward of the idea of reforming the Church by the help of the Imperial power, and accompanied by a reformation of the State, which was the main theme of Nicolas of Cues, and on the other hand tended to eviscerate to all intents and purposes the term "Kingdom of God," and apply it either to the state of the believer's soul, righteousness, peace and joy, or to a purely invisible and unorganised collection of beings, both living and dead. The invisibility of the Church is, in fact, to Luther the condition and the counterpart of the visibility of the State—which in its full sense is a new thing.

Luther's position, and that of other Protestants like Musculus, or Hooker and Whitgift, was only possible because our phrase—the conflicts of Church and State— is a misnomer when applied to the struggle between Popes and Emperors in the Middle Ages; it cannot be too often reiterated that the thinkers of the Middle Ages were not concerned with two separate and distinct societies, but merely with the relations between different officers or at most different departments of the society. Speaking generally the medieval mind puts the ecclesiastical officer at the head. Luther, following Wyclif and Dante, puts the civil at the head. Only later do we find, first in Presbyterians and afterwards in Jesuits, the distinct recognition of two societies whose relations are to be decided by some form of contract.

In any case we must not confuse Luther with Hobbes. It is true that the effect of the Protestant movement in Germany was to give the prince an entirely unwarrantable authority over the religion of his subjects, which he thought he had a right to change at his will. It is also true that Erastianism in its strict sense leads logically and practically to Erastianism in its developed sense, which makes religion the plaything of statesmen who may or may not profess any themselves. But the actual thought of Luther stops far short of this. All that he and his imitators asserted is the right of the most religious and gracious King " to visit, redress, reform, order, correct and amend all manner of heresies, errors, schisms, abuses, offences, contempts, and enormities whatsoever, which by any manner of spiritual or ecclesiastical power, authority or jurisdiction can or may lawfully be reformed, ordered, &c., &c., to the pleasure of Almighty God, the increase of virtue, and the conservation of the peace and unity of this realm." Their doctrine was that all coercive authority was vested in the prince by Divine Right; that the power of the State was absolutely vested in him; that no other separate organization could exist except by his fiat, or by his delegation. The hostility of Melanchthon and others to monastic communities is largely based on this, that they set up a different bond of society to that of the commonwealth; and possess a unity which is not of that of the civil State. No real social unities are to exist apart from the State; the medieval notion of a *communitas communitatum* gives way to the civilian doctrine of the omni-competent State set over against a mass of individuals. That this doctrine was dangerous is true enough; that it does not tally with the facts of life is also true; that it took generations to work out and is only now receiving its complete interpretation in the speeches of M. Combes, the Judgments of the House of Lords in the Free Church Case, and in the aims of Dr Clifford is also true! But that for the time and at the moment Luther and his followers only intended to assert that the lay power must be supreme, and that the unitary State was a self-subsistent entity, having therefore a Divine sanction apart from the ecclesiastical, is all that we can say. The freedom of the lay power from a clerical control, and hence the sovereignty of the prince—this is the sum and substance of their contention. This, as we know, worked out to mean the practical destruction of the Imperial authority on the one hand ; and the removal of all checks on princely tyranny on the other. Luther was far more revolutionary than he cared to admit or liked to believe. It is, however, against the unity of the Empire that his doctrines were subversive. In spite of his insistence on the duty of caring for one's neighbours, and of his condemnation of the evils of the newer capitalism, so far as concerned the peasants and the lower classes in general, Luther's supremacy worked for anything but amelioration. Above all, the dislike to the whole monastic ideal which characterised the reforming movement, helped to usher in that vulgar contempt for poverty, and the placing of comfort before character as an ideal, which is so distinctive of the modern as compared with the medieval world. This it is, perhaps, more than anything else that justifies Matthew Arnold's dictum that he was only a " Philistine of Genius. "

Luther is merely taken as typical of the whole movement of which he did not always do more than serve as the expression. The point is that with him the idea of the freedom of the lay powers to be found in Dante, in Marsiglio, in Wyclif, steps upon the stage of practical politics, and connects itself with that general tendency towards hereditary territorial sovereignty without which it could have had no lasting effect. His desire for a really omnipotent and reforming council puts him alongside of those Conciliar writers whom we discussed last week. He did but develop some of their views about the rights of the laity and also of national independence. We cannot understand the movement which succeeded without reference to those which failed. The unity and universality and essential rightness of the sovereign territorial State, and the denial of every extra-territorial or independent communal form of life, are Luther's lasting contribution to politics. Yet even the form which he gave to his ideas endured a long time. His return to the Scripture and the extremely literal interpretations which he favoured, coupled with his disbelief in ecclesiastical power, made that absolute reliance on the literal sense of the texts about non-resistance to temporal authority the *cachet* of all royalist writing for a couple of centuries. The idea that the " powers that be " could refer to ecclesiastical authorities (which we saw was the medieval gloss on an awkward passage) naturally appeared ridiculous, if the whole of the Papal authority was the wickedest of all usurpations. Luther's genuine belief in " Liberty " finds expression in the *Liberty of a Christian Man*, and he uses words about the necessity of consent to justify laws which might have been expanded into a programme of freedom. So far, however, as this was done by Karlstadt, the Peasants or the Anabaptists, Luther repudiated their glosses, and became more and more hostile to any claim to limit princely power. It was by transferring the notion of non-resistance from the Imperial to the princely, and from the ecclesiastical to the lay power, that Luther gave to the doctrine of the Divine Right of Kings such universal and enduring prevalence. Passive obedience even to the Emperor indeed was pretty nearly all that was wanted to enable Lutheranism to grow ; it was only when Charles was able seriously to undertake the subjugation of Protestantism, that some theory of princely resistance had to be found.

For the years immediately succeeding the Diet of Worms, the practice of passive obedience, *i.e.*, the mere non-fulfilment of the edict, was quite sufficient. So that for longer than he realized, Luther was able to believe both in the Imperial and the princely authority; eventually, rather reluctantly he had to give up the former and justify the League of Schmalkalde.

It is with Luther that the long catena of Protestant divines on the side of non-resistance quoted by Salmasius begins; and he fixed, in this respect, or rather expressed the attitude of mind, which remained distinctively Protestant in all those countries (except Scotland) where Protestantism was national in character.

Roughly speaking, what Luther did in the world of politics was to transfer to the temporal sovereign the halo of sanctity that had hitherto been mainly the privilege of the ecclesiastical; and to change the admiration of men from the saintly to the civic virtues, and their ideals from the monastic life to the domestic, and all this as a part of the Divine ordering of the world. It was largely an accident that for the next two centuries these ideals redounded to the advantage of monarchy, and made the prince an autocrat in his own country. It only needed a change in the depositary of the sovereign power to make the same conceptions of the holiness of the State and the duty of non-resistance apply to the citizen of a democracy unified according to the ideas of Rousseau.

We turn for a little to a teacher anything but religious. It would be impossible to gain any adequate notion of the intellectual forces, that made up the mind of the average European statesman from 1600–1800 if we altogether omitted a consideration of the influence of Machiavelli. This must be the cause for his introduction into this course of lectures; this and one or two other reasons to be noted presently. It is now generally recognised that it was not monarchy but efficiency for which Machiavelli cared, and that it was only as a means to an end that he recommended tyranny. His preference, as indicated in the *Discorsi*, was clearly for some form of republic or constitutional monarchy, of which he took the French to be an example[11]. It may, however, be pointed out that the ideal of efficiency, if it be *exclusive*, will almost invariably tend to become an apology for tyranny, whether that of mob or monarch. The moment a man begins to think of any particular reform as more important than any loss to human character that can accrue through waiting on the task of educating the public conscience to effect it, the moment, that is, he sets this or that object as an end itself irrespective of the men who are to reach it, he is bound to become impatient of average stupidity, contemptuous of all rules, legal, moral or customary, which delay the accomplishment of his ends. "The true type of Strafford was the revolutionary idealist hewing his way to his end without regard to obstacles." What is true of Strafford or Bacon, as apologists for despotism in their desire for the quick removal of abuses, is true of anarchists like Ravachoff or the Phœnix Park murderers, or terrorists like Robespierre, and many amiable socialists to-day. In all cases, the desire for some particular reform tends to remove that care for the gradual education of character, which is more important than any given measures, is always so easy to ignore or thrust aside in the enthusiasm of a great cause, and is yet at the basis of all true liberty, whether religious or civil. The cause for which Machiavelli laboured was, outside the religious sphere, as noble as a man could have, and the piercing eloquence of the last chapter of the *Prince* must find an echo in the hearts of many who denounce his system[12]. Yet, if once the safety of any particular country be set up as an end in itself, it is clear that any and all of the measures which Machiavelli approves may be not only necessary, but praiseworthy[13]. Moreover, as we now know, all he did was to express the actual and existing assumptions, on which the scramble of competition was carried out among Italian princes.

What we are here concerned with is so much of those assumptions as were to influence in the future the politics of Europe. For this purpose we may for the moment rule out as of secondary importance all the means which may be justified from Machiavelli in regard to the internal relations of a ruler and his subjects, presuming that here, as elsewhere, Machiavelli had the future with him, and that efficient extra-legal autocracy was to be the ideal and practice for the government of European States for the next two and a half centuries.

It is in International Politics, however, that Machiavelli has had his greatest influence. With territorialism dominant, and the unity, however vague, afforded by a single religious system with a recognised code of law, at an end, the relations between States became more definitely those of the "state of nature" than they had been since the early days of the Roman Republic; the struggle for existence became more keen, and less obviously subject to any rules than it had ever been

before among civilised peoples.   Now the remarkable
point about Machiavelli (and even of his adversaries) is
what he omits[14].   I do not think it quite true to say that
he is "inspired by the passionless curiosity of the man
of science[15]" ; for the question at the back of his mind
was never what is the true science of politics ; but what
rules of prudence may be garnered from history or contemporary experience to guide us here and now.   But
what distinguishes him from his predecessors is his
entire discarding of any attempt to found a philosophy
of right.   To speak generally, all political speculation in
the past few centuries might be described as directed
to that end ; to Machiavelli, however, the questions which
seemed of such importance to S. Thomas and the
innumerable other writers on the subject of politics,
whatever side they took, were simply beside the mark.
He did not, probably, consciously omit them ; it never
occurred to him to discuss them.   The practical end ruled
everything, and as has been said " he is the founder of
utilitarian ethics."   It is remarkable, too, that he expresses but the atmosphere of the Italy of his day.
Even a writer definitely hostile to him, like Botero, in his
work *Il Ragion di Stato*, yet makes very much the same
assumptions, and appeals to the same kind of motives.

What has vanished from Machiavelli is the conception
of natural law.   So long as this belief is held, however
inadequate may be the conception as a view of the facts
of life, it affords some criterion for submitting the acts of
statesmen to the rule of justice, and some check on the
rule of pure expediency in internal and of force in external politics.   The more, however, law comes to be
seen to be merely positive, the command of a law-giver,
the more difficult is it to put any restraints upon the

action of the legislator, and in cases of monarchical government to avoid a tyranny. So long as ordinary law is regarded as to some extent merely the explication of law natural, so long there is some general conception remaining by which governments may be judged ; so long, in fact, do they rest on a confessedly moral basis. And this remains true, however little their ordinary actions may be justifiable, however much they may in practice overstep their limits. When, however, natural law and its outcome in custom, are discarded, it is clear that the ruler must be consciously sovereign in a way he has not been before, and that his relations to other rulers will also be much freer—especially owing to the confusion of *jus naturale* with *jus gentium* which is at the bottom of International Law. The despots of Italy were, in fact, in the Greek sense, tyrants, and Machiavelli did little more than say so. What gives him his importance is that what was true of the small despots of Italy was going to become true of the national monarchs of Europe. To Machiavelli the State, *i.e.*, Italy, is an end in itself ; the restraints of natural law seem mere moonshine to a man of his *positif* habit ; and he substitutes the practical conceptions of *reason of state* as a ground of all government action, and the *balance of power* as the goal of all international efforts, in place of the ancient ideals, inefficient enough but not insignificant, of internal justice and international unity. Now no one can deny that very largely they have been ruling in Europe ever since ; just as it was only three centuries and a half after his day, that Italy herself reached, under the leadership of Cavour, the goal, which Machiavelli had set before her, by methods which his typical man of *virtu* would scarcely have disdained.

We have now to enquire how it was that this notion of *natural law*, which in some sense ruled speculation from Cicero to Rousseau, has disappeared so entirely before the gaze of Machiavelli. In the first place we must always remember his purpose. He was not writing abstract treatises on government, but looking at facts past or present with the hope of bringing peace to " the distressful country." He did not start from any ideals of government or desire to find them, he did not meditate on the philosophy of law. Social justice had to him no meaning apart from the one great end of the salvation of his country. He had the limited horizon and unlimited influence which always come of narrowing the problem. There is a sense in which it is quite true that *salus populi* is *suprema lex*; for laws and rules suitable for ordinary times are not always suitable for emergencies, *e.g.*, an interference with personal liberty at other times intolerable, or an executive justice in essence purely administrative, could be endured even by the British Philistine, if there were real and immediate danger of invasion. Every nation would allow that there are emergencies in which it is the right and the duty of a government to proclaim a state of siege and authorize the suppression of the common rules of remedy by the rapid methods of martial law. Now what Machiavelli did, or rather what his followers have been doing ever since, is to elevate this principle into the normal rule for statesmen's actions. When his books are made into a system they must result in a perpetual suspension of the *habeas corpus* acts of the whole human race. It is not the removal of restraints under extraordinary emergencies that is the fallacy of Machiavelli, it is the erection of this removal into an

ordinary and every-day rule of action. Machiavelli's
maxims are merely the paradoxes of self-defence—just
as the mildest householder may adopt a *ruse* to get rid
of a burglar, or defend himself with a revolver against
violence. It is the transformation of these paradoxes
into principles, that has been so dangerous. The net
result of his writings has been that, in the long run,
Machiavelli's principles have remained, as they ought,
as a mere *Deus ex machina* for internal politics ; but
have become a commonplace in International diplomacy.
They are of little harm if they are regarded, like justifiable homicide, as a necessary breach of the law ; but
when they come to be regarded as the law itself the
situation alters. Paradoxes only become dangerous
when they are transformed into platitudes. Machiavelli
actually saw in Italy that the restraints of law and
custom had broken down, and he strove to make the best
of the existing conditions. The mistake of his followers
is that they treat him as though he had been interpreting
and laying down rules of universal validity, which it is
quixotic even to desire to alter.

But this is not all. There can, I think, be no doubt
that the action of one community in its own real or
supposed interests must have had an influence on the
mind of the observer. The autocracy of the Papacy
was founded on a theory of sovereignty, which was with
Machiavelli beginning to pass over to the secular State.
The dispensing power proclaimed more clearly and more
universally than any other instrument that laws were
but the creature of the ruler and might be disregarded
at his will. The lines quoted by Pasquier show us how
widespread was the feeling already voiced by Nicolas of
Cues, that the crying need of the Church was that laws

should be regarded as having something more than a
merely positive sanction.

> " Je hay ces mots de puissance absolue,
>   De plein pouvoir, de propre mouvement ;
>   Aux saints Decrets ils ont prémièrement
>   Puis à nos loix la puissance tollue[16]."

It is true that the Pope was not supposed to
have the power to dispense with natural laws, yet
the jurisdiction for so long assumed and exercised
in the matter of oaths must have largely rendered
nugatory this restriction, and he was supposed to
be able to dispense with bigamy. For this matter is
decisive. It cannot be too often repeated that the fundamental difference between Machiavelli and Grotius is
concerned with this question. Grotius' contention, which
is denied implicitly and explicitly by Machiavelli, is that
human life is essentially a society, and that certain laws,
of which fidelity to plighted word is the most important,
are therefore as immutable as human nature) On this
notion he rears the whole of his system. Now it was
this system which had been shattered, or largely shattered, by the claims of the Popes to " interpret " the
obligation of oaths. It is interesting to note that one
of the most important instances of it was in direct
support of that autocratic power which Machiavelli did
so much to advance. Innocent III denied the right
of a king to diminish his regality, even though he had
sworn to the concession. This was erected by Bartolus
into a general principle of the inalienability of sovereignty[17]. It was exactly this notion, that charters
and liberties were matters of royal favour, leaving the
imperium unimpaired, which was at the bottom of the

dealings of James I with his Parliament, which was largely at the basis of those actions of Charles I, that made the Commons distrust all his offers, and which continued down to our own day to disturb the attempts to bind monarchs to constitutional government. It is against this that Talleyrand protested in writing to Louis XVIII, that the rights he guaranteed by the Charter must be recognised by him as inherent rights, not merely *octroyée*, and therefore presumably capable of being withdrawn. The *dispensing power* as a practice, the *plenitudo potestatis* as a theory, had for some time released the Popes from the restraints of law—which was only what Machiavelli did for the princes. It was, moreover, in the history of the Church more than elsewhere, that the complete subjection of the individual conscience to the interest of the community was demanded and often obtained. The danger of Machiavellianism is that it demands of the individual in the service of the community the sacrifice, not merely of his purse or his person, but also of his conscience. This we shall see exemplified (as indeed is inevitable) more completely in the history of the Church than elsewhere.

The Council of Constance had decreed in its dealings with Hus that faith was not to be kept with heretics; if for heretics we read enemies, and for Church read State, we have the whole of Machiavelli's system in this one decree. We must remember that the fundamental conception of a heretic is not a person who is in intellectual error, but a rebel against ecclesiastical authority, and hence the analogy to politics is even closer than might at first appear. Hus was condemned as a religious outlaw to whom human rights no more belonged. If the Church could do this there is nothing that the

State might not also do in its interests, provided of
course the existence of the State is a good thing[18].
Moreover it became customary to appeal to this decree
in justification of practices generally known as Machiavellian. In the *Satyre Ménippée* an instance is afforded.

Compare the spirit of this famous decree, which
practically declares the heretic a "rightless" person,
with the extremely grudging condemnation of the
principles of Jean Petit, who alleged that he had the
support of the greatest canonists in favour of his thesis
that a tyrant, *i.e.*, a traitor, may be slain by anyone at
any moment[19]. We shall see how strongly the tide has
been running in the Church towards making the Law,
whether positive or natural, a thing of nought where the
interests of the community itself are concerned. If it is
Machiavelli who declares that the end justifies the means,
what is most original in him is his *naiveté*. He says
what other people thought, and he regards the civil state
as an end in itself[20]. The hierarchical party regarded no
secular State as of such importance that it could dispense
with all obligations, but it tended so to regard the
Church although, as we have said, it did not expressly
deny that natural law was binding even on the Popes.

It is, however, undoubted that that complete supersession of the individual by the social conscience which
is the *cachet* of Machiavelli was carried to its highest in
an ecclesiastical community[19]. The Society of Jesus
expressly denies to the individual the duty of acting
upon his conscience where it conflicts with the orders of
the superiors[21].

If we take this in conjunction with the famous clause
about the individual being *quasi cadaver* in the hands of

the Society, we shall see how complete is the denial of any individual sense of right or wrong or at any rate its absorption in the social.

The point to notice is that in both cases the error arises from preaching the doctrine of self-sacrifice in an unreal and artificial form. From the point of view of Christian ethics self-sacrifice, which means the spirit of giving, is not at all identical with the self-annihilation which is the last word of the Pessimism of modern times, and of some systems of Oriental ethics. Love does not destroy, it enhances individuality. The gulf between the Christian ideal of Love, and the ideals of Buddha, Schopenhauer and Tolstoi, which mean the destruction of the individual, is at bottom irreconcileable; yet both by adversaries and believers, the mistake of confounding the one with the other is often made. Ethically what Machiavelli and the Jesuit Institutes alike demand is the complete absorption of the individuality by the social organism. Practically this will mean the tyranny of some one individual or group who can make the Society efficient. It makes no difference whether the community be religious or secular, except that the temptation to make the error is very much greater in the case of a religious body, whose ends are by all adherents recognised to be holy. The much abused morality of the Jesuits is only the most thorough-going form of an error, which will probably exist, so long as it is possible for men to conceive great ends, and to be impatient of the hindrances to their accomplishment. Still the fact remains that the principle leads commonly to the idealisation of an individual, who can promote these ends at the cost of ordinary rules of right; whether it be Cesare Borgia, Bismarck, or Frederic II in the civil sphere, or Gregory XIII striking his medal and illuminating Rome in honour of the massacre of S. Bartholomew, or Escobar torturing reason in the effort to make morality smooth to the worldly-minded. The Society of Jesus, perhaps, gives us in the development of probabilism the truest object-lesson in the inevitable consequences of the acceptance of Machiavelli's principles in regard to communities. These principles are, briefly, that right and wrong are terms that have no meaning in regard to the relations between societies, although in the ordinary view the moral code is to retain unimpaired its authority over private life.

The Society of Jesus, speaking broadly, transfers these principles to a religious body, *i.e.*, it recognises, not that the end justifies the means, a most important point not to be here discussed[22], but that the individual conscience is to be as nothing as compared with the commands of the community. The life of Parsons, the plot of Pius V against Elizabeth, and the actions of Garnet in regard to the conspirators of the Gunpowder Plot form the best commentary on this. This of course does not imply that the individual conscience ought not to be enlightened by the social reason. It is quite possible to think that Luther and Hus must have been wrong in carrying criticism to the point of rebellion. But that would not have made it right, for either thinking, as he did, of his duty to have acted differently. It may for instance be wrong to become an atheist; but it is not merely the right, it is the duty of a convinced atheist to act on his belief.

Having thus destroyed, in the interests of the Society (which is of course identified with those of religion), the individual conscience, men were driven on to destroy the

sanction of morality even in private life. The obvious
rule for conduct is assuredly that while a man is
responsible not only for what he does but for what he
thinks right to do, he is bound at any moment to carry
out the course he deems right, after taking every means
to enlighten his conscience. Probabilism directly denies
this, it asserts that it is morally justifiable for a man to
pursue the course, which he believes to be wrong, if only
he can find a single authority of weight who declares it
to be right, *i.e.*, if Guy Fawkes thinks treason a sin, he
is yet justified in committing it and still retaining his
opinion, if only he can quote Mariana, say, on the other
side. It is clear that this theory is entirely destructive
of all morality in a world where opinion is not unanimous,
for it takes away that individual sense of responsibility
for action which is its very basis. It does not even make
morality social. Yet this theory was so bound up with
the interests of the Society, although it was a Dominican
(Medina) not a Jesuit who invented it, that it gradually
became practically impossible for its members to express
any other view. Gonzalez himself made a heroic
endeavour in conjunction with Pope Innocent XII to
remove the stigma from the Society. It was all in vain,
however ; it was with the utmost difficulty and only by
the use himself of Machiavellian tactics, that he escaped
being compelled to hold a general congregation which
would certainly have deposed him, while every possible
effort was put forth by the "assistants" and others to
prevent the publication of his treatise against Probabilism.
The history of the Society of Jesus is not merely in its
common fame an exposition of the principles of Machiavelli ; it affords in its constitution the very completest
exposition of his doctrine ; which is that the individual

conscience is to be sacrificed to the community; while its most characteristic moral principle extends into private life the same destruction of moral responsibility, which the ordinary follower of Machiavelli would leave untouched[23].

Other evidences can be given, if need be, that it is impossible to remove the very notion of morality from international affairs, without in the long run undermining it in private life. The principles of Machiavelli have not as a matter of fact been confined to the sphere of State actions. Roughly speaking it may be said to have been the belief of ordinary statesmen from Machiavelli's time to the triumph of his principles under Cavour and Bismarck that the code of morals, and of Christian morals, is obligatory on individuals, but that in international matters any ideal of morality at all is not so much superfluous as pernicious, that "the Law of the beast" not only does but ought to reign unchecked with no attempt to interfere with the struggle of existence.

Now, as a matter of fact, this conception has had to be extended. First of all the obvious distinction between commercial and private life causes a similar assertion to be made in matters of trade. Business is business; and the "economic man" is held up, not as a mere rough generalisation from experience, but as the ideal of commerce. The evil wrought by the "orthodox" economists is not that they observed facts and deduced sequences of cause and effect, but that by so many of their followers, and still more by the average bourgeois their abstractions were regarded as *ideals*; and their delineation of what (with certain reserves) commonly is, was regarded as a statement of what ought to be in the best of all possible worlds. It is not the facts observed but their erection into an ideal, which is the cause, rightly or wrongly, of the humanitarian attack on the old economists, led by men like Ruskin and Carlyle.

The attack was directed against exactly the same notions as those of Machiavelli, only applied to commerce instead of the State. There was the same repulsion at seeing the meaner facts of daily life elevated into a principle; the same horror at the denial that moral obligations could have any meaning in regard to trade relations. In both cases there was the same attempt to assert some fundamental principles of human brotherhood and to claim that they are deeper than the apparently impassable exclusiveness of national or commercial individualism; and that at any rate the failure of men consistently to carry out the highest ideal is no reason for denying that such ideals ought to be striven for.

Our generation has seen one further step taken in the extension of the principles of Machiavelli. The doctrines associated with the name of Nietzsche are exactly similar to those of Machiavelli, except that they are now purely limited to individual ends; and that no sanctifying means in the thought of the community is allowed to interfere with the unchecked pursuit of individual strength. Machiavelli banishes the notion of right from politics. It is found impossible, however, to confine his principles within the limits originally allowed to them; and the economists or rather some of their followers banish ethics from commerce; and assert a still sharper distinction between family and business concerns than Machiavelli allowed between the State and the individual. Nietzsche goes one better and leaves triumphant, unashamed, the *Uebermensch* with his eagle of pride and his serpent of cunning, rejoicing pitilessly over the weak and suffering, and scorning the very notion of Love. The attempt of Nietzsche is to get rid of all ethical ideals which recognise the value of the sympathetic virtues. His frank return to the ethics of Paganism minus its better side is but the logical and inevitable outcome of the principles of Machiavelli when allowed unchecked predominance. For many generations of men it has been possible honestly to believe that all the notions of human life in society which underlie any claim to found an international code of ethics might be surrendered, while current ideals could retain their authority over the internal affairs of nations and still direct the conscience of individuals. This was an illusion inevitable perhaps in the general condition of affairs, but none the less an illusion. Nietzsche deserves the gratitude of all friends of humanity for the service he has done in tearing off the mask from human selfishness, and showing that the whole sphere of private life cannot in the long run be different from the ideals accepted in public affairs. Like Machiavelli too Nietzsche has the ill reputation which always attaches to one who removes that veil of respectability with which men love to disguise their real life. Nietzsche sees as Machiavelli saw the glaring and ridiculous contrasts between the high nominal aims and the actual life of most men; he sees in men like Napoleon a difference from the average man not in the dominating selfishness of his aims, but only in the intellectual force and practical genius with which he strove for their accomplishment. So he bids us once more worship force in the person of Nietzsche and crucify Love in the person of Christ. The principles of

Nietzsche are only the principles that animate the gods of the modern world, Jay Gould, Whittaker Wright and their numberless imitators ; only they are expressed with a scorn of convention and a savage contempt for the nominal ideas of men which the money worshipper has not enough lucidity of mind to understand. Just as Machiavelli sets up Cesare Borgia, as the ideal " saviour of society," and declares Christian ethics to be dangerous in their political effects, so does Nietzsche scoff at the very idea of a religion of Love, and bid us prepare for a " transvaluation of all values " in a world where selfish distinction is to be the supreme ideal force, and the only vice of conquering heroes will be their occasional magnanimity.

It is impossible to understand Machiavelli without comparing him with Nietzsche whose *Uebermensch* is but Machiavelli's man of *virtu* stripped of those public ends which make even Cesare Borgia less odious. There is indeed a difference. Nietzsche's savage and cruel scorn has still some of the Teutonic barbarism against which the culture of Italy and the Renaissance protested. He has not the level gaze of Machiavelli into the world of fact, and he proclaims his love of iniquity with an ineffectual shriek. Machiavelli was always considering the practical problem, how is Italy to be saved ? The problem of Nietzsche so far as it is practical is simply this, how shall I best exhibit my scorn for the contrast between men's lives and their profession, my distaste for their inconsistencies, my hatred of anything that is meant by religion ? But no less than Machiavelli does Nietzsche lay bare some dominant tendencies of our modern world ; no less than Machiavelli does he make it necessary for Christians to see that in the coming

century they will be combating, not a spirit which like
Mill denies the authority of Christ's Person, while
accepting that of his character; but *der Geist der stets
verneint*, the spirit which asserts that they are fools who
even admire Jesus, and that the morality of the Cross is
raving lunacy.

Having seen the extension of Machiavelli's doctrine
both into the highest spheres, religious community, and
into the lowest, private life, let us close by stating one
or two of the causes which have rendered him so difficult
to refute.   Here again a study of Nietzsche will be found
to help us.   It was not so much against Christianity, as
against Schopenhauer, that Nietzsche, originally a disciple,
wrote to protest.   In other words Nietzsche's attack is
effective because it expresses the rights of individuality
against those who would deny them.   As we have seen,
the ethics of Christianity do not and cannot mean the
annihilation of the self, yet the way in which they are
sometimes preached would imply this; the ethics are
really (so far as the individual is concerned) described
by Creighton "The perfection of character by effort."
In other words the end of man is the development of his
character, as Humboldt said: only Christianity tells him
that it cannot be developed in isolation and that the spirit
of giving is the true motive of life as against the spirit
of getting—or rather that all getting, whether money
or reputation or pleasure, is only a means to the great
end of giving.   This is the law of sacrifice, applicable
to family life, to commerce and to international relations,
e.g., Empire is only justifiable by the effects on the
character of nations.   If and so far as the English
retention of India stands for justice and liberty where
otherwise there would be cruelty and wrong, it is

justified on this ground, but Empire as mere possession used for its own ends is no more ethically worthy than private wealth selfishly enjoyed. But that there are real purposes in the life of a nation which it is meant to fulfil is at once the only justification of its continuance, while the affirmation of his own existence for high ends is the essential object of the individual. It is the denial of these ends in the interests of an exaggerated altruism by writers like Schopenhauer and Tolstoi, which is the excuse if not the justification of Nietzsche and his followers, who assert the right of the individual to be, and are instinct with genuine vitality. Against the travesties of Christian ethics which end logically in the denial of immortality Nietzsche did well to protest. Against a view which would destroy national conscience in a general cosmopolitanism and a sentimental humanitarianism, Machiavelli had his uses. At the moment when Machiavelli wrote, a thorough-going admission of international right could have been held to mean an affirmation of the only powers in any degree recognised at the head of Europe, the Pope or the Emperor; and would have produced more evils than it remedied. The fundamental truth in Machiavelli is the *Selbständigkeit* of nations, just as it is, though in a different form, in the teaching of Luther and the Divine Right of Kings. It is, perhaps, partly in the failure to recognise this, that is due the comparative futility of the replies to Machiavelli.

Further it is to be noted, that it is an error to assert, as some anti-Machiavellians have done, that there is no difference at all between *public and private morality*. The real value of Machiavelli is in his raising or causing men to raise the question, what is the difference? That there is such a distinction is clear alike from the general practice and common judgment of mankind, as Bishop Creighton says: "There is a difference between public and private morality."

It is, however, one thing to assert that there is a difference between the conduct of communities, or the relations of men in business and their private life, and quite another to assert that there is no rule of right at all in international matters. Here again Nietzsche helps us. The recognition of individuality means the definite repudiation of altruism, in the strictest sense, and exclusively considered. Moralists like Butler are right, not un-Christian, when they speak of a reasonable self-love in individuals; and the wholesale melting of Christian ethics into mere sentimental benevolence which in the long run is destructive of everybody's personality is an error. So with the State. A regard for its own existence, safety, and strength is not to be treated, as it may easily be, as a concession to an iniquitous selfishness; but as the right and duty of statesmen.

This implies the right of self-defence of war, of the ruses which accompany war, and the stratagems of diplomacy in a state of things bordering upon war. In fact, self-defence carries with it among nations the same or similar consequences as it does among schoolboys. Unless these things are recognised as legitimate, in any conditions existing or likely for some generations to exist, it will be vain that preachers and moralists will thunder against the immorality of politics or the selfishness of nations. The rights of national individuality correctly understood, and its corollaries in practice, are the residuum of truth in Machiavelli's system, which gives it its appeal ; just as the right to personal development and its corollaries is the residuum of truth in the so-called ethics of Nietzsche.

Also it must be recognised that in a state of things like international politics, where there is no recognised superior, and even International Law is but the voice of public opinion, the condition of affairs is very much more nearly akin to the state of nature as imagined by Hobbes than it is in relation of individuals.

In the actual world men have the defects of their qualities. In forming moral judgments we commonly and rightly grade men's faults differently according to their circumstances. Cowardice is the supreme fault of a private soldier ; and in return for bravery, other faults are treated as venial in comparison. So it should be in the historical judgments of statesmen. Patriotism, sincerity and devotion to the interests of his country are the *sine quâ non* for a statesman. If in the course of a career like Bismarck's, actions are committed which cannot be condoned, these actions are not to be admired, but are to be treated more leniently than any dereliction of his cardinal duty, devotion to his people. The error of Machiavelli and his followers is, that they assert such actions to be right ; the error of too many moralists is, that in their desire to secure the supremacy of the moral law, they assert that such actions are equally sinful with private vices. Assuredly the judgment of history ought to be that they are deeply blameworthy and not to be commended, but that they are to be regarded as the natural faults of a politician. We should in fact judge the statesman's crimes not as anything else but crimes, but still as crimes for which there is enormous temptation.

This consideration, I think, it is which enables us to decide for the author in the attack which Lord Acton directed against the judgment of Bishop Creighton in his history. Acton's theory, as stated there and more completely elsewhere, was definitely that "great men are nearly always bad men," and that ultramontanism was a doctrine of murder and that no one who even defends such a doctrine can be other than *ipso jure* damned[24].

The length to which he carried this view will be even more apparent when some of his letters to Döllinger are published. In the first place it may be pointed out that the actual doctrine is a peculiar one; because Newman (for he was included) and others either condoned persecution or praised those who did condone it, we are to make the assertion that they could not have been "in a state of grace." Acton is quite clear that what he condemns is Machiavellism in Church matters. But he uses the medieval notion, that we can know the condition of other men's souls in order to condemn these men for their failure to hold the modern notion of the duty of religious toleration.

Now this appears to be unreasonable; and entirely to lose sight of or rather to repudiate the consideration noticed above. It may well be that persecution is not only an error, but a crime; it may well be, as Creighton himself pointed out, that those who condoned or approved persecution cannot, except they are intellectual underlings, be acquitted of moral blame therefor. But it is one thing to assert that toleration both is and always has been a Christian duty, that the failure to see this is on the part of a thinker not merely an error, but a sin, that so far as history makes moral judgments it is to condemn him; and quite another to declare with

Acton, that it is a sin in a different category from all other sins, that it subjects the doer to the last penalty, and that we know that it does so.

Now it is the failure to perceive this, that runs through so much of the easily inflicted blame of statesmen's iniquities. Those who assert the inalienable supremacy of the moral law, and repudiate the principles of Machiavelli, are in the opinion of the writer not merely right, but asserting a truth, most eminently needed to-day, and needed especially by historians. For the first and most plausible temptation of the historical student is to accept the code of Machiavelli, and write accordingly; and in the long run such acceptance, if widely followed, must debase the national conscience. In later days when his smaller works are forgotten, it will probably be found that the most enduring of all Acton's claims to greatness was his passionate insistence on the need of moral law in the lives of nations and Churches, no less than in those of individuals. The protest which he made both in season and out of season on this subject is his real contribution to his time. But along with this there went an absoluteness of statement which the subject will not bear. He too had the defects of his qualities—and in order to ensure that we should not fall into the common error of average humanity and condone too readily the crimes of statesmen because they were successful, or those of Churchmen because they were sincere; he sweeps into one net of indiscriminate and unrelieved condemnation Newman and Fénelon, Rosmini and Dupanloup, and prophesies for them with certainty a future, of which he will not even profess to be assured in regard to the vilest and most criminal of mankind. With a deep reverence for the utterer of these condemnations, and for the general principles that guided him, I cannot but think that this extremity of over-statement injures the very causes he desired to promote and has a tendency to make it the ground of the too easy and too lasting victory of Machiavelli over all his adversaries.   In human judgment it is, I think, undoubted that the statesman and the ecclesiastic must be allowed to have the defects of their qualities.   While we are never to assert that these defects are merits (which is to justify Machiavelli) or that they ought not to have been avoided; or that right ought not to rule in politics as elsewhere; we are bound to admit that amid the innumerable temptations to which human nature is prone, there are certain more peculiarly dangerous to every condition of life, and that in considering the conduct of our fellows, we should be less rigid to those faults, whatever they may be, which are natural and incident to their position.

There is, perhaps, one more consideration which needs to be urged.   The code of morals considered as a code is in the Christian view not absolute.   The rules of conduct are but the rough formulae by which is expressed the fundamental fact of Christian life, devotion to a Person.   It may seem strange to seek in the very foundation of Christianity, love to God and man, for anything like an excuse for principles so universally execrated as those of Machiavelli or Escobar.   But we have to consider not merely the obvious fact that from the Christian point of view such principles are odious, but also the other fact that no principles are widely prevalent without their possessing some real ground or appealing to some truth, however distorted may be the form in which it is represented. Now the cause, if not the excuse, of all systems which casuistically interpret the ordinary rules of morality is that fundamentally morality is not obedience to a code of rules, but a life of loving devotion to a Person. As William of Ockham said, it is only the first commandment which is absolute, all the rest are positive and therefore may on occasion be relaxed. This is the supreme difference between Christian morality, and mere systems of ethics, like that raised on the Categorical Imperative of Kant. So far as I can see, all those systems readily succumb to the destructive dialectics of Mr G. E. Moore in his *Principia Ethica*. But the Christian system is left intact, because it is not (strictly speaking) a system at all. In his last chapter Mr Moore declares that " personal affections and artistic pleasures " are the only " true goods " in our experience. There is nothing in this incompatible with Christian ethics. The only difference between a Christian and Mr Moore is, that the former does, while Mr Moore (on grounds stated elsewhere) does not include among these the personal affection to God, and the Living Christ, which are at the basis of Christian living. It cannot be too often repeated that destructive criticism levelled at all the various schemes of ethics as immutable systems has no force against Christian ethics, of which the rules are nothing but inadequate and temporary *formulae*, expressing, in ordinary cases, the consequences in practical life of the love to God and our neighbour, which is their essence.

But this is a digression, however important. The point is that the rules of morality are not of the nature of eternal truths, immutable in their authority—but only rough statements of what in ordinary cases is man's duty.

Hence the need of some consideration of those extraordinary cases when they do not hold, and also the
extreme danger of making those exceptions into ordinary
rules.   As we saw, the real danger of Machiavelli is that
he or the system attributed to him makes the exception,
i.e., salus populi suprema lex, into a rule of action.   In the
same way the danger of systems of casuistry, as actually
studied, is that they inevitably direct attention to those
limiting conditions, in which the ordinary maxim does
not hold, or else to those doubtful cases, innumerable in
theory, rare in practice, in which it is genuinely difficult
to discern the right course of action.   Even Probabilism
would have no meaning, much less any danger, if there
were no cases in which the judgment was in a difficulty ;
for under these conditions there could be no differences of
opinion among authorities, and there could be no chance
for a man to take a course made tenable by some
authority, whose reasonings he did not himself echo.
Whether we like it or not, we cannot, in regarding
human experience as a whole, deny that there are cases
both in individual and national life in which circumstances
do alter cases, and in such cases for instance as the
favourite Jesuit case of a starving man and a loaf of
bread, or the public one of a statesman's ruse to prevent
an invasion, or an act of violence like Hodgson's murder
of the princes in the Mutiny.   In these cases it may be
true that there is no ground for relaxing the ordinary
code of morals (I am not speaking of law), but other
instances could easily be found in which there clearly is
such ground.   As long as this is the fact—and it always
will be the fact—it is idle to blame those who in cases
of this sort take a different view from the moralist as to
their duty.   The excuse of Machiavelli is that he wrote

in a time when for his country such a condition was a fact ; the condemnation of Machiavellism is that it raised these maxims of an unquiet time, dangerous enough even then, into a universal system, denied the obligation of right and wrong *in toto* in regard to international politics and so asserted the truth of the individuality of national life that it entirely denied or ignored the companion truth of the solidarity of humanity.

LECTURE IV.

THE *POLITIQUES* AND RELIGIOUS TOLERATION.

It would be misleading to pass from the ideas of non-resistance and the Divine authority of the ruler as defined by Luther, and the conception of the State as an end in itself superior to all rules of Law, natural and civil, to which Machiavelli gave currency, without some mention of that party in France, which in the sixteenth century carried these ideas to their fullest extent. It would be incorrect to give to the *Politiques* the attributes of a religious sect, although for the most part they were Catholics, and expressed what was for the next two centuries to be the dominant theory of Catholic princes in regard to the relation between the ecclesiastical and the civil State. Indeed the theory is undoubtedly still that of the foremost Roman Catholic States[1]. So much indeed was this the case that a Jesuit writer in the middle of the nineteenth century, seeking to restore the true conception of the relations of Church to State, declared that it had been largely forgotten owing to the prevalence of the ideas of the "regalist" writers[2]. These ideas come first into prominence in the *Politiques*, and find their next important expression in the writings of Sarpi and other Venetians against the claims of Paul V to interfere with the "natural liberty given by God unto the State." Although therefore the *Politiques* do not directly come within the scope of these lectures it seems necessary to consider them if our treatment is not to lack proportion. Moreover in view of the connection between Anglicanism in the seventeenth century and the doctrines of non-resistance and indefeasible hereditary right, it would be unreasonable to pass over in silence the first party whose very *raison d'être* was the assertion of principles associated by Englishmen with the Caroline Divines, with Filmer, and with James I. Besides, the importance of the *Politiques* in the development of religious toleration alone makes them worthy of notice in any sketch of the growth of liberty, nor would it be possible to discuss the opinions of Jesuits and Ligueurs without saying something of their most notable adversaries.

The writings of this party may be summarised as follows:—In the war of pamphlets initiated by the League we have the *Apologia Catholica* of Du Bellay (1586), written to maintain the claims of Henry of Navarre against the Guisian propaganda; the *Brutum Fulmen* of Hotman, written to denounce the interference of Pope Sixtus V in French affairs in his Bull of excommunication directed against Henry of Navarre, as a relapsed heretic; the *Vindiciae* of Servins, and other pamphlets republished in the third volume of Goldast's great collection. We must also include the *De Regno* of William Barclay, not a *livre de circonstance* but a complete treatise directed against all the Monarcho-machi, Buchanan, Brutus, *i.e.*, the author of the *Vindiciae contra Tyrannos*, and Boucher; the *De Republica* of Pierre Grégoire of Toulouse; the *Satyre Ménippée*,

and more especially the closing speech which is not
burlesque but gives the views of the loyal Catholics; the
Six Livres de la République of Jean Bodin, a scientific
treatise, but none the less the work of a thorough-going
Politique. The speeches of Michel de l'Hôpital and the
letters of the lawyer Pasquier throw valuable light on
the growth of ideas, especially in the matter of religious
toleration; the general feeling can be gathered from
Quatre Excellents Discours of the Sieur de Fay.

The rise and influence of the *Politiques* was indeed
the most notable sign of the times at the close of the
sixteenth century. The very existence of the party
testifies to the fact that for many minds the religion of
the State has replaced that of the Church, or, to be
more correct, that religion is becoming individual while
the civil power is recognised as having the paramount
claims of an organized society upon the allegiance of
its members. What Luther's eminence as a religious
genius partially concealed becomes more apparent in
the *Politiques*; for the essence of their position is to
treat the unity of the State as the paramount end, to
which unity in religion must give way. Luther neither
desired nor believed in toleration. It was the very
raison d'être of the *Politiques*, who for the most part
proclaimed the duty of loyalty to a sovereign of a
different religion, to proclaim the wisdom if not the
duty of toleration, and to assert the notion of indefeasible hereditary right. Their position in regard to a
Huguenot claimant to the crown was exactly that of the
Anglicans in regard to a Roman Catholic claimant in the
years 1679–81, when the Exclusion Bill divided parties
in England. Had James II followed the example of
Henri IV and made his Church a matter of policy

there is little doubt that he could have established a despotism, not inferior to that which Henri left to his successors. There is, however, this difference between the *Politiques* and the Anglican defenders of Divine Right. The former were, as their name implied, far more secular and utilitarian, more modern, more Machiavellian in the strict sense, than their English counterparts. It can hardly be said that there is a single argument that is not common to both sides, except those drawn from the Salic Law. But yet in England the religious duty of obedience, and if necessary of suffering, looms largest, while in France it is primarily of the unity of the State, and the actual evils of rebellion that we hear. The difference is one of degree and proportion rather than of theory and statement. But even here there is some difference. For the Salic Law, through which alone the Bourbons had a claim to the throne, compelled their supporters to develop the doctrine of legitimism in a far more purely legal spirit than was ever the case in England. It is indeed frequently said that indefeasible hereditary right is a "fundamental law." Acts like 35 Henry VIII. c. 1, which gave the King power to alter the succession, or 13 Elizabeth c. 1, which made it high treason to deny the power of Parliament to do so, are said to be *ipso facto* null. But this shadowy fundamental law is a very different thing from the definite words of the Salic Law, consecrated in its misinterpretation by the national struggle in the Hundred Years' War. This then is the first distinction between the *Politiques* and later and earlier apologists for the Divine Right of Kings. They are more legal in spirit—legitimism is the lineal descendant of the French monarchists,

just as Passive Resistance is the collateral heir o
the Anglicans. Legality is the watchword of the one
party—patience that of the other. The difference i
slight in appearance, but it goes deeper than is at firs
obvious. In the Anglican the Divine Right of Kings i
primarily a doctrine of the Church; it expressed at once
the tie that bound the Stuarts to Episcopacy and the
differences between England and Rome, between Prelacy
and Puritanism. To the *Politique* the Divine Right o
Kings was rather the natural right of the State, i
expressed his refusal to ruin the State for the sake o
religion, his nationalism as against an "alien invasion,"
his disgust at the flagrant illegalities perpetrated by the
League under the name of religion, the anti-clericalism
of lawyers like Pasquet, and the anti-regularism of the
secular priests.

Hence it is that the English believers in Divine
Right were the last to give up the theory of a uniform
State, in which religious liberty was forbidden, and
branded Hoadly as a heretic, not nearly so much
because of his theological heterodoxy as owing to hi
political liberalism, so that the issue between the famou
rivals in the Bangorian controversy was mainly tha
of religious toleration or its opposite[3]. The French
sticklers for the same doctrine were, however, in thi
period the main instrument in the movement agains
persecution. Under the son and grandson of Henri
after the State had won its victory, this phase passed
away. But in our period this is not so. The very
meaning of the party is the reverse of this. Driven by
the deplorable divisions of France to seek some shelte
for human life other than that afforded by ecclesiastica
sanction, some of the most moderate and far-sighted

minds discerned it in the one institution which both
parties could at least in words agree to reverence.
Nobody desired civil anarchy, or at any rate professed
to desire it, although Barclay in the *De Regno* tried to
prove that this was the real drift of the *Vindiciae contra
Tyrannos*. But unless religion could be removed from
the sphere of public policy, there was no likelihood of
anything but a continuance of this anarchy[4]. The most
crying evil in France was the ruin of all the nobler
elements of civilisation which followed in the wake of
religious animosities. The violent Catholics were hoping
for a restoration of peace and order, but only after such
a decisive victory as should result in the wholesale
extermination or banishment of their opponents. The
spirit which animates the writings of Louis d'Orleans
meant the destruction of unity in any State. Such a
prospect was repugnant alike on grounds of humanity
and policy to all those who were not wild partisans of
the old ideal of religious unity. The *Politiques* were
driven by the logic of facts to seek for a source of
national unity deeper than the ancient religious foundation. For this was irretrievably shattered or seemed
so, yet it appeared ridiculous to refuse the title of good
Frenchmen to some of the most illustrious houses
and some of the most industrious elements in the
country. Hence, beginning with the efforts of L'Hôpital[5],
enshrined for ever in his speeches, till after the
Politiques definitely became a party with S. Bartholomew, an event which exhibited in its most lurid form
the dangers of the ecclesiastical spirit, we find the
gradual development of the view that loyalty must not
be identified with orthodoxy, and that the State must, if
needful, be saved at the cost of toleration. The policy

F.   8

of Elizabeth was the same principle less completely
carried out; her statesmen claimed, and with substantial
justice, that political, not religious, motives were at
bottom of such persecution as they practised[6], nor was
there ever the same attempt to examine into thoughts
as was inherent in the Spanish Inquisition and the old
ideal of persecution for the sake of the heretic's soul.
We may trace the development of ideas as follows.
The medieval ideal regards civil and religious authority
as but two different aspects of God's grace of rule;
rebellion against ecclesiastical powers or heresy is thus
of the nature of treason, excommunication and outlawry
are convertible terms, a Church without the State may
be conceivable, but a State without a Church is not.
Religion must be the business of government which
merely wields the temporal sword for God's Church.
Persecution, too, is not merely practised on political
grounds, but in order to save the soul of the victim.
This ideal we call medieval.   It lingered on, however,
in the minds of many; and found, perhaps, in the
reign of King Jan of Leyden at Münster its completest
embodiment.   But it inspired the thought of Calvin and
Knox, was rarely absent from the minds of ecclesiastics
and was largely at the bottom of the Puritan revolution
and the acts of the New England Colonies; evidences
of this may be found in the words of the Solemn League
and Covenant[7].   The next stage is that forced upon the
Empire by the logic of facts and consecrated in the
religious peace of Augsburg, expressed in the phrase
cujus regio ejus religio.   In this stage unity in religion
is an element in the unity of the State, religious
differences must entail banishment; but an imperial
Church and a common religious law are abandoned.

each State goes its own way. This may be called *international toleration*. The next in order is the practice of Elizabeth, which is really tolerance for a consideration. Recusancy is allowed, but it must be paid for. The State makes a profit on its liberality and gives up the attempt to secure uniformity, except to the extent of forbidding all outward services or Churches which symbolise diversity. It is an attempt to secure the political advantages of religious uniformity, while reducing toleration to a *minimum*, and in a character-istically English fashion refusing to see what cannot be prevented. Dissent is put in the category of unrecognised but permitted vice.

Lastly we come to the toleration of the *Politiques*. Their theory asserts definitely that the State is in fact indifferent to religious unity and gives up the entire attempt to identify Church with State, never abandoned in England till 1688, and not altogether even then. It does not deny the right of the civil ruler to persecute or even his duty. It is not an assertion that toleration is in theory or in general the right course; but merely that it is a possible one, if circumstances make it expedient. It does not assert that persecution is always wrong, but only that toleration is sometimes right. This is the view of Bodin, Pasquier, L'Hôpital, and in general of their party. "Persecute by all means in the early stages of a heresy; keep it off, if you can, and if the cost in suffering or loss be not too excessive. But it may be excessive. In France at this moment it would be excessive. The new religion may be all its enemies declare it to be. But it is a fact. It is here. We can only get rid of it at the cost of deluging the country with blood, or replenishing the population of our enemies. Religious uniformity is a blessing; it is of the *bene esse* of a State. But it is not of the *esse*, and in case of need, we can live without it. Let us try and combine in the matters in which we have in common, the greatness and dignity of the national life, and allegiance to the sovereign. Let us endure as best we can the evil, real but unavoidable, of religious diversity. There are many evils like poverty and oppression which exist in a State, but do not destroy it. The Huguenots are of this nature. We do not like them. But we are loath to deny them all part or lot in the land. We must put up with them, and take precautions against any political dangers that religious independence might produce." This is the attitude of the *Politiques*, different from other parties in their own day, different from our views to-day. It would have approved the persecution of Nero, but condemned that of Diocletian. Toleration to them is not a virtue or duty or religion, as it has since become; it is a necessity, an experiment, a *pis aller*. What does come home to them with sacred authority, is the worth of the national life and loyalty to the monarchy which symbolises it[8].

Only in one or two thinkers such as Brown and Brentz and Castellio, Marnix (partially), and in one or two practical men like William the Silent, does toleration reach to the point of being regarded as a duty, and the tolerant habit of mind become an ideal[9]. Their day, however, had not yet come. And their whole attitude of mind is very different from that of the party we are considering. It may, however, be pointed out that while the *Politiques* desired toleration for the sake of the State, Brown demanded it in the name of religion. In order to preserve the State the *Politiques* would leave religion alone. In order to secure reforms, which were not desired or likely to be desired by the majority or the magistrate, Brown cries " Hands off " to the civil ruler, and preaches absolute independence of magisterial sanction. Thus when the *Politiques* had secured their object—order and national unity—their successors were free to destroy that very toleration on which it was based ; for the reason that their motive was never higher than expediency and national unity—and their bias in favour of kingly authority made it irritating to find any sphere of national life in which royal wishes were not obeyed. The theory of Brown, however, passed over in some degree to the Independents, and to Cromwell, and to Milton, and was to become the basis of the modern theory of toleration, as developed by Locke, Hoadly, Warburton and the ordinary Whig writers of the eighteenth century. Its distinctive note is its firm insistence on toleration as a natural right. The title of Hoadly's pamphlet, *The Common Rights of Citizens*, expresses the idea in the form it influenced modern life and procured the abolition of Tests. The originality of Brown consists in his recognition of the futility of expecting his own religious system ever to be universally imposed (this separates him from the ordinary Puritans), and in his clear enunciation of the private and individual nature of belief. In both these views he may be paralleled by some of the earlier Anabaptists, but they always showed themselves anxious when they had the power to make their religion as universal and persecuting as the Roman. So, indeed, did the Independents with but slight qualifications.

However this may be, it behoves us to recognise the

enormous work done by the *Politiques* in exalting the idea of the State as something which demanded sacrifices for its own sake, including a sacrifice of the ancient ideals of religious unity, and in making dominant the notion of the absolute and binding character of hereditary claims upon allegiance. Their ground for toleration was that same notion of making religion subservient to civil policy which resulted in Henry's submission to Rome, and perhaps inspired the ecclesiastical changes of William the Silent, and a good deal of the activity of Queen Elizabeth.

This trait, doubtless, it is which procured for the *Politiques* the nickname of Machiavellists. There were obvious grounds for so dubbing a party which made the monarchy its idol and avowedly put the interests of the State above those of religion, or at any rate religion organically living in a Church, and denied to it the right to determine political problems. Some of them also used language in regard to the assassination of the Duke and Cardinal of Guise at the States of Blois in 1588, which was in the usual sense of the term distinctly Machiavellian. As a general rule, however, the *Politiques* are scarcely to be charged with that entire supersession of morality by public policy, which is the usual connotation of Machiavellianism[10]. It is not natural law or the ordinary law which they desire to destroy, but the fundamental law of the French monarchy which they are determined to maintain. Their spirit is essentially legalist, which is the very opposite of Machiavelli.

This it is which makes them after Luther the protagonists of the Divine Right of Kings in its modern as distinct from the medieval phase, which was con-

cerned almost entirely with the Emperor and had little
to do with hereditary right. Like all those who found
politics endangered by ecclesiastical pretensions, they
asserted the immediate tenure of the crown from God
alone and indefeasible hereditary right. Indeed, the
situation of Henri IV made it incumbent upon the
Politiques to enunciate all the doctrines and arguments associated with this view. The strength of the
notion in the public mind is shown by the ridiculous
claim set up by the Guisian party, that all the kings
of the third race from Hugh Capet downwards were
usurpers, and that the Guises alone represented the
hereditary principle as being descended on the female
side from Charles the Great. This did not last,
for the fundamental principle of Ligueurs is the
sovereignty of the people, but it showed the extent
to which hereditary right was believed. Further, the
"monitorial bull" of Pope Sixtus V to Henri III,
and the assertion on behalf of the Cardinal of Lorraine of the principle of extra-territoriality, made it
necessary for the opposite party to assert the entire
Selbständigkeit of the civil power. We are treated
to all the usual arguments, the Scriptural, the legal,
the philosophical, the natural, in the *De Regno* of
Barclay; "by Me kings reign," and "they that resist
shall receive to themselves damnation," give the first,
and the civilian maxims of the prince being *solutus legibus*, and his sole pleasure having *legis vigorem*, the second.
The necessity of monarchy to secure the great end of
unity is reiterated, and the usual illustrations from bees,
geese and other birds are repeated with unconvincing
frequency. The special rights of the Gallican Church
as having no earthly superior are emphasized, and

recourse is had to the great decretal of Innocent III, *Per Venerabilem*[11], in which these rights are admitted. Pithou's great collection is a counterblast to sedition, quite as much as it is to Papalism. The claims of the Pope to control monarchs are ridiculed by Hotman in his *Brutun Fulmen*, and Servins in his *Vindiciae*. Servins, like Pasquier, was a lawyer. We must bear in mind that in England the "professors of that great and ancient mystery the Common Law" were on the side of Parliament, as Clarendon laments. In France, however, this was not the case, partly through the influence of the Civil Law, partly because the law was clearly on the side of Henri IV, and there was not, as in England, the deep feeling against the illegality of the proceedings of Buckingham and Strafford. The lawyers were in the main on the side of Henri IV, and the Parliament of Paris was imbued with a spirit hostile to the Ligue and still more to the Seize, whose most unpopular act was the "execution" of the first president, Brisson; and became for centuries the stronghold of opposition to ultramontane principles and Jesuit practices.

We may note that Barclay was a strong Catholic who began his work with an attack on George Buchanan, the tutor of James I, and only later on expanded it into its present form. He writes as definitely convinced that the true origin of the theory of rebellion is to be sought in the religious revolution, and runs back to Wyclif. So entirely one was the conception of European polity in the Middle Ages, that rebellion against its spiritual head is conceived to be the same thing as rebellion against its temporal authority. Barclay seems ignorant of the fact that Wyclif himself held a strongly

Erastian theory of civil government, and that when he talks of the duty of renouncing rulers it was of ecclesiastical rulers that he was almost exclusively thinking. The *De Civili Dominio* is directed not against temporal rulers or private property, but against ecclesiastical power and the temporalities of the Church, and the theory that gave the Pope the dominion of his " subjects' " property—a theory which the Franciscan doctrine of trusts had sharpened. It cannot be repeated too often that the animus of Wyclif's doctrine of dominion founded on grace is entirely anti-ecclesiastical, that he did not desire to interfere with the ordinary relations between lords and serfs, except so far as by enriching the former with the endowments of the Churches he would render oppression of their inferiors less necessary. The bias of Wyclif in theory and practice is secular and aristocratic and royalist; it is not really socialistic or politically revolutionary. So it is with Luther, only in a greater degree. Yet the Reformation was in itself so violent a loosening of the bands of authority that its supporters often unjustly were blamed with being adversaries of autocracy, which, as a matter of fact, they were forward to promote. Neither the credit nor the discredit which Barclay gives to Wyclif and Luther is justified by their theory, nor even by the definite and immediate effect of their influence. It has its justification, however, in the general state of mind which they expressed and intensified ; for it is that of a critical attitude towards existing institutions, and a spirit which is in essence revolutionary. So much more important in the long run are the real tendencies of personality than their conscious intellectual outcome. No amount of theorizing nor even of action on behalf of the temporal authority could prevent Wyclif or Luther being fundamentally revolutionary in spirit; and in the long run influencing even political freedom. This alone is Barclay's justification. Probably, however, his error, due in part to the conception of civil and ecclesiastical rulers as officers in a single society, was due more fully to the Calvinistic nature of the French and Scottish Reformation. Writing as a strong monarchist, Barclay naturally reprehends Calvin's expressed preference for an aristocratic form of government; it is, however, the disciples of Calvin rather than the master himself, who advanced the theory of resistance, and Calvin's own attitude was far more authoritarian than that of Luther. Luther's intolerance was merely that of an enthusiast, Calvin's was that of a strong ruler, who dislikes all obstacles in the way of a uniform system. Calvin's bigotry was that of a lawyer or an inquisitor, Luther's that of a preacher or a schoolboy.

It may be noted further that Barclay rightly discerns Buchanan's principles to be of universal import, and argues in the main on general principles, only devoting a couple of pages, out of the hundred which he gives to Buchanan, in refuting the special pleading he puts in derived from Scottish law and history. This alone should demonstrate the strange error of Ranke, who says that Buchanan's book is of particular and not general import.

One more very important characteristic of the *De Kegno* must be mentioned. Despite its array of other weapons, the main argument is utilitarian. It is clear from the frequency with which he returns to the thought that Barclay's own feeling was mainly aroused by a sense of the practical miseries of civil war. Over and over again he asks his opponents what possible advantage to the public welfare resistance to the ruler can ever bring? "Can the suffering caused by the worst of tyrants," he urges, "be equal to that produced by a single year of insurrection? Rate the evils of misgovernment as high as you will, still they are less than those of anarchy[12]." A somewhat similar thought is that of Luther, when he urges the priceless value of the security afforded by the law and the peace ensured by the civil ruler.

Now this argument so far as external evils are concerned is based on facts; and so far as temporary or minor tyranny is concerned has truth to support it. It is always safer to bear "those ills we have than fly to others that we know not of." This is the foundation of political quietism, and always remains the strongest support of any form of oppression.

The only way effectively to meet it is to transfer the argument for liberty from utilitarian to moral grounds. The evils of oppression and of despotism are not primarily to be found in the suffering, but in the deterioration of character which they produce. The problem of poverty in our own days is not the lack of bread and cheese, but the diminished opportunity of nobility of life, which the education of children in slums brings with it[13]. The eternal argument for liberty, which is also its limitation, is the right of human nature to reach the noblest. This was discerned by Savonarola, and is the reason why political liberty has as a matter of fact followed in the wake of religious animosities. The *Monarchomachi* who were the targets of Barclay's scorn would one and all have replied that for political liberty as such they cared either little or nothing. What they did demand was the right to that religious worship which formed for them the atmosphere of the highest character. Throughout the struggle of the sixteenth and seventeenth centuries, it was the right of their own Church to exist as a trainer of character which drove Jesuits, Huguenots, Puritans and Dutchmen to become often in spite of themselves the promoters of liberty ; and found perhaps its completest expression in the *volteface* of the Anglican clergy which alone made possible the revolution of 1688. For all these men character was bound up with religious system ; many of them did not greatly care and some of them definitely disapproved of religious and political liberty. But they were one and all driven to fight for the existence of that society, whatever it was, which was for them the true home of the spirit, and could alone direct it to the highest ends ; this they did in spite of all theories of the risks of rebellion, or the evils of anarchy, and sometimes in astonishing contradiction to the principles which in other spheres they maintained. It is perhaps true to say, not that civil liberty is the child of religious liberty, but that liberty, whether civil or religious, was the work often reluctantly, sometimes unconsciously, undertaken by communities of men who had an end higher than political, who refused to submit religion to politic arguments, who fought for ends never entirely utilitarian [14].

How feeble is the mere political argument for liberty can be seen from a work like the *Servitude Volontaire* of Étienne de la Boeotie. It is interesting as showing the influence of the classical spirit entirely apart from religion. It is valuable, too, as showing us an early form of the problem set himself by Rousseau in the first words of the *Social Contract*, that namely of discovering why if man is born free he is everywhere in chains. We note too an entire absence of the historical spirit in the judgment of the Roman Empire. To La Boeotie, as to others, Julius Caesar was a mere tyrant, and he can discern none of the conditions which made the Empire at that time the only possible form of government. The reason is, that he treats of an anti-monarchical condition as an end in itself, not the means to an end ; and hence cannot see that, under certain conditions, despotism may be the best school of character. Such a thought is the sole real justification for the British rule in India ; for it can surely be maintained that it has exhibited an impartial justice, an avoidance of the evils of Oriental despotism, which no other government in that country has produced. To base liberty upon moral grounds is to lay it on its only enduring foundation, but it makes it also something different from the ideal of a doctrinaire or a Jacobin, and relative to the condition of the human mind at the epoch considered. There is no such thought as this in *Le Contr'Un*. Liberty, *i.e.*, a republican government, is treated as the ideal, apart from all historical, natural or moral considerations. This pamphlet was a mere exercise, and had no practical influences[15].

Liberty was the work of enthusiasts but of enthusiasts for a different cause. It has lasted in England and the United States because it did not arise from purely political causes ; how far the liberty, equality and fraternity based on no other grounds are likely to be enduring, the future alone can determine.

To the almost intolerable dulness of the writings of the supporters of Henri IV, save those of Du Plessis Mornay, there is one exception. The *Satyre Ménippée*

is a Rabelaisian amalgam of prose and verse, describing
in burlesque the meeting of the so-called Estates of the
League at Paris in 1593 to elect a King of France.
Preceded by an allegorical frontispiece in which the
Jesuits, the preachers, the rabble of France, the Papal Le-
gate, and the Duchess of Montpensier are all facetiously
delineated, the writer or writers give mock speeches on
behalf of the various estates represented. There is much
wit and not a little coarseness. The *Satyre* closes with
a speech put into the mouth of D'Aubray, the representative of the Tiers État. It is an eloquent plea on
behalf of the ancient laws of France and the rights of the
natural prince. The motives real and imaginary of the
various actors are ably dramatised. The whole gives a
vivid picture of the various party passions and personal
interests which were for a time united in the organisation
of the League, but by their mutually exclusive pretensions
prevented any real agreement except for the purposes
of opposition.

From art we turn to science. Jean Bodin is, next to
Machiavelli, the most important political writer of the
sixteenth century. So early as 1572 he had defended
the cause of toleration ; for a time even he appears to
have been a Huguenot, but his great work *De la
République* proceeds from the standpoint of a scientific
enquirer, and may be said to begin the long series of
works written as scientific text-books on politics in the
sixteenth and seventeenth centuries. His book is the
first treatise on sovereignty in the strict sense and was
used very shortly after for lectures at Cambridge. All
subsequent writers from Hobbes to Sidgwick and
Professor Holland go back to him. His conception is
derived from the civilian theory of Imperial omni-

potence filtered through the Papalist writers; he tells
us that the greatest of all the Canonists, Innocent IV,
understood the subject profoundly[16]. His work has
been so much discussed that it needs little more than
mention. Suffice it to say that although in many
previous works adumbrated and clearly present to the
thought of such writers as Bartolus in regard to all States
non recognoscentes superiorem, the attributes of legal
sovereignty irrespective of forms or constitutions, omnipotent, indivisible, inalienable, are here set forth for the
first time with scientific accuracy. But Bodin is not
a purely scientific enquirer and has no doubt that
monarchy is the best form of government and that
France, England, Spain, are all pure monarchies with no
real underived powers in Parliament or Castes or
Estates. Like Filmer he cannot endure the " anarchy
of a mixed monarchy," and asserts the incompetence
of representative assemblies in any kingdom to give
more than good advice. Bodin, however, is more than
a theorist; he gives practical advice to governments.
He is strongly opposed to the confiscation of property
of persons attainted of treason, and traces the appalling
growth of criminals and bandits to this practice, for it
suddenly reduces to beggary persons accustomed to
luxurious living and incapable of practising or entering
a trade ; in days when all trades were "mysteries," to
which definite apprenticeship and membership were
necessary, it would not merely be want of training which
could bar the way. At any rate the world had not
discovered cheating at bridge as a refuge for the destitute.
We also find in Bodin speculations on the origin of
national characteristics and the beginnings of that theory
of climatic effects which played so great a part in Buckle's

notorious work. He was a free trader in an age of
bureaucracy, and, as we saw, a strong supporter of
toleration as it was understood by the *Politiques.* Michel
de l'Hôpital in his *Traité de la Réformation de la Justice*
is chiefly interesting for the evidence which his book
affords of the entire absence of the spirit of legality in
the tribunals of the day. The ideal of equality, which
always seems to Englishmen a little ridiculous in French
revolutionaries, is probably due to the fact that that
limited part of it known as equality before the law did
not exist in France before 1688. L'Hôpital laments
with reiteration and emphasis the way in which power is
able to hinder the doing of ordinary justice, and mentions
it as a special grace of Augustus that he only once
interfered to save a favourite from the condemnation of
the law. The need in the State, as it had been in the
Church, is not for laws but their impartial administration.
It was partly this sense that led to the idealisation of
monarchy as the only power which was highly placed
enough to prevent that oppression of interest and wealth
which was a normal feature of the time. It was not
merely the scientific theory of the modern State, but its
practical tasks with which Bodin and his contemporaries
were concerned. This is perhaps most evident of all in
the lengthy treatise of Pierre Grégoire of Toulouse, *De
Republica.* The author was a jurist, and it is from a
jurist's standpoint that he writes. As a sincere Catholic he
avoids awkward questions about the Pope, so far as may
be ; but he asserts distinctly the independence of the
civil power. The most noteworthy characteristic of the
book is the complete envisaging of the functions of the
modern State. Questions of marriage, the population,
education, are all treated ; we observe how the ideals of

Luther for the lay control of all civil matters are in substance accepted. For many of the questions here discussed would earlier have been considered merely to concern the spiritual authority. Although Gregory admits the right of the Pope to institute Universities he is clearly against any real ecclesiastical control of educational matters. We also find, as in Bodin, a certain amount of International Law. The dominating thought of Bodin and Gregory as that of Luther is the idea of the State as fulfilling the highest aims of the community ; politics is not for them, as for Jesuits and clericals, a mere secondary machinery, secular, utilitarian and mundane ; it might almost be described in Lord Acton's phrase as " the art of doing on the largest scale what is right." But there is no notion of self-government. The task of the State is to be effected by a bureaucracy ; the fundamental notions of James, still more those of Cecil or Bacon, are very similar. Indeed the whole development of governmental activity, the labours of Colbert and Pombal, even those of Frederic II and Joseph II, are a commentary on this work. The advent of the State, the possibility of a strong central power, general obedience to which was a fact or a dream nearly realized (Gregory wrote after the triumph of Henri IV), rendered it necessary for thinkers to consider what government ought to do ; whereas the task of the Middle Ages had been the struggle of the State for existence. The situation is somewhat similar to the change in English politics after the final admission to the franchise of practically the whole male portion of the nation in 1884 ; politics began to turn from political to social and economic questions—from the problem what ought a State to be men turned to the consideration what it ought to do. This to some degree was the case at the end of the sixteenth century. The struggle with clerical interference was or seemed to be at an end. All competing claims, feudal or federal, had disappeared. The inherent power of territorial kingship was assured in many countries and seemed to be in England, for Puritanism appeared a little cloud no bigger than a man's hand. The taking over by government of many tasks hitherto performed by the Church, the organization of industrial life, the development of trade, especially that over seas, the problems of the new capitalism, the promotion of culture, as understood since the Renaissance, might seem fit to task the energies of all statesmen, and to some extent did so. The age of the *grand monarque*, its culture and its brilliancy, its glory and shame was the natural goal to which the *Politiques* were approaching. It was the failure to imitate or carry out in England this ideal of all "gentlemanly" kings, that was the inner tragedy of the Stuart *régime*. The uprising of the modern idea of public spirit is perhaps the best phrase in which to describe the significance of the party.

One more related subject must be noticed. In Sully's *Économes Royales* we have something of an insight into the mind if not of Henri IV at least of his great minister.

The "great design" of the *Économes Royales* is in its oft-reiterated outlines, as easy of detailing, as it was visionary. Europe is to be divided into fifteen equal powers, so balanced that none shall find it possible to menace the liberty of the others. These States are to form a sort of Christian Commonwealth, with rules of arbitration so as to prevent war. There is to be a *universal freedom of trade,* and religious toleration. Now this design at first sight appears so chimerical, that it is hard to see how practical statesmen could have ever entertained it. There appears, however, to be no doubt that Sully really did think it worth putting forward. Even if we allowed that he had no other object than the desire to humble the House of Austria, we are driven to ask ourselves what it was in the general condition of things which made such means to reach the end conceivable. We notice first how the *residuary legatee* of the idea of unity of the medieval world is this conception of a body of States independent yet united by certain ties, whose action is to proceed by rules; in other words the idea of law as international ; secondly we notice how the practical principle of the balance of power is definitely put forward.

Political arrangements are in future to be based on an equilibrium of forces deliberately maintained. Sully may have been a visionary but he struck the key-note of European politics, until the era of force gave way to that of ideas with the Revolution of 1689[17]. The notion of the " balance of power " is indeed Italian and arose from the fact that Italy in the fifteenth century realized on a smaller scale those conditions which developed in Europe in the seventeenth. Hinted at by Machiavelli and always in the background of his mind, the principle formed the basis of the action of Wolsey and the inaction of Elizabeth ; was definitely appealed to by Marnix de S. Aldegonde, as a reason for Europe assisting the Dutch against Philip II, and at the close of the century finds its full expression in the design which Sully attributed to Henri IV.

Further it is to be remarked that the basis of the new

Europe is to be that of religious diversity but not complete toleration. The "great design" in fact takes the principle of *cujus regio ejus religio* from Germany and applies it to Europe at large. Here is no laying down of toleration as a principle; but since three forms of the Christian religion have come to stay, facts must be faced, and no more fuss made about the matter. That is the real position of Sully, and it corresponds to what we have seen to be the attitude of the *Politiques* towards the religious difficulty in internal politics.

The "great design" then is noteworthy as illustrating once more the fact that in the sixteenth century there came into definite though not final expression those principles which were to occupy the mind of Europe for two hundred years, and were to be the occasion if not the cause, of the groupings both of domestic and international politics.

LECTURE V.

THE MONARCHOMACHI.

IN the last lecture we saw how the enduring work of the sixteenth century was the modern State. Its legal omnipotence and unity, the destruction of all competing powers, separate or privileged, were assured, and a universal all-embracing system of law became possible. We have now to consider another result of the Reformation, popular freedom or rather its theoretical basis—for except in the British Isles and the Netherlands it disappeared in Europe, until 1789. It is not too much to say that political liberty would not now-a-days exist anywhere but for the claim to ecclesiastical independence.

It is the transformation of the desire to persecute into the claim to an inherent right to exist on the part of religious bodies that historically produces those limitations upon State action which are the securities of freedom. But this is not all. It was only by adding to political reasons a religious one, that the struggle for freedom in the sixteenth and seventeenth centuries ended in any but one way. As we have already seen, the forces in favour of absolutism and the general acquiescence therein were of immense strength; the universal desire for efficiency and legislative activity all made the same way; and a strong executive not only secured peace but was a necessity. With the decay of feudal and Papal influence there was one and only one motive, the religious, that could withstand the torrent of officialism, or in any way attenuate that orgy of centralisation which succeeded to the anarchy of feudalism. This may be seen first of all in the Church, which with the close of the Middle Ages became more and more a pure monarchy, until the rebellion of Luther deprived it of half its subjects and more than half its influence. It can be seen in every State in Europe, in none more obviously than in the Netherlands and England. The purely utilitarian argument was, for short periods, as we saw in our discussion of Barclay, entirely at the service of the central power and indeed always is[1]; the suffering caused by a day of civil war is always greater than that of a year of tyranny. The dangers of tyranny are, as Savonarola discerned, in their main moral, and it is the narrowing of character which is the most grievous result of oppression. Hence it is only some moral or religious motive that can in an age like the sixteenth century be at all available against the dominant tendencies. At bottom the claim of a religious body, however bigoted or unreasonable or exclusive its tenets or methods, is always the claim to maintain intact a particular type of character; and to maintain it by a right, which no argument from expediency can disturb.

In his latest and not least valuable work, Mr. Dicey shows how precarious is the plant of freedom when based on purely utilitarian grounds; he points out how dangerous Benthamite Liberalism has been to the very individualism by which it set such store; how by ridiculing all notions of inherent right in politics, and seeking to advance liberty under the cover of its utility which was supposed to be self-evident, Benthamism really prepared the way for that extension of the absolutism of the State which it abhorred, and forged those very chains of collectivism which fettered the freedom of its dreams. Now it was just this danger, or one analogous to it, from which both Rome and Geneva saved the constitutionalism of the sixteenth century. By basing the claim to freedom on Divine Right, it sought and on the whole succeeded in finding a refuge, where the assaults of the mere *Politique* could not touch it; so much so that monarchists had perforce to do the same. It is the influence of Luther or of Laud, not of Hobbes or Machiavelli, that is the real inspiration of Jacobites. Nelson might write of " *The Common Interest of Kings and People* " as being on the side of non-resistance, but the strength of royalism was the belief that it was a religious duty to obey " masters though froward." With such an argument, coupled with the general tendency to centralisation, the triumph of autocracy which as a fact was very general, must have been universal but for the claim of religious bodies to limit absolutism by their own existence or even their supremacy. What they desired, was not liberty or tolerance, but domination and independence—happily the power of the State proved everywhere too strong for their desire (except perhaps for a brief period in Scotland); but though they did not gain dominion, they secured, what has been better, tolerance. Political liberty is the residuary legatee of ecclesiastical animosities.

The Church was the first and last of immunists and the sects were likewise the first of Libertarians—but only in spite of themselves. The two religious bodies which have done the most to secure "the rights of man" are those two which really cared least about individual liberty, and made the largest inroads upon private life wherever they obtained the supremacy—the Roman Catholic Church and the Presbyterian. Their regard for their own supremacy or at any rate independence was so great that in countries like Scotland, where the government was either lukewarm or hostile to it, Presbyterianism proved a perpetual check upon the central power; while in France, where a long struggle between the two took place, each in turn was led by circumstances to put forth a theory of political liberty, which was the direct parent of the doctrines triumphant in 1688, and through Locke the ancestor of those of 1789. Moreover even when absolutism had triumphed in France the very man, who in the interests of uniformity had revoked the Edict of Nantes, when he attempted in those of nationality to set the Pope at defiance found a very real limitation upon the dogma that he was himself the State. Despite the sonorous declarations of 1682, and the solid advocacy of Bossuet, Louis XIV was beaten by the spiritual power, the Gallican liberties succumbed to ultramontane orthodoxy, the eldest son of the Church discovered himself to be subject to the correction of his father, and the most Christian King found that his title was the tacit condition of a contract which he was unable to repudiate. No triumph of the Papacy—except that of Leo XIII over Bismarck—was greater than the comparatively unregarded one which Innocent XII obtained over the *grand monarque.*

It was the struggle for existence of the Reformation sects, that compelled them to put forward a general theory of government which imposes checks upon absolutism, and to investigate and revive all ancient institutions which were or might be the means of controlling it.   Further than this the system of Calvinism was what neither Lutheranism nor Anglicanism nor Romanism was, a republican if not a democratic system. Practically it doubtless meant the oligarchy of the preachers or the tyranny " worse than Papal" of ruling elders; certainly it did not favour individual liberty; but it was opposed in theory to secular interference, and by its own methods to monarchical power; and hence in spite of itself Calvinism in France, in the Netherlands and Scotland became either in the world of thought or in that of practice the basis of modern liberty.   That it had of itself any such *penchant* is of course not the case; and illustrations of the fact may be found in Geneva under Calvin and Beza, in the Calvinistic principalities of Germany, in New England, in the very idea of the Solemn League and Covenant, and in the treatment of Episcopacy in Scotland after 1689.   Yet James I was quite right in his dislike to the system as fettering his freedom, for the organisation of Scotch Presbyterianism, borrowed from the French, did undoubtedly prepare the way for popular government. This can easily be illustrated from Scotch history in the years 1637–41, and from France in the years of the religious wars.   The point to note is that liberty is the result of religious competition ; otherwise it would have succumbed to the general monarchical tendencies.   It is, perhaps, best to avoid profitless discussions by saying that liberty in this chapter is used in no natural or sublimated sense, but according to the usage of Professor Dicey as comprising certain legal rights practically secured. These are the rights to freedom of discussion, worship, and person; to security against unlawful taxation; to some means of control over both legislative and executive. These notions were not new, nor, in principle, were the means by which they were secured—what was new in the sixteenth century was the strength of the forces, which everywhere threatened and in most places destroyed them. The destruction of the forces that made for anarchy was also a very real destruction of those that made for liberty, whether feudal privileges, or municipal rights. Even the Canon Law and the theory of the Empire made a sovereign, omnipotent, and unitary State impossible in the Middle Ages—except in the dreams of the extremer Canonists. As we have seen, however, all those competing or checking agencies had disappeared, and even in Catholic countries the claims of the clergy had ceased to make to any real extent an *imperium in imperio.* The civil law was triumphant. The conditions for a full theory of sovereignty existed and were active. There was a very real danger that this discovery—for it was a discovery—of a power that could not be bound by law because it could make law—would produce a more enduring tyranny than any hitherto known—and it did do this in some places, especially as in most States it was no assembly or republic to whose advantage this boon had come at last. In the next three lectures we shall be occupied with various phases of the struggle to set bounds to the *parvenu* and overweening renascence State. In many cases the struggle was unsuccessful except in the domain of theory—but we shall see forming the theory of limited monarchy and of public law, as it passed through the Whigs and Grotius to the Europe of the eighteenth century. We shall find in general the following facts to be universal.

(1) The *primum mobile* of all this struggle was religious. Civil rights are secondary, a means to an end, never successfully preserved either among Protestants or Catholics except where dangers to religious belief sharpen the determination to resist by a higher than utilitarian motive.

(2) The argument almost invariably makes a contract the basis of the State.

(3) It rests therefore on the conception of a law natural anterior to law in our sense. On the same conception the further structure of rules limiting the international irresponsibility of the State is raised.

(4) The conception of law which makes it the arbitrary command of an irresponsible sovereign, "one or number," is denied in concordance with the theory of law that it is "the voice of reason, the harmony of the world[2]," the foundation not the result of State authority.

Now the *nouveau fait*, which made it feasible to set up these claims, was the difference between the religion of king and people in an age of persecution. The king's power in the Middle Ages was subject to many limitations, especially to those of the ecclesiastical power. But though he might be admonished and even deposed by the Pope his religion never differed from that of his subjects; he might be a schismatic or excommunicate, he was never really a heretic—not even Frederic II was chargeable with this; his ferocious edicts in favour of persecution at a time when he desired to conciliate the Papacy are a proof at least of his *public* profession. But the Reformation changed all this. It made it possible for a king to be of a different confession from that of his people or from some influential section of it; and this in an age when all religious bodies proclaimed the duty of persecution, as incumbent upon the sovereign of a Christian commonwealth, and indeed as the mark which distinguished it from an atheistic, Machiavellian State. John Knox, Beza, Luther were on this point in agreement with Boucher and Louis d'Orleans, and out of sympathy with the ideals of the *Politiques*. Now it was only by some claim to a right of insurrection (unless a theory of toleration could be accepted) that there was any chance for a persecuted religion to preserve its existence. Hence the claims to a deposing power were revived by Rome in an age when otherwise they would have fallen into oblivion. The very idea of the Counter-Reformation is a restriction upon the omnipotence of the civil power, and in some sense a denial of international independence. Its thesis is that (1) Sovereigns may not do what they will with their own in religious matters, (2) States are not mutually independent entities, but parts of a wider order, a commonwealth bound by certain rules with which they are not at liberty to dispense. The struggle for liberty is always conditioned by the presence or absence of this determining circumstance—religious differences. They are the security alike of territorial sovereignty in Germany and (where they last long enough) of constitutional freedom in other countries.

For instance, in Germany, there was no growth either in theory or practice of liberty within the State; on the contrary, as we have seen, the whole trend of thought and fact is toward absolutism. The exception is the Anabaptist movement, which served but to bring

discredit on the ideas for which it stood, where it did
not, as at Münster, contradict them. The reason is that
inside the German States, religious competition was not
effective; the comparative tolerance of the religious
peace of Augsburg which substituted banishment for
burning as the punishment of heresy, and the fact that
exile did not mean leaving the Fatherland, rendered
it needless for recalcitrants to have recourse, like
Huguenots, to the theory and practice of rebellion. On
the other hand if we take the Empire as a whole, there
religious differences were truly effective and rebellion not
only became common, it became normal, and eventually
turned the prince into a sovereign and insurrection into
lawful war. When the peace of Westphalia is spoken of
as foundation of the modern public law of Europe, the
meaning of the assertion ought to be more closely ap-
prehended than it commonly is. What the treaties of
Münster and Osnabrück really did was legally to consecrate the international liberties of Europe, as they had
been secured by the religious revolution. The idea of
a united Christendom was abandoned. Internationally
religions were made equal. Pope and Emperor lost
theoretically what they had long lost practically, their
hegemony, and in a few years even the Imperial chancery
grants to national monarchs the title of "majesty." The
Canon Law ceased in fact to be international, which it
most distinctly was in the Middle Ages; became (subject
to concordats) merely the conceded machinery for regulating a department of particular States. Further the
sovereignty of the States of the Empire was admitted, and
struggles for existence between Habsburg and Hohen-
zollern would in future be wars not rebellions. In theory
the dogma that all States are equal begins to supersede

the medieval conception of a universal hierarchy of officials. Now all this was the direct and obvious result of religious differences; it could not have taken place had Emperor and princes all remained of one religious communion. Indeed had the Emperors become Lutheran, their power would probably have been consolidated instead of shattered; although there were, of course, many other than religious motives which contributed to princely preeminence. In this case we see the effects of religious difference in introducing liberty into international politics or rather making them international. We must bear in mind that this movement between States goes on *pari passu*, and is at least partly successful owing to the same causes, as the struggle between rival religions, inside the States, which emphasized that "division of power" on which liberty always depends.

In the Middle Ages liberty depended, wherever it existed, on the division of power between overlords and tenants-in-chief, or between secular and ecclesiastical rulers; in the conciliar era it was, or appeared to be, secured by the division of allegiance obtained by rival Popes; in the sixteenth century it either existed or was claimed effectively only when and in so far as political unity, always tending to uniformity, was broken by the struggle between Protestant and Catholic, or between Lutheran and Calvinist, or between Anglican and Puritan. Only because neither party could subdue, exterminate, or banish the other was toleration the result of the Revolution of 1688. If there had been no competitor with Anglicanism, James II's removal might have only led to a system as narrowly uniform as that of France under Louis XIV.

In the sixteenth century the whole course of the

Reformation in Scotland effected the liberty of the people and helped to secure popular government, because the king was always unsympathetic and sometimes hostile to the movement; but the very fact that it was general was unfavourable to true liberty, and the Episcopal Church was treated after 1688 with an intolerance which was nearly a century behind the treatment of the Nonconformists in England[2]. The Reformation could not have that result in England, but helped to increase the royal power, until a party arose, who disliked the Elizabethan settlement, and were determined to destroy it at the bayonet's point. The case of the Netherlands is yet more important; those provinces, in which the Catholic religion was dominant, did not find it necessary to carry their protest into proclaiming independence, and returned after a period of *Sturm und Drang* to the Spanish allegiance. France, however, affords the most striking object of the truth, as it is also the most important treasury of literature embodying it. There, so long as the question was undecided, the right to political liberty was proclaimed, according as circumstances dictated, alternately by the Huguenot and the ultramontane party. Eventually, however, the principle that the king must be of the same religion as the majority of his subjects was established by the submission of Henri IV. The struggle ended with the gift of toleration to the minority, but the apparent gain was more than counteracted by the triumph of the principle of uniformity in the interested Catholicism of Henri IV, to whom religion was a matter of policy; and eventually this principle ran its course till religious liberty was destroyed by Louis XIV in the interests of the unity of the State. In England a somewhat similar result obtained in 1688, but the security for freedom was greater in that, firstly, it was not merely local; secondly, the differences between the Church and Nonconformists were less far-reaching; and thirdly, the age of confessional conflicts was over, and rationalistic latitudinarianism was the dominant tendency in all bodies in the eighteenth century; fourthly, the connection of the party of freedom with aristocratic disaffection was less close than in France. At the same time we must bear in mind that even in England the *régime* of George III was comparable, if we allow for the difference of century and country, to that of Louis XIV, at least in its relation to already secured rights. George III threatened and for a time nearly overthrew those rights to personal liberty, freedom of discussion, and, at least in appearance, consent to taxation, which the settlement had apparently guaranteed; he was opposed to all those measures for the relief of Dissenters which were the logical outcome of the Revolution, and he succeeded in delaying, until the concession had lost all its grace, the merest justice to Roman Catholics[3]. In the strictest sense George III and Louis XIV and Philip II were national kings, they all alike represented with fidelity, the more admirable because it was unconscious, the most reactionary prejudices of their countrymen, all alike shared the limitations of *l'homme moyen sensuel*. But all alike illustrate the danger to liberty in a modern centralised state that lies in a government which has no deep source of division among its governing classes.

Let us now trace this development a little more in

detail. Ignoring the international aspects of the religious controversy let us keep to the internal politics of individual States. It was by the Protestants that the standard of revolt was first raised. Calvin the father of Presbyterianism was indeed very carefully guarded in his language, and avoids giving any countenance either to rebellion or democracy. He speaks with contempt of the mob. His own ideal was for an ecclesiastical oligarchy under the shadow of which he himself could rule. Theologically and politically he disbelieved in freedom. He declares himself abstractly in favour of aristocracy, but is very anxious to show that governments are relative to historical development, and in this he is very modern. He is clear that government of whatever form is to be obeyed as a religious duty, and he will allow no private individual to resist his prince. To estates of the realm, as the protectors of the people, he allows considerable power ; and he makes a remark about those States, where in fact "ephors" exist for a "check on tyranny," which was of great service for future disputants, whose use of the term is alone significant of Calvin's influence. Like others he adduces the instances of Ehud and Judith as cases of special inspiration, and thus leaves a loophole whereby such sanction could be claimed on the one side for the murder of the Duke of Guise, and on the other for that of Henri III. His conclusion, however, in favour of passive obedience is explicit, and he cannot and was not cited as an authority for the theory of rebellion. For Calvin this position was possible[4]. But to his followers in Scotland and France it was no longer tenable.

The course of the Scotch Reformation from the beginning to the deposition of Mary Stuart, and right

on through the Bishops' wars to the Revolution, affords,
perhaps, the most complete and consistent expression of
the duty of rebellion, alike in theory and practice, which
we possess outside ultramontane pamphleteering. In
each case there is a similar claim in the background
for an ecclesiastical independence which may mean
supremacy. John Knox, while he allows his monarchs
to play the part of Josiah, did not desire to tolerate any
idolaters ; and had he been powerful enough would certainly have made a "right faith" as much a condition of
legitimacy as did the Counter-Reformation. So far as
we can tell, his view of the office of the Christian
propagandist knew no limits either of morality or law ;
in other words his sense of the value of the particular
religious society was as strong as that of the Jesuits, and
like them he employed the means recommended by
Machiavelli to attain his ends ; among those means
murder and rebellion had a natural home in the
Scotland of 1555-80. In Goodman's treatise, the subserviency of political to ecclesiastical considerations
is yet more violently proclaimed ; he has a theory of
rebellion to justify Wyatt's insurrection in favour of
"that godly lady and meek lamb, Elizabeth," and would
clearly like to control not merely internal but external
policy by purely confessional considerations[5]. The same
is also the case with leaders like Melville a little later.
What they exhibit in general is first a theory of the
limits of the supreme authority which may, or may
not, become a theory of liberty ; and secondly the
purely religious and even ecclesiastical character of
this theory. This was the reason of James's dislike to
them.

The most generally important treatise on the subject is, however, George Buchanan's short dialogue *De Jure Regni apud Scotos*. Written to justify the deposition of Mary Stuart, it contains in a short compass the two main arguments which were to be at the service of the popular party until the French Revolution ; the argument from precedent and the argument from principle. There is the historical argument, which might be used in any nation, which had a constitution in the Middle Ages, that checks on the sovereign authority were ancient, customary and by no means merely nominal. It is an appeal to the law of historical development and was used even in the conciliar movement. We must not suppose it to be only true of England, because ours is the only country where these ancient checks have survived to become the foundation of modern liberty. It is as true or nearly so of medieval France as of England ; and the favourite formula of pamphleteers is borrowed not from Britain, but Spain. If the historical argument had less place in the German States, at any rate in the Empire it was strong enough ; and eventually successful. The independence of the sovereign prince of Germany is the final result, assisted by the Reformation, of a long historical development, which goes back to the very beginnings of lordship and service. In fact the triumphs of the historical principle are twofold: the territorial sovereignty and legal equality of small States is the crown of it in the one aspect ; the constitutional monarchy of England that of the other. The novelty is the absorption by the State in France or Spain of all competing jurisdictions on the one hand ; and on the other the destruction, even in idea, of any integral conception of Europe, more especially its religious unity.

The second aspect of Buchanan's book is the writer's theory of contract. In some form or other the anti-monarchical writers from this time forwards till Rousseau (and we can trace the idea backwards to Manegold of Lauterbach) all base their claim to check and if necessary to resist the monarch on the notion of the original contract. Once the notion can be popularised, that the obligations of government and protection are mutual and not one-sided, it is easy to protest effectively against tyranny, whether religious or political. The theory of contract raises to our eyes every possible objection ; it is unhistorical, abstract and self-contradictory. Not only does history afford no evidence of it, but of even a tacit contract the general consciousness in our own or any other age is unaware. Not only does the conception seem abstract and doctrinaire, but it seems very bad abstraction, and to imply a doctrine false to all our notions of political organisms and public utility. It contradicts the evolutionary theory of politics, and substitutes for a just reliance on the hatred of men to oppression a conception of abstract rights, which is as patient of real tyranny as it is often active against imaginary injuries ; for a prince might easily keep his contract and yet be a tyrant, *e.g.*, Philip II in Spain. Lastly, the conception is self-contradictory. For it assumes, as anterior to law, a purely juristic notion. If government is the result of a contract, what can make the contract binding, when there is *ex hypothesi* no sovereign authority to do so? These objections are all of them perfectly valid. Yet they must be used mainly as a means to help us to understand the condition of things which made such objections either imperceptible or inadmissible. Until the time of Filmer, and still more of

Leslie, the arguments on the other side were not at all of the character above noted, but rather concerned with showing the Divinely given authority of the ruler, and the religious duty of invariable non-resistance[6]. Leslie's criticism of Hoadly, indeed, has in it much in substance what might be written by a modern, such as Austin; as in form it is more brilliant and amusing[7]. But we have to consider the state of things under which such a theory seemed to many quite natural, and could be readily offered as an effective ground for practical action.

In the first place to that age the theory did not appear unhistorical and hardly was so. For it was the natural outcome of feudalism. Whatever be the defects of feudalism, it was a system which recognised the reciprocity of rights and duties in regard alike to political and economic power, in a way which, save in a limited sphere, it has been impossible to do since. We have, it is true, at length secured a recognition of the duties of government, but it is by an almost complete consecration of the rights of property, and an entire disregard of moral obligation of the owner, purchased by the absolute surrender of a portion of his wealth in the form of taxes. Now the feudal tie was essentially contractual; and it was easy to see in the coronation oath the recognition of a similar contract on the part of the monarch, and in the Baptismal vow a somewhat similar condition on the part of the Christian. At any rate, the theory of contract rested on two conceptions which were as a matter of fact operative in recent history, first, the reciprocity of protection and obedience implied in the coronation oath and indeed the whole religious ceremony, second, the nature of the obligations which bound lord

and vassal. We find writers like Du Plessis Mornay
actually appealing to feudal customs as a ground for
natural resistance. There is no doubt that as a
matter of fact the idea of the contract owes much to
the long prevalence of similar notions in all spheres.
We must bear in mind that in all complete copies
of the *corpus juris* there was the *Liber de Feudis*
For the Civil Law was not an ancient code that died
with Justinian, but a body of doctrine that developed up
to Henry VII. We may find further evidence in the
Baptismal vow ; by many this is treated as imposing an
obligation, which if the sovereign violates by heresy, he
may justly be deposed.

Secondly, the theory in the eyes of its supporters
gained rather than lost by laying stress on the idea of right
beyond that of mere utility. The influence of Machiavelli
was very great ; but a purely utilitarian theory of politics
was not to be thought of, and perhaps never *by itself* became influential until the days of Bentham. As was said
in the first lecture, we have seen the idea of right or
public welfare in general gradually supplant the notions
of rights in particular ; it has not been proved that the
change is beneficial. In some ways it tends to put
liberty at the mercy of sentiment and minorities under
the heel of majorities. Moreover the argument from
this side was, as we have seen, mainly on the side of
quiescence ; it is a very long view of public utility that
can ever justify insurrection. At any rate in days when
the claims of the Pope were based on ideas of Right
when those of his adversaries the kings were equally
based on it, when the connection of law with politics
was intimate and all action was conceived under legalist
forms, and the causes of rebellion were commonly re-

ligious, no view which did not make it legally right as well as expedient to rebel would have had any chance of convincing opinion or even of satisfying the consciences of the rebellious.   Theories are taken up, as a rule, to quiet doubts that perplex supporters, rather than to answer opponents.   The fautors of rebellion in Scotland, France and Holland needed to be assured that, in rising against the sovereign, they were not merely consulting their interests, but doing their duty and acting in defence of a legal right.   The same fact is shown by the rather ridiculous attempt in 1688 to quiet the difficulties of non-resisting Tories by the use of the word " abdicate " to describe the deposition of James II.

Lastly, and this is the most important point, the possibility of an original contract anterior to the State is significant of a world in which law, so far from being the offspring, was the parent of government.   The theory was possible because the whole world was conceived as governed by law, divine, natural or positive ; while the distinctions between these kinds of law are only of a secondary and subordinate character.   Law in its sense of universal rules of action is not confined to the merely private and municipal affairs of a definite kingdom ; but is descriptive of nearly all conceivable activities, human and divine ; the law of nature is literally a law of nature and in some minds is to be identified even with the instincts of the beasts.   But in any case law in the sense of a uniformity of action is the dominant and enduring notion ; that of a command is special, particular, modern or ancient, not medieval—at least not as descriptive of what is law and what is not.   The classical passage of Hooker breathes the whole spirit of an age, and serves to enshrine the legacy of our days, of the world

that was passing away.   It is doubtful whether God
himself can dispense with natural law ; while the whole
development of medieval Catholicism, with its legalist
conceptions of penance, and its legal system of the
canon law, served to implicate with juristic notions the
principles both of politics and ethics.

In one sense, then, the original contract is a theory
unhistorical, abstract and inconsistent—but these very
characteristics give us an insight into the historical
antecedents which produced it, the habit of political
philosophising on theological grounds which made it
palatable to the taste of the day, and above all into that
fundamentally juristic conception of the world, in which
all kinds of action and every sort of judgment was
expressed in legal phraseology, and in which the conception of law as the voice of eternal reason speaking
in the ways of God and in the works of man is so
general, as to disguise, if not to deny, that notion of it
as a mere command, which belongs either to the Roman
Church or the Renaissance State.   It is noteworthy
that Hotman, one of the strong supporters, though on
historical grounds, of the popular side, was a violent and
convinced " Germanist," strongly suspicious of the Latin
element in French civilisation.

Though Buchanan struck the key-note the tune was
largely of other composition.   It was the massacre of
S. Bartholomew which produced the most noteworthy
and valuable works from the Protestant side.   That
event caused, naturally enough, a violent reaction against
Machiavellian and Italian politics, for no one ever forgot
that Catharine de' Medici was an Italian.   The " liberals "
were, indeed, anti-Machiavellian : they were fighting first
for that notion of right in politics which Machiavelli

ignored, and secondly against that complete supersession of all other interests in that of political unity, which his system implies. We have from henceforward a mass of pamphlets which deal with the relations of governors and governed on very much the same lines as those of Buchanan. It should, however, be mentioned that the latter is alone or almost alone in granting to *individuals* the right of resistance and even of attacking the royal person. This was not the first time even in this century that attempts were made to limit the royal authority. Claude de Seysell in *La grande Monarchie de France* and Budé in the *Institution de Prince* had both expressed their sense of the importance of the states-general, and limitations upon royal power; while Étienne de la Boeotie in the famous *Contr' Un* had reiterated the attacks upon monarchy of classical antiquity. But these were either academic exercises or futile aspirations, had not the tocsin been sounded by *Le Reveille Matin des François* of August 24th. The pamphlet indeed of that name is merely a narrative of the facts, and says nothing of general principles like the other famous broadside *Le Tigre*, which is mere vituperation. The *De Jure Magistratum in Subditos*, by some attributed to Beza, may have suggested to Du Plessis Mornay the line of argument he adopted later; for it contains nearly all the arguments of the *Vindiciae contra Tyrannos* (which first appeared in 1576), although it is far less interesting and has none of the moving eloquence which makes the *Vindiciae* even now a live book. That work, of which the authorship is clearly to be attributed to Du Plessis Mornay and not to Languet, is the most important book on the subject, previous to Locke's work. It may be inferior in intellectual power to the work of Althusius,

but it had a deeper contemporary influence, just because
it is a *livre de circonstance* and not a scientific treatise.
The character of the argument may be briefly indicated.
Unlimited obedience is due to God alone; to the king as
his delegate a limited submission, always bounded by
God's law, is due. Between the Almighty on the one
hand and king and people on the other there is
an original contract, of which the covenant between
Jehoiada and the Israelites is the model; this contract
is on God's side one of protection; on that of the nation,
maintenance of the true religion. If the king violates
this covenant by persecuting the true religion, the people
are absolved from allegiance to their *mesne* lord by their
duties to God the overlord. A prince who persecutes
the faith is a rebel against God, no more a lawful sovereign
than a Pope deposed for heresy. It is evident how
greatly this theory of resistance on the basis of the
contract is framed for the express purpose of defending
religion; how the theory might be equally useful to
ultramontanes; how closely it is connected with feudal
conceptions. In detail the author shows the great
influence of the conciliar movement, for we find him
arguing from the rights of councils over Popes to those
of peoples over kings. Further, here, but still more in
ultramontane arguments on the same side, we note how
the medieval view of a Pope ceasing to be such *ipso facto*
in a case of heresy becomes the origin of the claim that
no Christian king is lawfully such who is heretical[8]; it is
not denied that infidel or Mohammedan sovereigns are
lawful monarchs, but they have no compact such as is
made by all Christians at their Baptism.

This contract, however, is not the only one which
the *Vindiciae* postulates. The writer goes on to another

instrument between king and people, which makes allegiance depend on good government, and places civil rights on a firmer basis than that of the royal grant. Here again we reach what was to be the main ground of struggle for a long time. The claim of kings, who had recognised the significance of sovereignty, was not so much to thwart the actual exercise of the national customs, as to claim that they were matters of grace not of right. It is against this claim that the idea of a contract proved so valuable—for it gave to the public the consciousness that their rights were no less rooted in the constitution of the country than were those of the king. The whole tendency of civilian lawyers was to deny this ; to treat as merely customary what hitherto had been regarded as legal, and to regard as readily alterable customs which had been treated as immutable. Some such theory as that of the original contract was needed to express the widespread consciousness that public rights and constitutional machinery were as much a part of the legal system as the admitted prerogatives of the crown.

The contract theory starts from the view directly denied by the theorists of Divine Right, that the people is the true source of royal power ; and in this our author and the numerous imitators were more indebted to Roman Law than some of them knew—for, as has been pointed out, the statements about the *Lex Regia* if treated as they were treated as a universal theory of government (there is a great deal of it in Barclay) imply that political authority springs from below—and to that extent favour the notion of the ultimate sovereignty of the people.

Both in this and still more in his theory of contract the author adopts and eloquently expounds that view of law which is common to him and many other writers, medieval and modern, which was noticed a little earlier, and makes of it something far higher than the positive edict of a transitory ruler. It has its relation to days when the legislative activity was either dormant or *in embryo*; and makes much, as it must, of custom as a source of law. It is concerned with the universality of law, its embodiment of principles rather than caprice, and pays scant regard to its sanction. Like the English followers of Coke and the common law, Du Plessis Mornay treats the idea as more venerable and majestic than any kingship. It is the voice of God; the king is but the creature of the law which is unchanged by time, unbiassed by passion, unmoved by fear; it knows no partiality and expresses no personal idiosyncracy, but is the utterance of universal reason, as against caprice and private interest. The *Vindiciae*[9] is a treatise which is elevated and impressive far beyond the run of political treatises, and breathes of the very spirit of liberty. Yet its author is nowhere so impressive as, nor does his style rise higher than, in those passages which extol the majesty of "Law," and express the ideas which through all vicissitudes were to distinguish the practical constitutionalism of the English people from the revolutionary system-mongering of Rousseau or Sieyès.

It is no anachronism to say that this treatise is very Whig, if by Whig be understood that body of opinion which is expressed in the writings of Locke and reflected in the Revolution settlement. Another evidence of the same character is the author's advice to individuals; all resistance on their part is rigidly condemned, prayers and tears are to be their weapons. Resistance must be orderly, directed by those estates which represent the kingdom rather than the king; or by those persons whose position is of public not private character. In this last provision we see how deeply the aristocratic spirit dominates the writer; for what he will not allow to the people he allows practically to nobles, even acting apart from any assembly[10]. There was little enough of democracy in theory or in practice among the Huguenots, and it is among the Jesuits and the Ligue that we must seek for thorough-going Jacobinism.

The historical element, which under various disguises is really at the bottom of the theorizing of the *Vindiciae*, becomes explicit in the *Franco-Gallia* of François Hotman. At first sight this work seems of an entirely different character from that of Du Plessis Mornay; the writer is not occupied with an ideal or universal theory of government but merely with an account of what the actual "law of the constitution" in France has been through the course of its development. He seeks to show that the nation of France is really one of free men.

But the two writers are alike in their conception of law and their reverence for precedent. And, when we bear in mind how entirely the possibility of such a theory as that of the *Vindiciae* is relative to the historical development of feudalism, we shall see that the spirit of the two is fundamentally the same, in spite of the deductive character of one work, and the inductive of the other. The contract theory is not really abstract, but a generalisation from the facts of the Middle Ages, just as the theory of sovereignty is an induction from the modern law-making State, and from the activities enshrined in the Canon and the Civil Law. In both the royal and the popular causes we are presented with a theory at first sight purely abstract and scientific, and in both cases the theory on inspection is seen to be relative to historical conditions and to owe its prevalence, not to intellectual curiosity, but to practical needs.

There are many other pamphlets, scattered through the *Mémoires des affaires d'état sous Charles IX*, and everything that Du Plessis Mornay writes is good reading, but there is little of substantial difference.   Daneau's *Politices Christianae* may, however, be noted, as crystallizing the whole into a scientific treatise.

The Huguenots, however, were not long in possession of the field; for they found in the claims of the Bourbon another and a better argument than theories of contract ; and the death of the Duke of Anjou in 1584 turned them into thorough-going supporters of legitimism.   Hereditary right and the Salic Law became their watchwords henceforth, and we must seek elsewhere for the succession to their older theories of liberty.

The Ligue inherited a double portion of this spirit. The Seize were the forerunners of the Jacobin Club, and Louis d'Orleans and Boucher were writers compared with whom the Huguenots were mild and moderate men. Both the organization and the doctrines of the Ligue were democratic—by preaching, and pamphleteering, by squibs, satires and poems it strove to appeal to all classes of the people.   Its object was to assert either in the Guise or the Spanish interest the main principle of the Counter-Reformation, that a heretic could never be a lawful king.   The principle was not really different from that of Knox and Goodman ; but it was laid down more universally, and attracted more attention.   Since even the Papalists admitted that a heretic Pope ceased to be such, and that is the view of

Gabriel Biel and John of Turrecremata, it is therefore obvious to assert with Reynolds that a Catholic king turning heretic becomes *ipso facto* a tyrant, and then by means of an argument analogous to that of the *Vindiciae* his deposition may be justified. There are many writings which express these views. The most important are the pamphlets of Louis d'Orleans, Jean Boucher's *Sermons de la Simulée Conversion* and the *De Justa Abdicatione Henrici Tertii*, Rossaeus' (Reynolds') *De Justa Republicae Christianae Potestate*. They are more violent and less original than the works of Hotman and Mornay, but Louis d'Orleans writes well. Indeed the *Banquet de Philarète* is full of imagination and a certain kind of eloquence. The *Dialogue du Manant et Maheustre* is also worthy of note ; it expresses the more theocratic and less unworthy side of the Ligue ; and is indeed an apology for the *democratic* Seize against the aristocratic adherents of the Duke de Mayenne. It is distinguished by an evident sincerity, and was written towards the close of the siege of Paris. On the whole, however, the theory laid down is the same as that of the Huguenots. Barclay makes it a reproach to Boucher that he has borrowed almost all his notions from the *Vindiciae*. It may be worth while giving a brief account of the longest of all these works, that of William Reynolds under the *nom de guerre* Rossaeus, entitled *De Justa Republicae Christianae Potestate*.

The author's argument is as follows :—He begins by showing the necessity and naturalness of civil government, and shows how men are driven to unite into a sovereign society. Then on a view of the varieties, both contemporary and historical, of the constitutions of

States he argues that no one form of government can have been originally established, but that the nature of the State and any limitations upon it are the result of the deliberate and purely arbitrary choice of the originally sovereign people. We find in Rossaeus what is also discernible in the *Vindiciae* and is the mark of all or nearly all the followers of this doctrine up to and after the Whig Revolution, the artificiality of the conception of the constitution. As against the theorists of Divine Right the libertarians are nearly all open to the reproach that they postulate a state of nature which is purely individualist and quite unhistorical, and that they make political constitutions the result of a conscious and definite choice on the part of a people supposed to have before their mind's eye the various forms of government and to have selected one as the best after due consideration. They prepare the way in fact for the rational savage of the eighteenth century, and have as little as he had to do with the history of social evolution. On the other hand we notice in Rossaeus a very definite adoption of the idea that political society is a *Genossenschaft*. In this he goes to the root of the matter, for the issue is really between those who take this view and those who derive all political power from above, and made a State primarily a *lordship*. This is the significance of the patriarchal theory as developed by Filmer. It treats society as purely a *Herrschaftsverband*. The contrast between the two ideas runs right back to the earliest times[11]. It is in this more than anything else that we are able to discern in the libertarians the strongly Teutonic element, just as in the theorists of Divine Right there is a marked Latin and civilian factor. In the second chapter on the *limited right of Christian*

kings Rossaeus makes use of this notion to declare (much
as the *Vindiciae* had done) that kingship must be bounded
by the end of its existence, *i.e.*, the security and freedom
of the subject. The individual could never have resigned his rights to the State except that he might
attain in return security for life and property. Thus a
condition is understood in all government whether or
no it be expressed: it must not contradict its own end[12].
This is the same conception as the conciliar party
had employed against the Pope. His power is given
in aedificationem, it must not be used *in destructionem*.
There is the statement of the limitations of all governmental theory very much as it afterwards appears in
Locke. Government is a pooling of individual rights
for the common needs of security; since it starts from
these rights its power is never omnipotent. This of
course is in direct contradiction to the doctrine of Hobbes
and Althusius, and later of Rousseau, who postulated
indeed a very similar origin for governmental authority
but gave it when formed unlimited, *i.e.*, sovereign
authority. All these united in taking their theory of
the origin of political power from one side, and its
nature and extent from the other of the combatants.
But Rossaeus is not content with these merely civic ends,
and proceeds, though by a different route, to the same
conclusions as those of Du Plessis Mornay. Governors
exist not only for life but for the good life; and the
encouragement of virtue is as much a fundamental condition of all government as is the security of life and
property[12]. This is proved by the practice of all nations.
Virtue requires religion for its adequate support, and
hence no government is legitimate without the admission
of the true religion. Even the governments of antiquity

allowed this as at once an extension and limitation of
their powers; and Christian peoples cannot be worse
off than Pagans or Turks. The inference to readers
who did not recognise toleration is obvious. No right-
ful prince can tolerate heresy; and a heretic king is
ipso facto a tyrant. The usual arguments from coronation oaths are employed. An interesting point is that
to the author the Spanish king is an example of a
legitimately limited monarch, while Henry VIII and
Elizabeth of course on the ground of their treatment of Protestantism are regarded as the worst of
tyrants ruling by no law but their own caprice[13]. Nor
was there, if the internal condition of Spain alone
be considered, anything particularly laughable in such
a view. Otherwise Mariana's famous book dedicated to
Philip III would not have been possible. Even two
centuries later that work could never have appeared
dedicated (except in irony) to George III without sub-
jecting its author to very considerable inconvenience.
The author then proceeds to an enumeration of the
characteristics of tyranny, which enables him to "deal
faithfully" with the last Valois. He considers that the
notes of tyranny may be reduced to three, (1) rapacious
oppression, (2) corruption of morals, public and private,
(3) hostility to the true religion. Under all these heads
Henri III is clearly a tyrant to be classed with Nero,
and Queen Elizabeth[14].

After this exhilarating chapter he devotes himself
to a candid examination of Protestantism which he
decides to be worse than Paganism; this, however, is
nothing to Calvinism, which is *longe detestabilior*. It is
noteworthy how he argues from the needs of human
nature as shown in all religious systems. His objection

to Lutheranism in regard to sacrificial doctrine and prayers for the dead is based almost entirely on the universality of these customs in some form or other[15]. The rest of the book is concerned with proving the right of deposition of heretic kings both by foreign monarchs and their subjects, and the fact that Henri is a relapsed heretic and that no faith is to be attached to his promises[16]. There is nothing especially noteworthy except the length—830 closely printed pages—with which these views are developed.

It is, however, worthy of remark that, in the argument about the disqualification of heresy, the author incidentally shows how even yet the doctrine of the *Selbständigkeit* of the nation has failed to penetrate. For he clearly considers the rules both of the Civil and Canon Law to be binding on individual States—the kingdom of France is, he makes evident, only a member of the commonwealth of the Church—and there exist to his hand the extremely severe constitutions of Justinian and others about the treatment of heresy[17]. We must bear in mind that the Corpus Juris in its complete form was not merely the law of the ancient world. Redacted posterior to S. Augustine, and under an Emperor half medieval, the conception of the place of the Church and the unity of religion, the notion of two powers equally from God, and the terms in which this is expressed, prepared the way for that development of ecclesiastical authority, which other causes concentrated in the hands of the Papacy and crystallised in the Canon Law. The usual examples from the Old Testament are employed by Rossaeus, and those from the Apocrypha; they are more skilfully used than by some authors. It is also to be noted that

the writer endeavours to show that Calvinism if allowed
to run its course will be as hostile to all secular power
as ever was Rome, and will destroy the aristocracy.
He makes out, as was easy, the strong case there was
for fearing under developed Presbyterianism a clerical
tyranny, and in this he may be compared to later
Anglican writers. He also demonstrates the way in
which the organization of "the religion" had been
practically worked so as to make a State within the
State, a new kingdom. He is eloquent on the revolutionary character of heresy, which will require all other
institutions to be made new in accordance with its
general spirit; and makes great play with the earlier
insurrectionary literature of the Huguenot party[18].

The book is not interesting nor eloquent nor particularly well argued, and is greatly marred by its
absurd exaggeration of style. But it affords as good
evidence as any other of the way in which similar ideas
of the nature of government were developed by either
party; of their subserviency to religious or ecclesiastical
purposes; of their dependence on views which go back
through the Middle Ages to the later days of the
ancient Empire; and on that general conception of
a universal Church State which is at least as old as
S. Augustine. Orthodoxy is a fundamental law of the
State in the real view of all these controversialists[19].
Speaking generally it may be said that the Ligue writers
are both more democratic and more theocratic and more
violent than the Huguenots[20]. They tend to say more of
tyrannicide. The murder of Henri III was received
with a chorus of delight. Boucher in the appendix to
the *De Justa Abdicatione Henrici Tertii* can scarcely
contain his transports. But the Huguenots never

admitted that they were really resisting the king, and are ridiculed by their opponents for their pretence—to be followed in England—of separating the king from his council. The same, however, was the case with the Ligue, until the murder of the Duke of Guise drove them definitely to throw off allegiance to the tyrant and made the act of Jacques Clement in ridding the world of "the worst king of the worse race that was ruled" the consistent outcome of their declared principles. We cannot, however, really separate between the principles of Ligueurs and Huguenots. Both assert the cause of civil liberty; both do so on the basis of an original contract, and combat the notion of absolute power responsible to God alone; both develop their argument on religious lines and treat heresy or rather heresy combined with persecution as a proof of tyranny. The Ligueurs treat the national State as but a part of a larger whole, and in this perhaps lies their main difference from the Huguenots, who go no further than to demand foreign princes' help in favour of "the religion"; they did not and could not talk of a Protestant Christendom.

The purely religious or at least ecclesiastical motive of both parties is of course obvious; but with religion intermingled there were political grievances over taxation and denial of justice to the people. Of course the pamphleteers were purer in their reasonings than the political leaders. The Ligue was doubtless largely a mere cover for the ambitious designs of the Guises. But that does not alter the fact of the predominantly religious character of the motive to which it was necessary to appeal. To all parties government is largely a theocracy—it is *Politices Christianae* which all affect to seek. The mere notion of utility is not enough to justify an insurrection. Right must be proved. Hence arises what we remarked, the predominantly legal character of the argument. Every pamphleteer is occupied in proving that *his* party is *de jure* resisting somebody who by his own or others' action is usurping authority of which he is no longer legally seised. This is the animus no less of royalists against the Pope than of Huguenots and Ligueurs against an absolute monarch.

What is clear throughout the discussion is the dread of the new absolutism of the State; the determination to resist the notion of its universal authority; to assert that there are spheres of life and bonds of association which do not arise from its fiat and cannot be dissolved by it; and the practical connection of this with some interest, real or supposed, of religion. Even the theory of Divine Right was from one point of view, as Whitgift saw, an admission of ends higher than those merely political in civil society; for the lowest view of the State was taken only by professed Machiavellians, and those who divorced it in idea from all but immediate ends except in so far as it is inspired by the Church with a higher life. The conception of the State as purely secular was, however, more completely realized by that body whose theories we shall consider in the next lecture.

LECTURE VI.

THE JESUITS.

FROM the Monarchomachi we naturally pass to the Jesuits, the real agents of the Counter-Reformation, and partly also of Spanish aggression. Nearly all the Jesuit writers of importance in the earlier years of their existence are Spaniards, or Philo-Spaniards. We must regard their attitude as partly, at least, determined by national feeling—even in spite of their professed aims. The complete recognition of the sovereignty of the non-Imperial States would perhaps—indeed almost certainly—not have been a feature of Jesuit philosophising, had they sprung from a German origin. In that case there would have been an attempt to reinstate in its ancient prerogatives the Imperial Crown. As it is, however, they criticise Bartolus, and assert the complete equality of sovereign States and, in temporal concerns, the relatively independent character of royal power. They are thinking of their masters. The Spanish character of early Jesuitry is illustrated by the famous book of Juan Mariana, *De Rege et Regis Institutione.* This book was burnt by orders of the Parliament of Paris, and aroused a violent controversy on account of the tone in which it discussed the murder of Henri III. It was always declared that the Society was not responsible for the doctrines, and in the second edition slight alterations were made which did not materially affect the passages incriminated[1]. But Lossen is of opinion that the Society is not really to be identified with this book of a man who by no means approved of the methods of Jesuit government, and wrote a treatise to point out its defects[2]. This view, I think, is well founded. The book is *sui generis.* It is unlike nearly all the treatises, whether occasional or philosophic, which the Jesuits produced in such numbers. Nor is it really of the same order as the books considered in the last lecture. Indeed it is easy to parallel Boucher with Becanus or D'Orleans with Parsons or Cardinal Allen; and there is a very considerable resemblance between the Jesuit *livres de circonstances* and those of the Ligueurs. But except in practical conclusions this is not the case with the *De Rege.* Its whole tone is different; it is very individual, very Spanish—indeed it is not a Counter-Reformation pamphlet at all. It is far more comparable with the work of Sir John Fortescue, *De Laudibus Legum Angliae,* or Sir Thomas Smith's *Commonwealth of England,* or Claude de Seysell on the government of France, than with the pamphlets and treatises produced in such seething haste by the religious wars—although it of course alludes to them. It is of especial interest, for it shows us the way of thinking that was natural to a Spaniard and the kind of atmosphere in which the greater works of Molina and Suarez, Vasquez and Salmeron were reared. It will then be convenient to consider this book which is short and interesting before we proceed to the great mass of writing.

The book is dedicated to the young prince of
Asturias who was afterwards to be Philip III, and is
in this respect a work of the same order as Budé's
Institution du Prince or, to go back to the original, the
De Regimine Principum of Egidius Romanus. It is
tutorial, and contains practical guidance for a good
prince and the way to train a man for the *métier
du roi*.

Mariana opens with a description of the state of
nature which in its sentiment heralds the day of
Rousseau and the eighteenth century.

The idea of a golden age, however, gives way not to
internal individual greed, but to external danger; and
families must coalesce for defence. So arises the State,
and by their voluntary surrender the multitude choose
a ruler for certain ends. These ends are the measure
of his power, and the writer goes on to argue against
absolutism. Mariana makes it quite clear that he does
not regard the King of Spain as having any rights of
arbitrary taxation or legislation, and expresses his regret
that some of the powers of constitutional freedom are
falling into disuse. He of course denies the competence
of the king in ecclesiastical causes, but says little of
the Pope (as Lossen remarks), and regrets the wholesale
secularisation of Church property that had been proceeding in Spain, no less than elsewhere. The chapter *De
Tyranno* is what gave the book its fame and its infamy.
Mariana followed nearly all writers since Bartolus in
dividing tyrants into the two classes of usurpers, tyrants
in the Greek sense, and legitimate sovereigns ruling
oppressively; but he makes less of the difference than
most, owing to his taking a stronger view of the rights of

individuals in regard to those of the second kind. For
nearly all are agreed that a tyrant *absque titulo* may be
slain by anyone. This was a very practical point. For
it involved on the Protestant side the justification of the
murders of the Guises and the Cardinal of Lorraine and
in theory of Catharine de' Medici—as may be seen from
the *Vindiciae.* In the Papalist view, Elizabeth and William
the Silent were tyrants (they had no title to rule), while
to the Ligueurs Henri IV was *le tyran de Béarn.* Mariana,
however, and Buchanan are almost alone in allowing to
the individual the right of tyrannicide against a legal
ruler who is an oppressor. Both, in the last resort,
permit to dispense with the formalities of a public
deposition ; and Mariana's justification of the murder
of Henri III treats him as a tyrant of this sort. He
decides that a tyrant may be killed both openly and
by craft but objects to poison when the victim drinks
or eats it because this compels him to become a
suicide. There is no harm in poisoning him through
clothes or cushions. This distinction goes back to John
of Salisbury's *Policraticus*, the earliest medieval apology
for tyrannicide.

In regard to other matters it is worthy of note that
the writer in his chapter on "the Poor" definitely
demands a regular poor-law, would like it imposed upon
each municipality and recommends a more liberal
employment of monastic and other ecclesiastical revenues
for this purpose ; he disapproves loudly here and
throughout the book of any secularisation of Church
property, but he would see with pleasure the ancient
fourfold division of tithe or something like it reintroduced,
and the mass of indolent and luxurious clergy dimi-

nished. In the chapter on "spectacles" he expresses himself with Puritanical strictness on the evils of the modern stage, but unlike the Puritans recognises the necessity of having regard to the conditions of the public mind, and recommends that the stage be regulated, and the young, so far as possible, be kept away from it. In regard to the choice of Bishops he is content to leave it practically to the king, so long as he will choose men of light and leading. The most remarkable chapter, however, is the closing one, which is against the toleration of more than one religion in *the same province*. The argument is hardly theocratic at all, and distinguishes the book as perhaps the least ecclesiastical of all the books on this side in the period. The reasons for prohibiting more than one religion are that heretics cannot be relied on to keep their promises, and without this fundamental good faith societies cannot exist. The argument is the same in a different form as that of Locke, that atheism must not be tolerated, for that destroys the basis of the original contract, and removes the obligation to keep the pact. Mariana goes on to point out the practical impossibility of men of competing religions agreeing, and the extreme danger to the government of favour and even fairness between two bitterly hostile parties. This of course was true in an age when religious parties all believed in the duty of mutual extermination. In regard to the argument so often used that the Turks managed to tolerate other religions than their own and many of them, he declares the Turks no models for Christians, but goes on to point out that they did so only on the basis of denying all civil rights to the subject populations, and that, *if that condition were accepted by heretics*, toleration might be possible. This passage, and indeed the whole tone of the chapter which is eminently political, shows how far the author is from the reckless bigotry of Rose or Boucher, or the colder fanaticism of Beza or Cartwright. Probably deliberately, he avoids any mention of the Roman claims, and any examination of heresies. There is far less of the idea of a universal state of Christendom than in the ordinary Counter-Reformation treatises; but of imperialism there is a good deal, as was to be expected, and a certain amount of very sound advice anent the treatment of provinces according to their customs and modes of thought and character. The author is clearly not in favour of a merely centralised despotism; while his knowledge of Spanish history and patriotism is so great that he is never at a loss for an instance. Quite apart from the chapter on the treatment of tyrants the work is a very remarkable one to have been published with an imprimatur in the heyday of the Spanish monarchy, and during the reign of Philip II; it is a political treatise with references to religion, not a pamphlet in favour of a religious community under a political guise like the *Vindiciae*. There is more of the historian than of the Jesuit in the book. If it has not the impressiveness and eloquence of Du Plessis Mornay it has a charm and a freshness that are all its own; and is perhaps even stronger in its recognition of the sovereignty of the people as fundamental to the State. Perhaps it is this recognition more than any other characteristic that assimilates Mariana's work to the ordinary treatises of the Jesuits on political matters. These treatises are not the least important effect of the renewed scholasticism, which it was the mission of the Jesuits to further. In form more often

than not they are a commentary, by way of dialectic
discussion, on those parts of the Summa of S. Thomas
which treat *De Justitia et Jure*, and embrace the topics of
the origin and nature of law and therefore a civil society,
the limits and the competence of the law-giver.
This is the case with works like those of Vasquez or
Salmeron entitled commentaries, or Molina's *De Justitia
et Jure*, and indeed with Suarez' *De Legibus*, though that
starts less directly from S. Thomas.   A little later,
we have works like those of Petrus de Lugo and
Sanctarelli, and even in Jouvency are found similar
ideas awakening similar controversies.   In addition to
these we have controversial works like those of Parsons
and Allen in England, or Tanner, Bellarmin and
Suarez in reply to Sarpi and the other defenders of
Venice against the Pope, besides the whole host of
writers led by Bellarmine, who fought against James I
and his apology for the oath of allegiance.   In some
of the treatises of moral theology it is also possible
to find discussions of the right of tyrannicide.   All the
writings give one an insight into the mind of the Jesuits
on political questions so long as the Counter-Reformation was still proceeding.\ From the close of the
religious wars in 1648 we may almost date their tacit
surrender of the claim to pronounce on these questions,
and their enlistment on the side of royalism, of
which the most marked example was their support of
Louis XIV, although this was conditioned by their
controversies with the Jansenists.   The views of these
writers though similar are not always identical, and
they are never official; not only was the Society no more
publicly committed to them than it was to Probabilism,
but Aquaviva at the request of the French court issued

an order in 1614 that they were not to meddle with politics at all[3].

It remains however true that the Jesuits were everywhere regarded as the main supporters of the deposing power and the opponents therefore of the Divine Right of Kings; that the easiest way of condemning Dissenters in England was to dub them Jesuits on the ground that they shared their views as to the rights of subjects to resist their sovereigns, and that this activity only ceased with the practical cessation of the opportunity of destroying heresy by arousing insurrection. The only chance left was that tried in England to reintroduce Roman Catholicism by despotic power, instead of exterminating Protestantism by an appeal to national traditions allied with religious conservatism.

Of pure nationalism indeed the Jesuits were not and could not be the promoters—except so far as it meant the Spanish Empire. For they were the upholders of the old idea of the unity of Christendom in a new form. It meant no longer a civil unity: there was to them, as Spaniards, no universal Empire except the Church; no final authority but the Pope. But their treatises are full of the idea of the law that is more than national;—in spite of the recognised independence of States men like Suarez clearly regard the *Corpus Juris* as the common form of law, and though it is sometimes admitted that Roman Law as such does not bind, yet it is clearly a part of the general heritage, no less than is the Canon Law in matters ecclesiastical. The whole force of their appeal rests on the conception of a law that is higher than merely national custom. The Jesuits are far from being the sole, but they are the cardinal instance of that conception of law, as the embodiment of eternal justice which is everywhere struggling against the modern conception of it, as absolutely the command of the law-giver. This might not indeed apply to the Pope, a true sovereign, but in their view it did apply to everyone else. The most interesting thing in Suarez' great book is its table of contents; what should make a man include under the same title so many kinds of law to our thinking nearly as disparate as the laws of cricket and the laws of political economy? It is because, while differing in every other point, sanction, incidence and origin, they are yet alike in all, expressing in some form the idea of right ; in other words they are concerned with *some* notion of justice, an ethical conception anterior to the law in the stricter sense. For this very reason their thought of law is of wider import and more universal than ours ; and enters far more into theological or ethical discussion. It cannot be too often repeated that the only possible intellectual foundation for all the " liberal ". conceptions of politics in those days and the form which they took is the prevalent legal atmosphere of discussion of every form of practical activity ; and also a belief in the eternal significance and the universal validity of those conceptions of right and justice, involved in the idea of law, which it was the work of Machiavelli, Hobbes and the royalists to disengage from it. Throughout these pages, long and tedious with dialectic, there runs the claim that law may be nullified because it embodies injustice as against the more modern view, that anything the law-giver bids or forbids is good law merely by his fiat. The confusion between ethics and law may be erroneous from the theoretical, yet from the practical standpoint, their entire separation was equally dangerous. At any rate it was some sense, that law

was in its nature more than a mere command, that it
implied justice and a right recognised but not created
by it that gave all these writings their significance and
their effect. Liberty was preserved where it was
preserved, because right and law were identified in
language, and not distinguished in thought—or in other
words because the moral element in legal obligation
was not forgotten.

It may seem that the last people likely to effect such
results would be the Latinist lawyers, with their study of
a system so eminently "imperative" as the Civil Law, but
it must be pointed out that the *content* of the system
had become so much a part of the organization of life
that any other arrangement in many private concerns
was and has remained unthinkable, that there are phrases
at the very outset which strongly emphasize the ethical
aspect of law, that the Canonists had further developed
this notion (in spite of their insistence on the Papal
sovereignty), and that the Canon Law made a
natural bridge to connect legal rights with ethical and
theological discussions. Besides this the *jus gentium*
was the common law of nations. Modern "liberal"
maxims are the result of an amalgam of law, ethics and
theology. Moreover the system must be considered as
a whole. On the one hand there is the Pope to whom
all the attributes of a sovereign law-giver may be
ascribed, and whose despotism by Divine Right framed
the model for that of other absolutists, as we have
already seen. On the other hand, and this is where the
Jesuits impressed the theory of popular liberty even
reaching to such men as Algernon Sidney, there is the
ordinary king, whom they conceive as the mere creature
of popular choice, the minister not the master of his

people, the *dispensator* not the *dominus* of their goods.

It is indeed, as we have seen, largely the conception implied in the argument from the *lex regia* on which Jesuits and others rely for their theory of popular sovereignty. The king is head. True, but how? Simply because the multitude transferred their power to him of their own accord. His authority springs from below, from the community; he is its delegate. It is this which the Jesuits emphasize; they do not indeed omit altogether the notion of a contract, but it is a matter of minor importance compared to the purely popular origin of power. Once this be admitted, all absolute claims are easily refutable, and indefeasible hereditary right becomes an impossibility. With Suarez and Molina political power is the inevitable result of the determination of men to live in a society[4]. In fact political authority arises out of the nature of a community as such. It is a contradiction in terms to talk of joining a community and giving it no power. If men live in a community, that community must essentially possess certain powers of organization. In other words a corporate body is something more than the sum of its members; the greater Jesuits are on their way to the conception of the *personality* of corporate bodies, if they have not reached it. The nature of their own society would certainly teach them this. Nor must we forget in the development of the contractual theory the influence of monasticism. A "Leviathan" like that of Hobbes formed by the deliberate choice of its members, with absolutely sovereign rights, and no power of renunciation of obedience, was more nearly paralleled in a monastic order than in any "national" State; when Melanchthon says that the true communal life is that of the State and not that of a religious order, he shows that the analogy of monastic institutions to the State was one that naturally occurred to the mind; and it is possible, though it can hardly be proved, that the artificial theory of the State may have owed something of its prevalence to those bodies, in some respects states in themselves, which did arise by deliberate choice and contrivance. Anyhow the original sove reignty of the people is a cardinal doctrine of the Jesuit thinkers, is more emphasized by them than by Protestant controversialists; and if not separated in practice from some notion of a contract between the depositary of power and his subjects, is separable from it in thought. They prepared the way for Althusius and therefore for Rousseau. The governing thought of Suarez is that the community has its power immediately from God as a result of the fact of its being a society, in other words of something like Rousseau's social contract The governing thought of the *Vindiciae* is that individuals come together to form a State for certain ends, and surrender some powers but not all to the body so formed. The Whig State is in fact a limited, the Jesuit and Jacobin State is an unlimited liability company.

Molina, though he declares the State to derive its power not from a pact but immediately from God, yet denies to it absolute rights. On the other hand Suarez while he asserts for the community rights *per se* distinctly affirms that the government whatever it be is appointed under conditions. He ends in fact pretty much where the Whigs began[5].

But their object is nearly always ecclesiastical They desire to emphasize the difference between ecclesi-

ɪstical jurisdiction, which comes from above, and civil,
which springs from below. The Pope has his power
from God, he is his immediate vicar; not so kings and
emperors, theirs is from the people, their right is only
Divine so far as all things natural and worthy are
Divine; but to say the same of the Pope is to commit
the heresy of conciliar agitators; and the two must be
distinguished. This is the meaning of the deeply interesting treatise of Lainez on the right of Bishops[6].
His object is to deny that their powers of any sort
have any other origin than the Papal grant; and to
this end he distinguishes sharply between secular and
ecclesiastical governments.

Lainez brings out what, as Gierke says, is to be
found in most Jesuit writers, the absolutely secular
character of their conception of the civil power. It is
a purely human institution for the worldly ends of peace
and riches. It might be said that taking the civil
State as a separate entity, they accepted a purely utilitarian view of its activity. It is to them non-moral.
Its laws have a merely outward sanction; although
it is a duty to obey them, in so far as they do not
conflict with higher ends. Their idea of the civil power
is, in fact, that of Locke and the individualists who
regard the State as necessary for certain indispensable
ends, but as in itself dangerous if unchecked, and
rather evil than good in its activities. The Jesuit view
is that the end of the State being purely external, it
cannot be in the last resort worthy of high reverence;
and must be kept under tutelage, if man is to reach his
highest. They separate sharply the civic life of man,
which is external and partial, from his religious, which is
internal and all-embracing[7].

Since, however, men are not merely creatures of this world, their unworldly interests need protection and this is the office of the Church. The door is thus opened for the Papal claims, and the deposing power can be justified in the usual way. The point to notice is that they conceive the civil power as *purely* secular ; and to a certain extent as independent. This is at once similar to the view of Presbyterians like Cartwright or Melville, rebuked by Whitgift for their " Turkish," "Machiavellian " theory of the State ; and opposed to the Protestant doctrine of Luther or the Anglicans who consecrate the activities of the State by treating the Church as its other aspect and entirely repudiate the dichotomy raised by Jesuits and Presbyterians. The one theory descends through Whigs to English individualism. The other is the ancestor of modern socialism, for Luther is the true forerunner of Hegel in his political views.

The Jesuits were not great originators. Their view of the State was not new ; it is the hierarchical doctrine adapted to new circumstances. We find even in their views about tyrannicide little that is not an expansion of older views. Just as Probabilism was invented by a Dominican, although it became the *cachet* of seventeenth century Jesuits, so their view of the relation between civil and ecclesiastical powers, like that of the nature of law, can be found in other writers. The conceptions of law entertained by Soto, Navarra, and Covarruvias are fundamentally those of Suarez and Molina. Of the theory we have now to discuss it is the popularisation rather than the invention that is to be ascribed to the Jesuits.

This theory is generally known as that of the indirect power of the Pope in regard to the civil ruler.

The Jesuits and others who hold the view do not claim for the Pope the monarchy of the world; they do not assert that States are without a real being and some independence of their own; the Pope is no longer universal ruler. The claims of the canonists and writers like Bozius to make him an Emperor are deliberately surrendered; and the *Unam sanctam* undergoes careful interpretation. Bellarmine's treatise on the subject was actually put on the *Index*, because it only allowed the Pope an indirect power[8]. This is Bellarmine's own account; even if the reason be not the true one, the fact that he could say so alone proves that from the ecclesiastical point of view he was regarded as an innovator. Now when we consider that his book was condemned by the Parliament of Paris as scandalous and inimical to the independence of kings and the Gallican liberties, it is clear that some explanation is needed. The truth is this. Under the mask of an indirect power, which is to interfere in politics in order to prevent laws being passed contrary to ecclesiastical liberty or against the virtue of the people, and may depose a monarch, if he attacks the immunities of the Church, it is clear that practical activity of the most dangerous kind might be exercised by the Popes; and that the doctrine if carried to its extremes might be so used, as to mean a temporal sovereignty for the Pope, or at any rate an irritating suzerainty[9]. That with the Jesuit order triumphant it could have been so used is probable enough; and all the evils of the Ligue might at any moment be repeated. This was obvious, and is the cause of the anger of the Parisian lawyers and later on of James I.

But there is another aspect, and this must have struck

the Pope. If the Pope's power in politics be only
indirect, the civil power must have its own existence
assured by rights other than Papal; it is in idea
independent. Moreover, the Pope may interfere to
protect his own subjects, but so may the ruler of
any State in the interests of his subjects who are
residing abroad or even if they are not. In other words,
while the Pope may interfere, it is as ruler of an
independent community, not as head of the whole
organization of which the civil State is but a part. And
this is actually used as an argument by more than
one writer to justify such interference.

In a word, the relations of Church and State are
international; the Pope is no longer the head of one
great community, of which the kingdoms are the
provinces[10]. Whether Bellarmine quite saw this is doubtful, whether he even meant more than a verbal concession
to the other side cannot be proved; but taken in
conjunction with their view of the different origins of
civil and religious power, and the facts of the case in
regard to Roman Catholics in England or Germany, and
the depression of the Holy Roman Empire in favour of
national States, there can I think be little doubt that the
Jesuit view was really paving the way for a great change.
No longer was Christendom a whole. That had disappeared absolutely with the religious peace of Augsburg
and would be recognised finally in 1648. No longer was
the great Church-State with its twin heads even an ideal.
But (and this is true even of Catholic States) there are
now a multitude of communities possessing within themselves complete independence; only "the liberty of each
must not hinder the equal liberty of all," and so the Pope
as head of one of these communities must interfere where

necessary for his subjects. It is true that in this case the members are scattered throughout the other communities, and are identified with the same physical persons as the subjects of the civil States. But we have henceforth two communities brought into relation; no longer, as in the medieval view, one community with separate departments. The Jesuits are not always consistent, and sometimes, as was only natural, hark back to the older view. But the theory of the "indirect power" marks the change from the idea of one commonwealth with different officers to the modern conception of Church and State as two distinct social entities. In this sense it is epoch-making. It is true that the Gallican mind attempts but with little success to show that the "medieval" Papalists really meant no more, save in a few instances[11]; but the problem has been how to get out of the political dangers aroused by the principles of the *Unam sanctam* without denying its verbal statements. This process went on until in our own day the theory of the Church as a *societas perfecta* was worked out again by the Jesuits, Palmieri and Tarquini[12], and in the Encyclical *Immortale Dei*[13] was proclaimed official. What it really does is to substitute for the claim of supremacy a claim to independence, which, under a system of toleration, never need mean any more; and permits as complete a recognition of State power as is seen on the part of Roman Catholics in the United States or Prussia. At this time men were only feeling their way to such a notion, nor could it be realized until an age of toleration.

But the theory of the Church as a *societas perfecta* was expressed even at this time by Simancas and is given by a conciliar writer as a ground for deposing the Pope— *i.e.*, the Church as a perfect society must have the power

of purging itself from within, and therefore getting rid
of an impossible Pope. On the Jesuit side, what is most
remarkable is that they admit, grudgingly and reluctantly
it is true, but still they do admit the State to be a *societas
perfecta*; or rather, confining that expression to the
Church, they admit the State to have an existence
independent of the Church, with its own origin, end, and
limits. It is indeed to be kept in its limits, reminded of
its origin, and confined to its end by the Church. But
still it has independent rights and powers.

Barclay makes use of the theory as against Papalist
claims and is rebuked by Bellarmine for going too far in
developing the independent rights of the State. It is,
of course, always the power on the defensive that is most
anxious to assert these rights, whether Barclay and Catholic
royalists, or in our own day the Jesuits, for the power in
possession is clearly a *societas perfecta*, if there be such a
thing in nature; what needs to be proved is that it is
not the only one, *i.e.*, that there are one or more other
communities complete in themselves, whose powers are
not derived from and not dependent on the other *societas
perfecta* but merely recognised by it; just as one State
recognises another. In ecclesiastical matters the difference is that the same person is a member of both bodies.
In the Middle Ages, in all controversies, the State, if the
term is to be used, means the hierarchy of lay officials,
the Church that of ecclesiastical; the contest is not
between Church and State but between *sacerdotium* and
regnum. Later on the State means the whole community,
clerical and lay, and the Church the same persons in the
religious aspect; so that whereas in the medieval controversies the struggle, if it be ever correct to regard it as
between two societies at all, is between two separate

departments consisting of different persons, but each within the same society, in modern times the controversy is always one between two communities in which it may be that the same persons are members of both. The reason why it was possible to make the Civil Law and the Canon Law in any way harmonise, was that they were each conceived as laws regulating the members of the same society, while further the very decay of Imperial power in practice rendered both laws rather a set of ideal rules than entirely obligatory legal systems of the modern kind. At any rate until the "reception," the acknowledged force of local customs or laws makes the whole Roman system rather a general norm to which law should try to conform than a purely positive juris- prudence; all this helped the assimilation of legal, ethical and theological ideas, out of which grew both modern politics and international law.

The conception of Church and State as two separate communities was not completely carried out among the Jesuits; so far as the Papal power was concerned they were still under the influence of the ideal of a universal State of which the kingdoms were members; and it was only gradually that they were forced to that admission of non-Catholic States as individuals, which though not the only, is the surest basis of the claims that both are perfect societies. In England it is only after the Toleration Act that in Churchmen like Warburton the idea comes up. But the Jesuits lay definite claim to the Church being a perfect society, they admit the same for the State in general, and they deny any final authority to the Empire; thus making it a necessity to formulate in the future a distinct notion of two societies to be mutually recognised by Concordats.

This idea was at the time carried furthest by English and Scotch Calvinists. In this they borrowed from the French. Not only was the organization of the Huguenot Churches the model for those of Scotland and England—for they had the same problems, *i.e.*, to make the system of Calvin national not merely municipal, and to do so from within, not as in Germany from above by princely authority—but the conditions of the religious wars made it possible and even necessary for the ecclesiastical organization to be largely used for civil purposes, to communicate with foreign princes, raise armies, levy taxes, and indeed perform much of the business of a government. Hence we find Rossaeus abusing the Huguenots and Coligni for their organization of an *imperium in imperio*, while of course the Ligue was similar. In both cases it was not even an organized Church in the medieval sense of the official hierarchy, but a community in which lay and clerical elements worked together; and it cannot be doubted that both Huguenots and Ligue helped forward the notion that Church and State were two distinct kingdoms, which might as corporate persons enter into relations with one another, but which differing in end and meaning were never the same, never merely separate aspects of one society, even though every member of the commonwealth, as was certainly intended in England and to some extent accomplished in Scotland, should be a member of both.

However they came by it, it is certain that this notion of two distinct commonwealths, both visible, both coercive, both complete and self-sufficient, yet one with an earthly, the other a heavenly end, is to be found in the leaders of the Presbyterian movement in

England, Cartwright and Travers, and in the second stage of the Scottish Reformation. Mr Lacey has pointed out that this idea which is to be found in Melville is not in Knox, who held the view that Church and State were merely the different aspects of the same society, or, to be more accurate, that the civil and ecclesiastical powers were each magistracies of that which in one aspect is called the Church, in the other the State. The real recognition is that of a corporate personality; the end is the differentiating conception, and we are helped forward towards the idea of a "general will" which in the commonwealth, even if composed of the same persons, is different from that in the Church. In this respect Jesuits and Presbyterians work together, owing to the sharply ecclesiastical character of the theory of both parties, and to the actual fact no longer seriously to be denied of the *Selbständigkeit* of the State. In an age of increasing secular power and of competing religions, the Church as an organized community has to formulate afresh the notion of its significance; for it is rapidly ceasing to be even ideally true that kings are its officers, and the dream of a universal State had disappeared with the failure of Charles V to secure the Empire for his son. The danger of the House of Austria to Europe might be greater, but the new Europe was clearly not going to be organized on any rearrangement of the old Imperial theory.

The Spanish origin of the dominant neo-scholasticism cannot be too greatly estimated as an element in this process of the freeing of the State, and the distinguishing of it from the Church. For Spain was a new power, and could not claim, like French Ligueurs, any ancient Papal recognition of temporal independence, *i.e.*, their

theory must be general, not particular. It was, then,
a necessity to formulate for the Pope a theory which
should leave him a position as head of the Church, but
deny to the Church any claim to be a State including
other States; hence the importance of the recognition of
the separate ends of the two, and the indirect nature of
Papal authority. For this indirect power might, though
it need not, be interpreted to mean no more and
no less than that of any official exponent of ethics
or theology, who *must* at times claim to deal with
the basis of political authority, even if all he does
is to tell people to obey the law on grounds of religious
duty. In theory the Pope after this doctrine need be no
more than a Professor Green expounding "the principles
of political obligation." It has indeed been attempted
to show that the medieval claims meant no more than
this, but in face both of statements and of actual facts
this attempt can only be recognised as ingenious rather
than convincing.

But this is not all. With State and Church recognised as independent societies, with the definitely declared
recognition of national freedom, with territorialism more
and more rampant in Germany, some theory of the
relations between these bodies was a necessity. This
theory was to take the form of international law in
the next century. The Jesuits and the other Spanish
philosophers, Navarra, Soto, Covarruvias, prepared the
way for this; they did this by frank recognition of the
separateness of States, combined with their belief in the
law natural as the basis and real authority of all laws,
and with their inheritance of the amalgam of Civil and
Canon Law as a body of ideal rules, not merely of positive
obligation. The Spanish mind completes the amalgama-

tion of laws divine, civil and ecclesiastical into a single system; it contemplates the universe as subject to the reign of jurisprudence, and Suarez' treatise is not only of laws, but of God the legislator; he knows many kinds of law, eternal, natural, positive, but no distinction between them that is really fundamental; his ethics is essentially legalist, and hence the danger of casuistry and the possibility of "Probabilism" which is not necessary to a system with no confessors. By easy stages he passes from law in the strictest sense to those portions of the Civil Law not enforced in Spain, but still felt to be law; to Canon Law which if partly ecclesiastical positive law shades off frequently into practical morality; and to the law natural, the dictates of reason and conscience, which alone gives to municipal laws their enduring validity, and lifts jurisprudence from being the science of individual litigation into a philosophy of the universe[14]. This was the atmosphere in which International Law grew up, and without which it was impossible that it should have grown up. It means at once the prevalence of Roman Law, yet its ideal character, the lingering conception of Christendom as a unity, coupled with the practical recognition of territorialism and the impossibility of making the Pope or the Emperor international arbiters. We find in Bartolus the beginning of this; he emphasizes the independence of those cities *non recognoscentes superiorem*, and formulates from both civil law and morals some of those rules which are to regulate this intercourse. But to him Emperors and Popes are true lords of the world; and it is heresy to doubt it. What he did for Italy had in the seventeenth century to be done for Europe. We have seen what is really a single attempt at a practical scheme in the great design of Sully. I forbear to cite the classical passage from Suarez. It is too familiar to need more than mention. The Jesuits laid the foundations of a new system partly because of their modernity and partly owing to their conservatism. They combined the new recognition of political facts with ancient ideals of unity, and the older conception of law, as an eternal verity. These two elements of thought were both to be found and were necessarily found in the system of politics of that day. Without the one the conception of States as juristic and equal persons is impossible, equal not in power any more than are individuals, but in the fact of being able to direct themselves to conscious ends ; without the other the notion of a unity of these persons, and a bond binding them together, and certain limits of activity they may not overpass, would not have been possible, or would have taken longer to discern. The persistence of the notion of law natural, coupled with the actual facts of widespread and increasing prevalence of the Civil Law, its purest outcome, and also of the general reorganization of the Canon Law, formed the only possible atmosphere for that notion of the legal obligation of contracts which as we saw was the necessary condition and the true explanation of the popularity of the doctrine of the original contract, and is also at the very bottom of the whole system of Grotius in regard to international affairs.

LECTURE VII.

THE NETHERLANDS REVOLT.

THE triumphant figure of the latter half of the seventeenth century is that of William the Silent. The assured independence of the Netherlands is a greater achievement than the defeat of the Armada or the Battle of Ivry or the deposition of Mary Stuart. Henri IV sacrificed half of the principles for which he stood in order to secure success; William the Silent sacrificed nothing but his life. In spite even of the religious intolerance of the Synod of Dort and persecution he would never have approved, the Netherlands were to the seventeenth what the England of the Revolution was to the eighteenth and early nineteenth centuries, a working model of free institutions, and the centre of light for the rest of Europe. Laud complains of the way in which books which he disliked got themselves printed in Amsterdam. In the struggle between liberty and authority the possession of a hostile printing press becomes of capital importance. It is not in any novelty of ideas, so much as in their practical accomplishment, that the influence of the Netherlands was so important. Hitherto we have spoken of movements like the Conciliar or the Huguenot, which ultimately failed, however fertile in ideas ; or the Jesuits whose early excursions into popular politics were forgotten by the age which connected them entirely with the *ancien régime*. These movements, as we saw, had all their influence on the future, and were not merely heralds but makers of our modern world of thought. But it was the Netherlands that gave them the leverage which rendered them effectual—until that was done even more powerfully by England. The Dutch revolt gathered up the various tendencies against absolutism, and made them effectual as a practical force and operative in the future ; its success enabled them to crystallize and take philosophical shape, just as the success of Henri IV made the same process possible for the theory of royalism, and was the condition *sine quâ non* for such writers as Pierre Gregoire of Toulouse or Barclay. Dr Cunningham has taught us to look to the Dutch as the source of our commercial improvements in the seventeenth century. That "conscious imitation" of them of which he wrote is no less conspicuous in regard to politics. For they appeared to have solved the problem which others were discussing. They had shown how to combine liberty with order in a modern State, they had secured control over their own government, too much control as was afterwards apparent. During the early years of their revolution, the ideas of toleration had found deliberate expression, and if these were afterwards deserted, the example of William the Silent remained. They had paved the way for federalism ; and their existence rested on the principle of nationality, no less than on that of the right of resistance to tyranny ; the status of their leader was that of a small sovereign prince, and prepared the way for the recognition of the equality " before the Law " of all States, while their

position in regard to the Emperor, like that of the Swiss,
served still further to emphasize the passing away of the
old European order. Their government was rather a
limited monarchy than a republic. Ideas, which might
otherwise have been buried for all time, could influence
future developments because there was now a modern
place where they could be seen actually at work—not
the relict of two Empires like Venice, nor the cast-off
clothes of feudalism like Poland, but a living, growing
community consciously occupied with modern problems,
and shaping its destinies in accordance with principles
destined after long obscuration to become generally
recognised.   The   Dutch   succeeded   because   they
represented such different tendencies.   On the one
hand their success in throwing off the foreign yoke of
Philip and organizing themselves as a territorial unity
under a prince must be regarded as analogous to the
process whereby the other German princes became
sovereign and independent of the Empire. A great deal
of the feeling against Philip was national. The case was
stronger than that of Huguenots or Scotsmen, because
the oppressor was always regarded as foreign, and some
of the motives which in Germany made for princely
absolutism were conjoined with those ideas of the rights
of subjects against the prince, which were the watchwords
of the Huguenots and the Ligue. In addition to this,
there was the motive of European independence as
against the overweening influence of the Spanish branch
of the Habsburgs, and the danger of a universal monarchy
—of which it was believed that not only Spanish generals,
whether military or Jesuit, were the herald but the Pope
was the servant. The cause was not merely that of local
independence or political liberty ; European freedom was

interested[1]. Just as in the War of Liberation royal rights, national feeling and constitutional freedom all combined to unite Europe and England against universal monarchy and foreign absolutism in the person of Napoleon, so in the Netherlands revolt there were mingled with the ideas of the rights of individuals and the original contract the motives that inspired England against Spain, the *Politiques* against the Ligue, and some of the German princes against Charles V. The resistance was successful because it combined European, national, religious, and popular arguments for freedom in a single movement. The result is that, after it had settled down, we find expressed by the Dutch mind all these various tendencies, and reduced to system. Its European side finds expression in the system of International Law devised by Grotius; its nationalist Protestantism in the attitude of the government towards the Remonstrants, and in the general belief in the rights of the secular prince to control religious ceremonies and suppress heresy, in which Grotius approaches English Protestants like Selden, and generally the low as opposed to the high view of Church power[2]. The same side is also shown in the territorialism of Grotius and his strong views about non-resistance. The popular theory of power becomes crystallized in Althusius.

We must bear in mind, that if ever there was an instance of the superiority of intellect to force in human concerns, it is to be found in the success of the Dutch. It was not, as the oleographic theory of history teaches, because Philip was a monster of wickedness that he lost the Netherlands, but because like most kings, *e.g.*, Louis XIV and George III, who have been thoroughly representative of their peoples, he was stupid, and typified the Spanish character in its least tactful elements. He was opposed by a man who, whatever his faults, was above all things quick and adroit at using opportunities. The Dutch, indeed, were placed "in the Thermopylae of the universe"; and but for their resistance it is almost certain that European liberty would have succumbed to the universal aggression of Spain, and even England would have been endangered. In the days of their triumph the Netherlands became the University of Europe; if we remove from the first half of the seventeenth century the thinkers, publicists, theologians, men of science, artists, and gardeners who were Dutch, and take away their influence upon other nations, the record would be barren instead of fertile, despite the great name of Bacon. They form a natural conclusion to this series of lectures, for they carry on the tradition to the seventeenth century, and further than that exhibit the beginning of the gradual disentanglement of political from theocratic arguments, which was only completed at the close of the age. Stained at times with intolerance, which even the spectacle of their sufferings should not lead us to ignore, with leaders clever but opportunist, of whom it is well said that "only the extravagance of partisanship can make him a hero," exhibiting already some of those faults of obstinacy, avarice, and slowness, which a century later ruined them as a great power at the close of their most victorious war, with a fanaticism equal to the ultramontanes and a "provincialism" in itself as ignoble as that of Castile, they remain the pioneers of liberty in modern as distinct from medieval Europe, the one oasis in the desert of absolutism, the great source of intellectual and moral enlightenment, in the age of which the typical statesman was Richelieu, with

his view of popular poverty as a source of strength to
tyranny, and the typical Churchman Bossuet, *le grand
gendarme*, or our own Laud, who with all his greatness,
could not see any way but that of force for the promotion of righteousness ; while the typical political
philosopher was Thomas Hobbes, in whom the
meanest of all ethical theories united with unhistorical
contempt for religion to justify the most universal of
absolutisms.   Again, as in the case of the sects and their
influences, we shall see how it was rather in spite of
themselves than for any other cause that the Dutch
possessed the influence they did.   Their supreme object
was their own independence of the foreigner, and the
preservation of their own religion and of local rights.
The first object had nothing to do with political liberty
proper, for it is secured equally well and often more effectively under a national absolutism.   The second in no
way meant the toleration of other forms of faith, and even
in their hours of direst distress, the Prince of Orange
had the utmost difficulty in securing decent treatment
for the Catholics.   The third, indeed, had a connection
with liberty and may have been the main cause which
prevented a thorough absolutism.   Certainly it helped
towards a theory of federalism.   But the real importance
of the Netherlands lay in their success ; in an age when
all the tendencies were the other way, and the Counter-
Reformation had at least half conquered even in France,
the Dutch were there—a people who had united themselves, had chosen their own head, had resisted at once
their own sovereign, and the cause of universal monarchy,
and proclaimed, if not tolerance, at any rate bounds to
the progress of the Counter-Reformation.   On the one
hand this fact helped to inspire the princes in the Thirty

Years' War, the last great effort at once of the Counter-Reformation, and of Imperial authority—in other words the last attempt to restore the old order temporal as well as spiritual.   On the other hand over England their influence was enormous; there is no doubt that the Puritans feared (doubtless wrongly) that the movement led by Charles I and Laud was merely a part of the Counter-Reformation; and the mere provision of the Netherlands as a place of refuge for malcontents was alone important, while the Dutch influence in the real attempt to produce a Counter-Reformation here is too obvious to need pointing out.   What does need pointing out, is that our Revolution was only the culminating triumph of the Dutch mind ; that it was the final achievement of forces that had been at work for a century; that England owed at least a few peerages and pensions to the representatives of the nation, which had by both example and precept prepared her for constitutional liberty.   It was not the defeat of the Armada but William of Orange who finally conquered Philip II.   The House of Orange may be regarded as the educators of England When she had trained this country to keep alight the torch of liberty and enlightenment, her *welthistorische* mission was over, and she sank into a second-rate power.   To estimate our debt to Holland is hard ; to over-estimate it is harder.   The supreme fact is that it was a free State in a world rapidly tending to a uniformity of absolutism, a Calvinist Teutonic federalism, unlike anything else—for Geneva was a Latin city-state, and its influence was over in France, until the days of Voltaire and Rousseau.

Let us trace for a few moments the way in which the Dutch prepared the way for posterity.   This work was

so enduring because it was so slow. Like the English
Parliament, the States-general only gradually, and
almost in spite of themselves, threw off their allegiance.
They began like the English—and so did Huguenots and
Ligueurs—by warring against evil counsellors. They
never reached the violent republicanism of the Ligue.
They endeavoured to reconcile rebellion and loyalty by
the assertion that their insurrection was justified by
fundamental laws, and that if only he would give them
ancient liberty and remove the troops, they would show
to the king more loyalty than his own Spaniards. We
can trace these ideas throughout the works of Marnix de
S. Aldegonde, and the official documents, many of which
he drew up—*e.g.*, the famous compromise of 1565,
announcing a political resistance against the introduction of the Spanish Inquisition, declaring that in such
cases no guilt of rebellion is incurred, for their action is
solely due to holy zeal for the glory of God, the majesty
of the king, the public peace and the security of property.
The terms both here and in the French troubles are
remarkably similar to Parliamentary pamphlets in the
early stages of the Civil War. Even when the States
threw over Don John of Austria, and invited the Arch-
Duke Matthias to assume the government, it was rather
to secure to the elder branch of the House of Habsburg
its ancient rights. The Union of Utrecht in 1579 did
not abandon allegiance to Philip but was merely an
agreement of the States to protect each other against any
force that might be brought against them ; it arranged
the government of the provinces, and above all laid down
the independence of each province (not individuals) in
regard to religion, and thus asserted generally the idea
of freedom of conscience. The loss of the Walloon

provinces was the greatest loss possible to religious toleration, because, had they remained, a general toleration or at least local option in religious matters must have been a permanent principle of the federal State, not a mere temporary expedient.

In the Apology of William the Silent, rebellion is a little further justified. It is noteworthy that William like others rests a good deal on the deposition of Pedro the Cruel in 1369 in favour of Philip's ancestor Enrique, and demands pertinently, if that resistance were lawful and Philip's title acquired by it is good, how the action of the Netherlands can be impugned. The truth of course is that indefeasible hereditary right was a new doctrine, that royalty having escaped the fetters of feudalism desired also to remove those of popular rights. The Netherlands revolt was indeed, to some extent, feudal in spirit; it was at least partly due to the dislike of mesne lords to the suzerain becoming direct and absolute sovereign—we may include municipalities in this—and in this way forms another link between the medieval and the modern theory of liberty.

Not till 1581 did the States definitely depose Philip[3]. They alleged that it is notorious that if a Prince who is a Shepherd treats his subjects as though they were slaves, and destroys their privileges, he is no longer to be held their legitimate prince ; and especially after a public resolution of the States of the country they may abandon him. When petition has failed, they have no other means of preserving their ancient liberty, for which they are bound to expose themselves by the *Law of Nature*, especially when the Prince has solemnly undertaken to observe certain customs and *on that condition alone* obtained their allegiance. It is to be observed that this document is at once more emphatic and more general in its tone than is our Declaration of Right a century later. Its publication in several languages is alone proof of its wide influence. We must remember how important the Dutch press was as a means of publishing foreign heterodoxy[4].

This is the general line taken by the Dutch defenders of their liberty. I think, too, it can hardly be doubted that Barclay and perhaps Pierre Grégoire had them in view, in the one exception which they allow to the universality of the duty of non-resistance. One pamphleteer definitely puts the case on feudal grounds, arguing that the causes for which a vassal may lose his fief apply also to the lord. William argues from Philip's own action in making war against the Pope because he had not kept his contract as overlord of Naples. The *joyeuse entrée* of Brabant was also used as a proof of the original contract, and might almost have suggested the notion.

By the close of the sixteenth century the independence of the Netherlands was practically assured. It remained for the Dutch to consolidate their victory and to crystallize into systematic treatises the principles of the movement. For our purpose we may confine ourselves to two writers, who on different sides expressed these principles —Althusius and Grotius. The former was not himself a Netherlander, but he came to reside within the territory, was clearly influenced by the facts he found before him at Herborn and may be regarded as the representative publicist. His work *Politica Methodica Digesta* is, with the exception of Bodin's treatise, the most important of all works for the scientific student. Dr Gierke in a work, compared with which everything else

on the subject is but prattle, has demonstrated the value
of the book and traced its influence backwards and
forwards. Perhaps, indeed, Treuman is right in saying
that he rather exaggerates the importance of the book.
There seems to be no proof forthcoming that it directly
influenced Rousseau—although the likeness of ideas is
so great as to render that a highly probable conjecture.
M. Dreyfus-Brisac, who quotes the relevant passages in
his edition of *Le Contrat Social*, appears to think not
proven the charge of plagiarism.. Althusius writes as a
professor not a pamphleteer. His book is emphatically
not a *livre de circonstance*, and is perhaps for that
reason charged (and I think justly) by Dr Gierke with
a certain insipidity of tone. It has not the eloquence or
the appeal of the *Vindiciae contra Tyrannos* and is less
readable.

More, however, than any other writer does Althusius
sum up the whole thought of the day. Like Albericus
Gentilis he both quotes and knows the words of all
previous publicists, and he appears to have been
considerably influenced in the structure of his work
by the dull and flat lucubration of Lambertus Daneus[5].
He makes considerable use of Gregory of Toulouse,
Salamonius and of Patricius of Siena, a renaissance
scholar who wrote a book—*De Republica*—with reference
to the Italian city-states. He criticises Bodin, but he
is indebted to him; and in this as in other ways
prepared the way for Rousseau, who combined with
the royalist conceptions of legal omnipotence popular
theories of the origin of power.

Now this is just what Althusius does. If he does
not accept quite *ex animo* the legal theory of sovereignty
he is far nearer to it than are the Huguenots or the

Whigs, who always—as we have seen—endeavour to deny the existence of any power in the State above the law, whether royal or parliamentary. The reason of this is that for them contract is a bond between governor and governed, which settles the relations of each and is therefore above legal review.

To Althusius, however, the contract is social, it is the mutual agreement of all to live in an ordered society. His view is not essentially dissimilar from that of Suarez or Molina. There may indeed be another contract between whatever ruler the people, which is now a single power, may agree to set up, and themselves. In this he is different from Rousseau, who allows only a single contract—the social; but the practical result is very similar. In both cases the rights of sovereignty belong not to the ruler, whether one, many, or few, but to the members of the association. And the sovereignty of the people becomes the foundation of the State. Althusius does not display the profundity of the deeper thinking Jesuits, like Suarez and Molina, who evolve sovereign power from a community by the mere fact of its existence without any deliberate pact; and thus prepare the way for the true theory of corporations, in which authority and self-dependence are inherent essentially, and not dependent on any agreement, since they arise from the nature of the case. But his doctrine of a social contract is far less artificial than that of the original contract, as ordinarily propounded; and it escapes the logical absurdity which made Whigs even as great as Locke or Hoadly the legitimate sport of writers like Filmer and Leslie, who were never weary of pointing out that law-makers must have existed before laws, and that the conception of the constitution of a State as unalterable was unthinkable. On Althusius' theory it was quite possible, as indeed on that of Rousseau, to assert the limited nature of all actual governmental authority, without making the formal error of declaring that laws could not be altered even by the legislature.

By another conception, however, Althusius' system was preserved from the great practical danger of that of Rousseau, the enunciation of the sovereignty of the people in so violent a form, that there is nothing to check the tyranny of the majority or even a plebiscitary despotism. This defect was inherent in Rousseau's system, and appears in every modification of it, owing to the absolutely unitary conception of the State, entertained alike by Rousseau and by royalists, which is a legacy of the Roman Empire through the Papacy. Alike under the theory of Hobbes and that of Rousseau, or (in regard to the Church) under that of the Canonists or the Jesuits all power is ultimately concentrated at a single centre, and every form of right or liberty is of the nature of a privilege, tacitly or explicitly granted by the central authority, which may be king, nobles or people.

The last three centuries have witnessed the victory of the principle that, so far as individuals are concerned, some rights or liberties shall always be practically, even if not theoretically, recognised by the modern State— though even here the liberties of the subject are less fully assured than often seems the case. Yet the struggles in England, and still more the declaration of the rights of man, proclaim these liberties as the universal limit upon the practical exercise of the legal omnipotence of the central power. But owing partly to the very sharpness of the idea of a legal sovereign, partly to the long struggle to destroy illegitimate immunities, and to the arrogance of the Churches, partly to the influence of theories originally derived from city-states, partly even to the very recognition of those individual rights above mentioned, there is nothing like the same recognition of the reality of corporate communities apart from the fiat of the State.

In other words, in spite of all actual Parliamentary institutions, the modern unitary State is still conceived as a *Herrschaftsverband* rather than a *Genossenschaft*. The controversy over the right and the nature of Trades Unions, the Associations' Law in France, the ecclesiastical difficulty in Scotland, and even certain aspects of the education question all alike turn at bottom on the question whether the State creates or whether it only recognises the inherent rights of communities ; whether in the Jesuit phrase there may not be a *societas perfecta* besides the more obvious one of the State ; or whether in modern German phrase the corporate union be not real rather than fictitious personality, *i.e.*, possessing its own inherent life and powers that may be checked, but cannot in the nature of things be destroyed. This position is rendered the more important by the growth of federalism real in the United States, Switzerland and Germany, and quasi in this country. A conception of law and sovereignty which may fairly fit the facts in a unitary State becomes increasingly difficult of practical application to any developed federal community, and ceases to have any but a paper value. It may indeed be argued that the victory of the North in 1866 was really a victory for that idea, for it decided that the rights of the States were not ultimate, and went a step towards abolishing them except as delegations of the supreme power. But it may be replied that just as individuals may have rights recognised by a State, which yet crushes a rebellion, so may societies.

But the point to notice here is that this federalistic idea is to be found in Althusius and through him connects itself with the medieval theory of community life. There is not much difference between that idea of the *communitas communitatum* which the Middle Ages meant by the commons, and Althusius' notion of the State as above all else a *consociatio consociationum*. He definitely protests against those who refuse to consider the smaller associations such as the family as anything but economic. The novelty in him is his view of the State as entirely built up on the principle of associations[6]. Indeed the change of the connotation of commons from the view delineated above to the modern one of the mass of common people is significant of the whole development of thought from medieval to modern times, a development which in part will have to be retraced in face of the actual facts. In other words the *Selbständigkeit* of the individual, as against an omnipotent State, has been the battle-ground of liberty for three centuries; this has now given place to that of the *Selbständigkeit* of societies. What the issue will be or when it will be decided it may not be possible for a historian to say before nineteen hundred has become three thousand. What these lectures have endeavoured to point out is that, as a matter of fact, this achievement of individual liberty was never attained and except for the short period of the Benthamite movement never sought merely for its own sake. Its achievement became feasible only because it was connected with the recognition of the right to exist of some society usually religious, which the civil magistrate did not desire to exist. It is often agreed that religious differences are the ground of modern liberty. It is a mistake to suppose, as we have shown, that this is because as a rule any or all religious bodies cared about such liberty. What they desired was the right to be, what they denied was the right of the State to suppress them as societies, and in standing up against State omnipotence they secured individual liberty in spite of themselves. Indeed they secured it so well that we have forgotten how it was secured and have to learn once more the lesson, that the State is something more than a mass of individuals. What is needed now-a-days is that as against an abstract and unreal theory of State omnipotence on the one hand, and an atomistic and artificial view of individual independence on the other, the facts of the world with its innumerable bonds of association and the naturalness of social authority should be generally recognised and become the basis of our laws, as it is of our life.

Now, if Gierke at all exaggerates the importance of Althusius, the reason is doubtless because he is nearer than anyone else to those ideas of "realism," so dear to the great jurist's heart. Here, as in other matters, Holland led the way. Its government was federal. The rights of each province and even each town were recognised as inalienable. Hence, we find that Althusius starts, not, like some writers on politics, from the top, but from the bottom; the unit of civil life is for him not the individual but the family, and he rises by a series of concentric circles from the family to the town, to the province, and the State. His State is a true *Genossenschaft*, a fellowship of all the heads of families, and he takes care to prevent the absorption of local and provincial powers into the central administration. It is not merely that he allows rights to families and provinces; but he regards these rights as anterior to the State, as the foundation of it, and as subsisting always within it. He would no more deny or absorb them than a hive of bees would squash all the cells into a pulp. Only, be it remembered, it is not separate and equal cells, but differing and organic limbs of the body politic which he contemplates. He admits indeed the need of a central organ. This is to the whole like soul to body. It is significant that the old symbol of the relation of ecclesiastical to civil power is used to signify the relation of government to society.

Into his doctrine of the influence of ephors, who are to prevent excesses of government, we need hardly go, as there is nothing here but what is paralleled elsewhere. The dependence of the theory on the peculiar facts of the Netherlands and on the nature of the struggle with Spain is fairly evident. The strength of the communal burgher element; the federalistic tie; the deliberate agreement to throw off the Spanish yoke; the choice of the House of Orange—all had their influence in shaping the theory, and in influencing future generations. How far American federalism was developed from these sources it would be hard to say. But the close connection of Puritanism with Dutch Calvinism must have prepared the ground. In England a pamphlet of 1642 in praise of the Dutch system quotes almost verbatim the words of Boucher in favour of the rights of subjects.

Even in his theory of contract Althusius, as we have seen, combines elements that are found commonly opposed in the sixteenth century; with the general conception of the State entertained by the Dutch thinkers, the same is true. But for the Netherlands it might have seemed that there was no *via media* between the exaltation of royal power, and the general attitude of suspicion of the State and denial of sovereignty which characterised the Huguenot and Ligue and English Presbyterian writers and passed by them through the Whigs to the *laisser-faire* school of Radicals.

There was also the controversy between the ideas of those who, recognising with Luther or the *Politiques* the sanctity of the civil power, were prepared to go all lengths in establishing the claims of the prince to deal with religion, and that other view typified by Jesuits, but held also by Presbyterians, that the State itself was a mere contrivance, of purely temporal significance, needing for inspiration the guidance of the Church, or at any rate unable to compete with the superior claims of the kingdom which, though not " of this world," was so very much in it, that its behests were paramount on any question involving morals. Now, as we saw, the development of the theory of two societies was due to the peculiar circumstances of the Huguenots in France, of the Presbyterians in England and Scotland, of the Roman Church as against an encroaching State. It was by no means bound up with what is ordinarily known as Calvinism, or with the practical working of it in Geneva, which was definitely a Church State. So in the Netherlands. In spite of the toleration originally proclaimed by the Union of Utrecht, the ideal of religious uniformity eventually triumphed. Toleration was undoubtedly the ideal of William the Silent, who was essentially a *Politique* : and it was appealed to by the Arminians in the controversy of 1614. But they were allied with the party of the burgher oligarchy, and Maurice seized the opportunity of strengthening his power by making use of the Calvinist predilections of the populace. Exile and confiscation were then proclaimed against the Remonstrants; and Calvinism, which had thus become a conservative force, attempted, just as it did in England, to repress by the strong hand the invasion of wider and more rational views. The party of Arminians in both Holland and England was the party of liberty or at least of change as against the authority of Calvinism, which, after it had been first an inspiration in the sixteenth century, and then in the seventeenth became a tradition, in the eighteenth died down into a prejudice. Now in Althusius, despite his federalism, we have no hint of any sort of independence for the Church; it is not envisaged as a separate society. Its officers are merely a part of the general machinery of the State[7]. The latter, indeed, is conceived as holy; and the author's view of the State is thus definitely that of Luther, the Anglicans, Zwingli, Erastus, as opposed to that of Jesuits and Presbyterians; the difference being that in his case the sovereignty over religious matters is inalienably vested in the people, for the original contract of association can only disappear with the State, whereas the others as a rule vest it in "the godly Prince." The point to note is that Althusius holds a high not a low view of the State; it is something consecrated, the embodiment of justice. His most frequent tag is that from S. Augustine, *remota justitia, quid regna nisi magna latrocinia?* The rights of the State extend over all persons and all causes; there is no conception of a contract between Church and State, or an alliance between them. Grotius, who was imprisoned in the Arminian controversy, yet strongly maintained the Erastian view; and in his lengthy treatise, *De Jure Regni apud Sacra*, he develops it in the ordinary way. But while it is the idea of a Christian commonwealth that rules the thoughts of both writers, it is more of the political than the theocratic side that they are thinking. The notion of a Church-State may be interpreted so as to lay emphasis on either one or the other aspect. It may become a pure theocracy, like the Anabaptist kingdom at Münster, the Puritan *régime* in England, and to some extent Laud's system; or it may be a body politic in which uniformity of religious worship and the paramount authority of the secular government are the main elements. It may fulfil the ideas of Calvin or Savonarola; it may express the aspirations of a Selden or a Bacon. Now the animus of both Althusius and Grotius is distinctly political. It is not a Church with civil officers that they mean by a Christian commonwealth, but a State with ecclesiastical among other ministers; and in this respect again they display their kinship to other German princes. It is the ordered life of the community as a whole, consecrated to civil ends, with education, like religion, cared for, with all possible provision for leading the good life, and for correlating the smaller activities of town and provincial life with that of the State, which Althusius contemplates. Combining elements from both parties, in his conception of governmental activity, in his idea of the inalienability of sovereignty, in the whole notion of the wide competence of the State, Althusius is really more akin to bureaucratic statesmen of the type of Pierre Grégoire and Bacon, than he is to the enthusiasts of revolution. It is of the life of the community organized on a recognised basis of popular sovereignty that he is thinking far more than of the rights of subjects against their rulers. Hence his treatise had little or no influence on the next revolutionary movement, that of England ; and the Whig ideal is more individualistic, more suspicious of government, more akin to the *Vindiciae contra Tyrannos*, than to anything to be found in Althusius. Only with the development of American independence and the reaction of the ideas it expressed on the Continent had Althusius (or at least his ideas) a chance in Europe. The indebtedness of Rousseau to Althusius may or may not be demonstrable ; that the conceptions of the two writers *with the significant exception of federalism* are similar and in some respects identical, there can be no doubt.

If we turn to the final work of Grotius we see at work principles which at first sight are the opposite of what we should expect, but nevertheless are the result of the Netherlands revolt. With the rules of International Law these lectures are not concerned, with its foundations they are. It is indeed astonishing how large a space in the works of both Albericus Gentilis and Grotius' *De Jure Belli* is occupied by the discussion of questions merely political ; nor must we forget that Albericus Gentilis wrote three dissertations on behalf of royal power, as against the theory of resistance. Here we observe how the territorialism, which was an element, though commonly overlooked, in the Dutch revolt, becomes an integral part of the system of International Law. Not only is territorial sovereignty a necessary assumption of International Law, but Grotius goes out of his way to condemn the theory of resistance, to show that by the *lex regia* popular power is wholly transferred to the prince. He admits indeed a rare exception ; but so did even a royalist like Barclay. His definition of the cases in which resistance is justified is so narrow that it may be doubted whether any case but that of the Netherlands ever fell within it. It is the world of seventeenth and eighteenth century diplomacy which Grotius contemplates, with absolute princes for the most part, territorial sovereignty and the equality of the juristic persons of International Law. This latter doctrine, which we have seen in a more concrete form in the *grand dessein* of Sully, was closely connected with Netherland influences ; for William the Silent in his apology appeals against Philip II to the fact of his being a *sovereign prince*, as good as he was[8]. The juristic equality of sovereigns was not beginning to be a fact until the close of the sixteenth century.

With the general assumptions on which the system of Grotius rests, we were concerned in discussing the Jesuits. The fundamental basis of the whole system of Grotius is the claim that men are in a society bound together by a natural law which makes promises binding. This is also, as we saw, at the root of the doctrine of the original contract. It is the same with writers like Vasquez and Suarez and Albericus Gentilis, whose fundamental ideas are similar to those of Grotius. Albericus Gentilis indeed in his treatment of the social nature of men and his citation of authorities lends strong support to the view of Mr A. J. Carlyle, that the most decisive change in political thinking is that which came some time between the days of Aristotle and Cicero, and proclaimed the fundamental equality of men—a doctrine ever since asserted, denied in our own day once more by Nietzsche and by others who are facing the problem of brown and yellow races. All these works are the true anti-Machiavel. They strike at the roots of his assumption; which is that of the absolute separateness of States, the fundamental badness of human beings, and the universal prominence of self-interest and fear[9].

A study of Albericus Gentilis reveals an interesting link between Vasquez and Suarez and Grotius. In both Albericus Gentilis and Grotius we observe that their real originality lies not so much in their acceptance of Roman Law as a basis, as in their selection from it of only such parts as were suitable and really made for a higher morality. In this respect the value of the canonical jurisprudence was incalculable. Albericus Gentilis constantly appeals to general notions of equity, and to principles of the canonists, as against those who would decide by a mere pettifogging sophistry. In both cases we see, as we saw in our discussion of the Jesuits, how the Roman and Canon Law, and the maxims of theologians and philosophers were all combined in the system actually set forth. Had the Civil Law stood alone, its system was too hard and sometimes too narrow for a code of international morality to have been founded on it; nor did it, except here and there, contemplate international relations. But it did not stand alone; for centuries men had been expounding it in conjunction with another system believed to be of equal or higher authority, and that system led on to the introduction of principles from any other sources[10]. Moreover, except in Italy, and in Germany only after the "reception" so recent as 1495, Roman Law was not authoritative, it had to make its way; it was everywhere, France, Scotland, Spain, half accepted, *i.e.*, its principles were generally regarded as decisive; they could be employed when nothing prevented it; but very often feudal rights and private privilege or local custom or national habit did prevent it; and so men were familiarised with the notion of a law universal in scope, commanding general reverence and awe, but yet not everywhere and always decisive like a modern statute or the Code Napoleon. All this, while it probably assisted the various nations to employ as much of the Civil Law as they could assimilate and no more, was also in favour of the foundation of a system like modern International Law which partly was and partly was not law in the sense of ordinary positive law.

It is in a world of such conceptions that International Law was born and alone could be reared. It was not possible to frame it from a purely English system, and there was—unless Selden be an exception—no English lawyer of note in the days when men like Puffendorf or Vattel were names to conjure with.

Into the merits of the controversy raised by the idea of International Law, we need not enter, especially as Professor Westlake has recently said nearly all that needs to be said on the matter[11]. But it may be pointed out that the theoretical question is admirably debated by Albericus Gentilis when he says that there is a sense in which right is claimed for public actions, and in which condemnation of non-omission is not the mere universal hostility to acts of cruelty or ungenerousness—in other words, that in the relations of States there are, by general consent, certain causes of action to which the definitely legal stigma of a breach of obligation is attached, and *vice versa* : if this be admitted there must be some sense in which the word law is rightly used[12].

Lastly, the practical value of the work of Grotius was

very great. The danger of Machiavelli was not that he dissected motive and tore the decent veil of hypocrisy from statesmen, but that he said or implied that these facts were to be the only ideal of action ; the service of Grotius, his forerunners and successors is not that they produced a scientific system under which State action could be classified, but that they succeeded in placing some bounds to the unlimited predominance of "reason of state." Machiavelli's was a rough generalisation from observed facts ; and, like all theories based on the universality of low motives, it contained a minimum of truth with a maximum of plausibility and was of great immediate practical utility. For its success it unconsciously assumes the existence of other motives, *e.g.*, the religious, whose existence as a real power the whole system denies. The object of Grotius was not to make men perfect or treat them as such, but to see whether there were not certain common duties generally felt as binding, if not always practised, and to set forth an ideal. As Albericus Gentilis points out, he is concerned not only with what men do, but what they ought to do, and the jurist has ever to remember that *jus* is *ars aequi et boni.*

The founders of International Law did not stop, they regulated the struggle of existence. That famous pamphlet *The fight in Dame Europa's school* rests for its verisimilitude on a conception of Grotius and implies a contradiction of those of Hobbes and Machiavelli. International Law is like schoolboy honour or good form, it does not destroy selfishness or quarrelling or cheating ; but it proclaims that certain things are to be avoided and others are obligatory, and it unites even those most sharply divided as members in a single society. It does not solve the problem of man in

society, but it recognises it.   Now the theory of
Machiavelli and Hobbes at bottom is the reverse of
this; it teaches that men are not in society at all except
by accident and artifice; and with all its superficial
attractions it fails to reach the true facts; that even
hatred implies a relation, and that neither States nor
individuals can have differences unless there be some
atmosphere which unites them[13].

At any rate, I hope that enough has been said to
point out how the intellectual no less than the
practical conditions which made the work of Grotius
possible and necessary were the result partly of age-
long influences, partly of the peculiar effects of the
religious revolution.   The former explain the continued
and ever-growing influence of the Civil Law, the
ideal of the Holy Roman Empire, its connection
with the Canon Law, which makes International
Law a sort of legacy of the Middle Ages[14].   The
foundations both of International Law and modern
politics are the residuum which the medieval world
passed on to its successor ; and the same may largely be
said of the connection between feudalism and the
contractual theory of government.   But it was the
religious revolution alone which produced the actual
conditions to which all this was applied.   On the one
hand it helped in Germany and England towards that
development of national unity, royal omnipotence, and
administrative universality, which was to be the common
form of the continental State till 1789 and the ideal of
English statesmen for a long time.   On the other hand,
by the division it produced (*a*) between Emperor and
princes, (*b*) between princes and subjects, and (*c*) between
State and State, it shattered for ever the ancient

conditions even as an ideal, and prevented the notion of
international justice taking the form of a reconstituted
Empire. This process was further assisted by the
division between the two branches of the Habsburgs
and the predominance of Spain, the conditions under
which the early Jesuits imbibed their ideals. These
general conditions assured the predominance of territorial sovereignty, the recognition of the non-religious
basis of the State or at least of the multi-religious
nature of the European State-system[15], while the unity
of humanity, which had been taught in some way from
the time of the Stoics and impressed as an ideal on
every generation from the time of Augustine to the
Renaissance, prevented the final and deliberate outward
recognition of the view that States have no duties to one
another and that the international polity is a fortuitous
concourse of atoms. It was these conditions compacted
of the ancient ideas of human society and the immutable
authority of the law natural, coupled with the modern facts
of State independence and self-sufficiency and religious
differences, that made International Law in the form
which it took possible, *i.e.*, it made it truly international
and in the form of its expression really law. It made it
a system fundamentally secular although it was in origin
ethical and even theological. Of both the international
and the municipal commonwealth the basis was becoming though it had not become frankly secular—and the
most remarkable advance towards this end was made in
the theories of the *Politiques*. But religious divisions
everywhere and the establishment of the Dutch Republic
helped towards this end, while the latter, more than
anything else, contributed towards the change of the idea
of political authority from a lordship into an association;

this again was assisted both by Jesuit speculations on society in general and the actual nature and constitution of their own community.

One final truth may be noticed. The doctrine of the unity of history is more impressively realized in a study of political thought than of any actual constitution. Lord Acton was of opinion that here more than anywhere else a continuous development could be demonstrated. If the pages of a writer like Grotius, or still more Albericus Gentilis, be studied carefully, it will be seen how to him the world was always one; that true principles in politics are to be found partly by reasoning, but still more by the distilled essence of thought ancient and modern, by something akin at least to the comparative study of institutions and by the wise selection of historical instances which as in Machiavelli are valued always for their significance as parts of a system. International Law is indeed a philosophy of history in the idea of its early exponents—just as the "law of the beasts" is in that of Machiavelli, only while the latter like modern "naturalism" gives to its system the superficial clearness of an induction from a narrowed basis and an assumption of low motives, the former recognises that however imperfect its realization in fact some notion of righteousness had always regulated men's judgments of value, even if it had been belied by their action. Alike in international relations, in popular theory, and in absolutist apology, the idea of law and right is upheld in some form, and utility merely and purely as such is repudiated by all except avowed followers of Machiavelli and Hobbes. In this indeed lies the connection of all these doctrines both with theocratic assumptions and with medieval life; the gradual supersession of these notions by that of immediate and perceptible utility took two centuries to develop, and was largely helped by the general secularisation of life which followed the destruction of religious unity and the *Aufklärung* of the eighteenth century. What is to be noted is that only through this revolution did ideas no less than facts take the shape in which they influenced the modern world.

NOTES.

INTRODUCTORY.

(1) The claim was set out by Innocent III in regard to the dispute between King John and Philip Augustus. His words are worth quoting, for they put in a nutshell the whole argument for Papal supremacy, and show how, on a purely legal theory of Christianity, the moral teacher was bound to elevate himself into a supreme judge in both private and public matters. They show also how foreign to the ideas of the time are modern notions of International Law. As the greater part of the letter was embodied in the *Decretale*, its principles became a part of the Statute Law of the Church. They are to be found in *Decretale* II. 1, 13. I quote the most important part :

"Qui scrutator cordium est, ac conscius secretorum, quod charissimum in Christo filium nostrum Philippum Regem Francorum illustrem, de corde puro et conscientia bona, et fide non fictâ diligimus, et ad honorem et profectum et incrementum ipsius efficaciter aspiramus, exaltationem regni Francorum, sublimationem Apostolicae sedis reputantes, cum hoc regnum benedictum a Deo semper in ipsius devotione permanserit, et ab ejus devotione nullo unquam, sicut credimus, tempore sit discessurum : quia licet interdum hinc inde fiant immissiones per Angelos malos, nos tamen qui Satanae non ignoramus astutias, circumventiones ipsius studebimus evitare, credentes quod idem Rex illius seduci fallaciis non se permittet. Non putet aliquis, quod jurisdictionem illustris Regis Francorum perturbare aut minuere intendamus, cum ipse jurisdictionem nostram nec velit, nec debeat impedire. Sed cum Dominus dicat in Evangelio : 'si peccaverit in te frater tuus, vade et corripe eum inter te et ipsum solum : si te audierit, lucratus eris fratrem tuum : si te non audierit, adhibe tecum unum vel duos, ut in ore duorum vel trium testium stet omne verbum : quod si non audierit, dic Ecclesiae : si autem Ecclesiam non audierit, sit tibi sicut ethnicus et publicanus.'

Et Rex Angliae sit paratus sufficienter ostendere, quod Rex Francorum peccat in ipsum, et ipse circa eum in correptione processit secundum regulam Evangelicam, et tandem quia nullo modo profecit, dixit Ecclesiae : quomodo nos qui sumus ad regimen universalis Ecclesiae supernâ dispositione vocati, mandatum divinum possumus non exaudire ; ut non procedamus secundum formam ipsius ; nisi forsitan ipse coram nobis vel Legato nostro sufficientem in contrarium rationem ostendat ? *Non enim intendimus judicare de feudo, cujus ad ipsum spectat judicium, nisi forte juri communi per speciale privilegium, vel contrariam consuetudinem aliquid sit detractum : sed decernere de peccato cujus ad nos pertinet sine dubitatione censura, quam in quemlibet exercere possumus et debemus.* Non igitur injuriosum sibi debet Regia dignitas reputare, si super hoc Apostolico judicio se committat, cum Valentinianus, inclytus Imperator, suffraganeis Mediolanensis Ecclesiae dixisse legatur : ' Talem in pontificali sede constituere procuretis, cui et nos, qui gubernamus imperium, sincerè nostra capita submittamus, et ejus monita (cum tanquam homines deliquerimus) suscipiamus necessario velut medicamenta curantis.' Nec sic illud humillimum omittamus, quod Theodosius statuit Imperator, et Carolus innovavit, de cujus genere Rex ipse noscitur descendisse : ' quicunque videlicet litem habens, sive petitor fuerit, sive reus, sive in initio litis, vel decursis temporum curriculis, sive cum negotium peroratur sive cum jam coeperit promi sententia, si judicium eligerit sacrosanctae sedis Antistitis, illico sine aliqua dubitatione (etiamsi pars alia refragetur) ad Episcoporum judicium cum sermone litigantium dirigatur.' Cum enim non humanae constitutioni, sed divinae potius innitamur, quia potestas nostra non est ex homine, sed ex Deo, nullus qui sit sanae mentis ignorat quin ad officium nostrum spectet de quocunque mortali peccato corripere quemlibet Christianum : et si correctionem contempserit, per districtionem Ecclesiasticam coërcere.

Quod enim debeamus corripere et possimus ex utriusque patet pagina Testamenti. Cum clamet Dominus per prophetam : ' Clama, ne cesses, quasi tuba exalta vocem tuam, et annuncia populo meo scelera eorum' : et subjungat ibidem : ' Nisi annunciaveris impio impietatem suam, ipse in iniquitate, quam operatus est, morietur : sanguinem autem ejus de manu tua requiram.' Apostolus quoque

nos monet corripere inquietos : et alibi dicit idem : ' Argue, ob-
secra, increpa in omni patientia et doctrina.' Quod autem possimus,
et debeamus coercere, patet ex eo, quod dicit Dominus ad prophetam, qui fuit de sacerdotibus Anathoth : ' Ecce constituo te super
gentes et regna, ut evellas et destruas et dissipes et aedifices et
plantes.' Constat vero quod evellendum, destruendum et dissi-
pandum est omne mortale peccatum. Praeterea cum Dominus
claves regni coelorum Beato Petro Apostolo tradidit, dixit ei :
' Quodcunque ligaveris super terram, erit ligatum et in coelis, et
quodcunque solveris super terram, erit solutum et in coelis.'
Verum nullus dubitat, quin omnis mortaliter peccans apud Deum
sit ligatus. Ut ergo Petrus divinum judicium imitetur, ligare debet
in terris quos ligatos constat in coelis. Sed forsan dicetur, quod
aliter cum Regibus aliter cum aliis est agendum. Caeterum scriptum
novimus in lege divina, ' Ita magnum judicabis, ut parvum, nec erit
apud te acceptio personarum.' Quam Beatus Jacobus intervenire
testatur : Si dixeris ei qui indutus est veste praeclara : Tu sede
hic bene : pauperi vero, Sta tu illic, aut sede sub scabello pedum
meorum.

Ideoque universis vobis per Apostolicam sedem mandamus, et
in virtute obedientiae praecipimus, quatenus postquam idem Abbas
super hoc mandatum fuerit Apostolicum executus, sententiam ejus,
imo nostram verius, recipiatis humiliter et faciatis ab aliis observari ;
pro certo scituri quod si secus egeritis, inobedientiam vestram
graviter puniemus. Licet autem hoc modo procedere valeamus
super quolibet criminali peccato, ut peccatorem revocemus a vitio
ad virtutem, ab errore ad veritatem, praecipue cum contra
pacem peccatur, quae est vinculum charitatis ; postremo cum inter
Reges ipsos reformata fuerint pacis foedera, et utrinque praestito
proprio juramento firmata, quae tamen usque ad tempus prae-
taxatum servata non fuerint ; nunquid non poterimus de juramenti
religione cognoscere, quod ad judicium Ecclesiae non est dubium
pertinere, ut rupta pacis foedera reformentur ? Ne ergo tantam
discordiam videamur sub dissimulatione fovere, praedicto Legato
dedimus in praeceptis, ut (nisi Rex ipse vel solidam pacem cum
praedicto Rege reformet, vel saltem humiliter patiatur, ut idem
Abbas et Archiepiscopus Bituricensis de plano cognoscant, utrum
justa sit querimonia, quam contra eum proponit coram Ecclesia
Rex Anglorum, vel ejus exceptio sit legitima, quam contra eum per
suas nobis literas duxit exprimendam) juxta formam sibi datam à
nobis procedere non omittat."

(2) A recent and most significant instance is the Scotch Church case, which, whatever its practical difficulties, is of the utmost theoretical interest. The official edition of the Appeal shows how the House of Lords, in spite of itself and under the conception of merely interpreting the terms of a trust, was forced into a discussion of the doctrinal questions and the meaning of self-identity when predicated of societies. Hegel in the Law Courts is no inadequate description of Mr Haldane's speech. The following altercation with Lord James is irresistibly comic:

Mr Haldane :—" Your Lordship is assuming, if I may respectfully say so, an anthropomorphic conception of the Supreme Being. It is very difficult to discuss these things, but I must say your Lordship is really assuming that the Supreme Being stands to a particular man in the relation of another man—a cause external to him in space and time acting on space and time and separate from him as one thing is separate from another. The whole point of the speculative teaching has been that that is not so; the whole point of the Church has been that that is a totally inadequate conception, and that, at any rate without resorting to any explanation, they have to hold the two things as in harmony and reconcilable."

Lord James of Hereford:—" Mr Haldane, till you told me so I had not the slightest idea that I was conceiving that."

Mr Haldane:—" I am afraid, my Lord, theologians would deal severely with your Lordship's statement " (p. 504).

Lord James of Hereford:—" I am much obliged to you."

Further on we have an illustration of the way in which the whole case turns on the idea of the inherent life of a community which is not the State and does not arise from its fiat.

" The Church is like an organism; to use a metaphor I used before, the organism parts with every part of its material every few years, but its identity consists in this that it assimilates and parts during the period of its life with the old material and takes in fresh material; so the Church does not consist in the identity of its members. It is not A., B., and C. coming together and entering into a contract with each other which is to bind them and their estates; on the contrary, it is the formation of an organisation which is to remain, like the life of the organism, notwithstanding the change which takes place in the constituent members. Now that that was the scheme or doctrine of the government of the Presbyterian Church is perfectly plain. You begin with the congregation, which is a set of people who worship in a Church in a particular building, that is to say, under a certain kirk government. That kirk government is the government of the kirk session, which consists of the minister and elders; there is also a deacon's court, which deals with secular matters, but the minister and elders are the ruling body" (p. 514).

Mr Haldane:—"Well, my Lord, my argument at your Lordship's bar is this, that if you ask what is the test of identity, the test of the personal identity of this Church lies, not in doctrine, but in its life, in the continuity of its life as ascertained by the fact that the majority have continuously kept on doing these things which are within their competence, according to our opinion" (p. 518, Orr's *Free Church of Scotland Appeals*).

Observe, that the House of Lords did not deny this power of development to a society, if such power appeared in the terms of the trust, only it refused to consider the Society except under the form of a trust, while Mr Haldane's argument is for the inherent life of a society. It is in fact, that idea of Suarez and Molina which he stands for, as against a notion which contemplates only the State and a mass of individuals. The meaning of the judgment is the refusal to consider a Church as anything but a mass of individuals. Individual rights are untouched; but the life of non-State Societies is to be denied.

(3) Treumann, *Die Monarchomachen*, 23.

(4) M.G.H. *De Lite*, I. 365.

Nonne clarum est, merito illum a concessa dignitate cadere, populum ab ejus dominio et subjectione liberum existere, cum *pactum pro quo constitutus est constat* illum prius irrupisse? Nec illos quisquam poterit juste ac rationabiliter perfidie arguere, cum nihilominus constet illum fidem prius deseruisse. Ut enim de rebus vilioribus exemplum trahamus, si quis alicui digna mercede porcos suos pascendos committeret, ipsumque postmodo eos non pascere, sed furari, mactare et perdere cognosceret, nonne promissa a mercede etiam sibi retenta a porcis pascendis cum contumelia illum amoveret?

There is an account of Manegold in Mr R. L. Poole's *Illustrations of the History of Mediaeval Thought*.

(5) Augustinus Triumphus in *Summa de Ecclesiastica Potestate* ed. 1473, Quaestio XXVI. 5. Mr Poole gives an admirable account of the views of this author in his chapter on "the hierarchical theory of the State." *Op. cit.*.

It is only, however, by perusal of a treatise like this or that of Bozius, asserting the world-monarchy of the Popes, that the real difference between this theory and that of " indirect" power can be seen. To Augustinus kingdoms are merely the *stipendia* of princes for wielding the temporal sword of the Church. This illustrates the notion of the Church-State as a single society; it is only inside a part of it, *i.e.*, the nation, that State and Church properly speaking compete. The State in fact is a specialised term, the secular organisation of the Commonwealth.

(6) *De Ecclesiastica-Potestate,* Qu. XXIII.

(7) S. Thomas deals with the subject of politics in the *Summa* II. I. 90 sqq. and also in the *De Regimine Principum,* of which only the first book and the first six chapters of the second are by him; the rest was added by Ptolemy of Lucca.

On the influence of the Aristotelian spirit and the addition of " *naturrechtliche* " ideas to those purely theocratic, see Gierke, in Professor Maitland's translation, Cambridge, 1900.

(8) Cf. Lossen, *Die Lehre von Tyrannicide in der Christlichen Zeit.* He argues that, except Mariana, the Jesuits did not really do more than develop the views of S. Thomas, although in regard to tyrants they laid too much stress on an isolated and early passage.

(9) Even Augustinus Triumphus makes this reservation, XXII. It is very general.

(10) See on this point, Carlyle, *History of Political Thought in the West.*

(11) This oath of Aragon is to be found in Du Hamel, *Histoire Constitutionnelle de la Monarchie Espagnole,* I. 215. It runs thus : " Nos qui valemos tanto come vos, os hazemos nuestro rey y señor, con tal que nos guardeis nuestros fueros y libertades: y sino, no."

(12) The actual text in the Code is as follows :

Cum enim Lege antiqua, quae regia nuncupabatur, omne jus omnisque potestas populi Romani imperatori translata sunt potestatem. C. I. 17. I.

It is well to have the terms of this before us, as it is at the bottom of a great deal of discussion on the origin and limits of sovereign authority.

In Salamonius we have the definite statement of the universality of politics :—Phil.: Principatus ipse est a natura sine hominum constitutione, et ideo ubique sibi ipsi similis tam apud Romanos quam Parthos, Scythas, Medos et alias nationes omnes. Jur.:

Talis est qualis suo cuique placet populo....Phil.: Jure ergo principatus illa competere dicendum quae populo placuerunt. Jur.: Convenit. Phil.: Ex his, si diligenter consideraris, palam sit. Jus principatus nihil aliud esse quam jus quoddam populi, et per hoc jure populi et auctoritate, quisque principatum agere ac leges constituere nec plus posse et valere quam ejus potest populus. 16. He goes on to declare that "Princeps se subjiciat non sibi, sed *personae se subjicit Civitatis*." He goes on to argue that laws are of the nature of compacts, and that civil society is founded on a voluntary pact.

(13) C. I. 17. 1.

Nos vero sanctionem omnem non dividimus in alias et alias conditorum partes, sed totam nostram esse volumus ; quid possit antiquitas nostris legibus abrogare ?

Here is a very frank expression of the truth, that it is only by the recognition of the sovereign power of the legislator that the danger of a reign of the dead can be obviated.

(14) C. I. 14. 4.

Digna vox est majestate regnantis legibus alligatum se principem profiteri; adeo de auctoritate juris nostra pendet auctoritas.

(15) D. I. 3. 31.

(16) D. I. 4. 1.

(17) Cicero, *De Legibus*.

(18) C. v. 59. 5.

There is an error in Stubbs' admirable note on the subject, *Const. Hist.* II. 132; the title is not 56 as there stated but 59. What Stubbs says in the text of Edward transmuting a "mere legal maxim into a great political and constitutional principle" is capable of a much wider extension, for it is typical of the whole way in which the medieval and Renaissance mind envisaged the Civil Law. It became, as we shall see, right down to the beginning of modern politics, not so much a jurist's code, as a compendium of political philosophy, and could be appealed to at any moment as an argument. The very first condition for understanding the rise of modern politics is that of realising how Scripture, Aristotle and the Corpus Juris, and above all this last, united to form the seed-plot of all political ideas.

(19) See the use Bracton makes of this *De Legibus Angliae*. The point is further developed in my *Divine Right of Kings*, p. 24. To take a further illustration, it was because private and

public rights were still partly undistinguished, that International Law was able to arise in the way it did. Grotius argues for War from the right of justifiable homicide, and the same is true of the application of many other principles, such as *usucapion* to the action of States.

(20) Cf. Pollock and Maitland, *History of English Law*, I. 512.

(21) In M. G. H., *Libelli De Lite*, III. 663:

"Auctoritate divina simulque sanctorum patrum institutione reges in ecclesia Dei ordinantur, ut habeant potestatem regendi populum Domini, genus electum, gentem sanctam, qui est ecclesia sancta Dei. Ecclesia quippe Dei quid aliud est quàm congregatio fidelium Christianorum in una fide spe et charitate in domo Dei cohabitantium?...Quem quidem principatum ita nonnulli distribruunt, ut dicant sacerdotem habere principatum regendi animas, regem vero regendi corpora, quasi animae possunt regi sine corporibus et corpora sine animabus. Quod nulla potest fieri ratione. Necesse est enim si bene regantur corpora, bene regantur et animae et e converso, quoniam utraque ideo reguntur, ut in resurrectione simul utraque sal ventur....Quae cum ita sint manifestum est quod rex habet principatum regendi eos qui sacerdotali dignitate potiuntur. Non ergo debet excludi rex a regimine sanctae ecclesiae, id est populi Christiani, quia ita divideretur regnum ecclesiae et fieret desolatio."...He goes on to anticipate Wyclif: "Sacerdos quippe aliam praefigurabat in Christo naturam, id est hominis, rex aliam id est Dei. Ille superiorem qua equalis est Deo patri, iste inferiorem qua minor est patre." *Ibid.* 666.

Rex principaliter sequitur Christum ex ejus vice et imitatione, episcopi vero interposita vice et imitatione apostolorum. 670.

(22) This growth of utilitarian argument though it first became prominent in Machiavelli gained greatly in extension owing to the Benthamite movement. The appeal to the notion of right, when there is apparent chance of lessening suffering by disregarding it, is treated as almost immoral by many 'advanced' thinkers. Cf. Dicey, *Law and Public Opinion*, for the way in which Benthamism brought this habit into prominence, and left it as a legacy to the Collectivism of our day. Perhaps it is truer to say that it is the legal idea of right which has given way to one of the general welfare; this is in accordance with the general change of political thought from the ideas of the Whigs, symbolised by Burke, to those of the Jacobins, expressed by Rousseau. From the modern reformer back to Machiavelli and even the Conciliar party "rights" are regarded with suspicion, as the enemies of Right or National

Welfare, and whereas the Whig movement was an attempt to secure legal consecration for limitations on the sovereign power, the great tendency of all thorough-going reformers is to sweep away the vested interests, which masquerade under the name of legal rights, and to magnify the one power, whether King or Parliament, that can promote true justice.

(23) Pollock and Maitland, I. 68.

(24) Op. cit.

(25) See Augustinus Triumphus.

(26) It may be worth while quoting the first few lines :

Bonifacius...dilectis filiis Doctoribus et Scholaribus universis Bononiae commorantibus...salutem. Sacrosanctae Romanae Ecclesiae (quam imperscrutabilis divinae providentiae altitudo universis dispositione incommutabili praetulit Ecclesiis, et totius orbis praecipuum obtinere voluit magistratum) regimini praesidentes, assidua meditatione urgemur; ut juxta creditae nobis dispensationis officium, subditorum commodis jugi, quantum nobis ex alto concessum fuerit, et sollicitudinis studio intendamus.

Amplectimur voluntarios labores ut scandala removeamus ab ipsis, et quas humana natura lites cotidie invenire conatur, nunc antiquorum declaratione, prout nobis est possibile reprimamus... Universitati vestrae igitur per Apostolica scripta mandamus, quatenus librum hujusmodi...quem sub bulla nostra transmittimus, prompto suscipientes affectu, eo utamini de caetero in judiciis et scholis; nullas alias, praeter illas quae inferuntur aut specialiter reservantur in eo, Decretales aut Constitutiones à quibuscunque nostris praedecessoribus Romanis Pontificibus post editionem dicti voluminis promulgatas, recepturi ulterius, aut pro Decretalibus habituri.

(27) II. 1: Licet Romanus Pontifex (qui jura omnia in scrinio pectoris sui censetur habere) constitutionem condendo posteriorem, priorem, quamvis de ipsa mentionem non faciat, revocare noscatur ; quia tamen locorum specialium et personarum singularium consuetudines et statuta (cum sint facti et in facto consistant) potest probabiliter ignorare; ipsis, dum tamen sint rationabilia, per constitutionem à se noviter editam (nisi expresse caveatur in ipsa) non intelligitur in aliquo derogare.

With regard to local customs being mere matters of fact, Bartolus used exactly the same principle in respect of the Emperor.

(28) Goldast. This dialogue is in I. 58—229. In a relatively brief space most of the arguments for and against regal and Papal sovereignty are therein set forth.

(29) The matter is discussed in Maitland, *Canon Law in England.*

(30) Seculares judices qui....personas Ecclesiasticas ad solvendum debita....dampnabili praesumptione compellant a temeritate hujusmodi per locorum ordinarios censura Ecclesiastica decernimus compescendos. II. 2. 2.

(31) *History of Political Theory in the West,* Chap. I.

(32) *Development of European Polity,* Chap. 22.

(33) Creighton, *Papacy* I. 32.

(34) Clement V in his decision about the "Unam Sanctam" only goes so far as to say that it made no difference ; the French king and people are no more subject than they were before to the Roman See. Thus an ample loophole was left for the development of future ultra-montane pretensions ; for it was easy enough to allege that the principles of the "Unam Sanctam" dated from at least the eleventh century.

Extrav. Comm. V. 7. 2.

(35) This dialogue is in Goldast, Vol. II. 396—957.

(36) The book is edited by M. Langlois, Picard 1891.

I may refer to a brief account I wrote of Pierre Dubois, entitled *A forgotten Radical,* in the *Cambridge Review,* 1899. Renan has a long study of him in his *Études sur la politique religieuse du règne de Philippe le Bel,* and there is an article in the Victoria University Studies.

(37) Bozius was an Oratorian. His treatise *De Temporali Ecclesiae Monarchia* appeared in 1602.

(38) See the Bull of Condemnation in Shirley's edition of the *Fasciculi Zizaniorum.*

(39) *e.g.* his defence of the outrageous act of John of Gaunt in regard to the Sanctuary at Westminster. It forms a good part of the *De Ecclesia.*

NOTES TO THE CONCILIAR MOVEMENT.

(1) The wording is as follows :

Concilium generale faciens et ecclesiam catholicam repraesentans, potestatem a Christo immediate habet, cui quilibet cuiuscunque status vel dignitatis, etiamsi papalis existat, obedire tenetur in his quae pertinent ad fidem. Mirbt 155.

The decree only refers in terms to the Council of Constance and the affairs of the moment. It is only by inference that it can be extended into a general assertion of conciliar omnipotence.

(2) In John of Segovia.

(3) Cf. the phrase of Cajetan in his argument for Papal autocracy, printed in Rocaberti.

(4) A very recent work brings out this fact with great ability. M. Gabriel Pérouse in his *Le Cardinal Louis Aleman* shews how among the main causes of the failure of the Council of Basle two were most prominent, (1) The Council, ignorant of the distinction between control and administration, attempted without training, knowledge or cohesion to grasp the whole governing activity of the Church, judicial, executive and legislative. It failed in the same way as the English Parliament failed in the seventeenth century ; owing to the extreme democratic tendency of some of its members, anything like leadership was distrusted, and even small committees were attacked and hampered. (2) Aleman was working for the medieval system as against the Roman Curia which was organising the modern Papacy. The book is so new that a phrase or two may be worth quoting.

"Escorté de théologiens scholastiques et de moines errants, lui-même et jusqu'au fond homme du moyen âge dans sa foi passionnée, dans sa croyance à l'unité chrétienne...il combattit vainement l'éclosion de cette ère moderne, où les papes italiens entourés de leurs humanistes diserts et de diplomates habiles aux compromis, allaient réorganiser l'Eglise au moyen d'ingénieux concordats, au profit de leur pouvoir propre et des princes séculaires, aux dépens des vieilles institutions médiévales les chapitres, le lien métropolitain, le principe électif des monastères" (pp. 498, 9). Cf. also, "Tandis en effet que le nonce et la cour de Rome cherchaient à hâter la moderne organisation de l'Eglise, la majorité des Pères s'inspirait des principes de l'âge précédent... Pouvoirs judiciaire et administratif, législatif et même exécutif, tout était revendiqué par les Pères, comme le droit exclusive de convoquer le concile suivant." (196.)

On page 169 the author shews that the real purpose was "d'ajourner indéfiniment aussi la dissolution du Concile, et de s'ériger en jurisdiction permanente, but inavoué des vrais disciples de Constance."

The parallel to the Long Parliament is obvious.

(5) If the deposition of Richard II be studied, it will be seen how far Parliament was from asserting any such definite theory of popular sovereignty as that proclaimed by the Council. The articles are in the *Rolls of Parliament*, vol. v.

(6) See the decree in Mirbt 155. It should be read in connection with the later refusal of the Council of Basel to be dissolved without its own consent. In theory this was preserved even at the surrender in 1449.

(7) For the literature of this and the other chapters, my Bibliography to the last chapter of Vol. III. of the *Cambridge Modern History* may be cited.

(8) Conrad is one of the earliest writers. His letter is in Martène and Durand's *Thesaurus*, vol. II. 1200—1226. It contains some interesting expressions.

(9) Henry of Hesse and most of the writers will be found in Dupin's Gerson, vol. II.

(10) Hubler has pointed out, how the Conciliar writers start partly from the notion of precedent, developing their constitutionalism in the same way as Hotman in France, as Coke and the common lawyers in England ; and partly from universal principles of political reasoning applicable to all societies, and more perfectly to the Church. The antithesis of this attitude is that of Étienne de la Boeotie. He is mainly interesting as shewing the way in which pure renaissance sentiment, unmixed with any flavour of medievalism or notions of historical development, might produce an abstract republicanism. To him, as to Machiavelli, the only history worth quoting is Roman, while he is of course without the Florentine's extraordinary keen insight into facts and existing tendencies. His general attitude is not unlike that of Shelley. Government to him is simply an American trust exploiting the masses in its own selfish lust. The one thing needful is to awaken the consciousness of the masses whose numbers will alone secure victory. He might almost have written the lines :—

> Rise like lions after slumber
> In unvanquishable number !
> *　　*　　*
> Ye are many, they are few.

(11) It is, I think, remarkable that in the recent discussion about the position of the laity in the representative Church Council more attention has not been paid to the very strong assertions of the rights of laymen made by the Conciliar leaders both in Constance and Basel. We find these persons, who were undeniably both orthodox and nationalist, with sympathies not dissimilar to English Churchmen, asserting very strongly the right of the lay power to be presented in the person of Emperor, Kings

and their ambassadors. It must be remembered, that in a democratic government like the English, elected members would naturally take the place of the ambassadors. High Papalists, like John of Torquemada, complain of the powers claimed for laymen.

The documents quoted as Chapters XVI and XVII in the Consultationes printed by von der Hardt are among the most important bearing on this point. The first is attributed to the Cardinal of Cambrai, the second to the Cardinal of S. Marco. I quote the most important passages, interesting for the appeal they make to early Church history.

"Sicut patet in Actibus Apostolorum et in historia Eusebii quae Actibus Apostolorum immediate subnectitur, quandoque in Conciliis congregabatur *tota communitas Christianorum,* quandoque Episcopi Presbyteri Diaconi, quandoque soli Episcopi sine Abbatibus, quandoque cum Episcopis Abbates, quandoque Imperator convocabat et congregabat Concilium. Sicut haec varietas potest probari jure naturali et divino et ex historiis praedictis. ...Item, eadem ratione, qua supra, non sunt excludendi a voce definitiva Sacrae Theologiae Doctores, ac juris Canonici et Civilis. Quibus et maxime Theologis, datur auctoritas praedicandi aut docendi ubique terrarum, quae non est parva auctoritas in populo Christiano, sed multo majus quam unius Episcopi vel Abbatis, ignorantis et solum titulati....Item quantum ad materiam terminandi praesens schisma et dandi pacem Ecclesiae, velle excludere Reges, Principes aut Ambasiatores eorum...a voce seu determinatione etiam conclusiva non videtur justum ac pium aut rationi consonum." von der Hardt, II. 224.

Perhaps the most moderate attitude is that of the Cardinal of S. Marco:

De ambasiata autem Regum et Principum clarum est, quod in iis quae conveniunt universalem Ecclesiam, utpote unionem Ecclesiae et fidem, admittendi sunt. Sed stare debent determinationi peritorum et doctorum in his quae sunt fidei. *Ibid.* 230—1.

Zabarella's views in the *De Schismate* are very similar.

(12) It is hardly necessary to say that in the eyes and the phraseology of the canonists the flock whether of Pope or Bishops are "subditi," even more completely than a nation is the subject of its King in common speech.

(13) Simancas, *De Papa* (Rocaberti XIII. 277):

Cum respublica spiritualis perfecta sit, et sibi sufficiens, ut se ipsam indemnem servet, potest ea omnia facere, quae necessaria fuerint ad suum finem consequendum exercendo etiam jurisdictionem in eos, qui in rebus temporalibus alioqui sibi subjecti non essent. *Quod quidem naturali jure cuicumque Principi facere contra aliorum rempublicam licet.*

A similar view is in Bellarmine, *De Rom. Pont.* v. 7.

This passage is alone proof of the error made by the Bishop of Exeter in his *Regnum Dei*, wherein it is asserted that the notion of the Church as a "societas perfecta" is only modern and Jesuit.

See the document in Denziger, *Enchiridion*, pp. 405—422.

(14)   A few of the more notable phrases of Nicolas may be here cited.

"Pulchra est haec speculatio, quomodo in populo omnes potestates tam spirituales in potentia latent, quam etiam temporales et corporales." II. 19.

It is nonsense to say "omne id jus esset quod Romanus Pontifex vellet,"—for the Pope is subject to the canons, and these are under natural law, *contra quod etiam princeps potestatem non habet*, II. 14. Even the decretals owe their authority as much to long acceptance, as to Papal institution. We may compare with this a Gallican argument, that the French Church does not accept all decretals of the Pope *ipso facto*, but merely those consecrated by time in the *corpus juris*. II. 3.

"Multa concilia etiam rite convocata errasse legimus."

These passages serve to shew how the idea of natural law, partly embodied in the more general maxims of the Roman jurisprudence, partly in the intellectual atmosphere, was the real milieu, in which the constitutionalism of the day could alone thrive. This remained true right on to Rousseau.

"Omnis constitutio radicatur in jure naturali ; et si ei contradicit, constitutio valida esse nequit." II. 14, and again

"Cum natura omnes sint liberi, tum omnis principatus...*est a sola concordantia et consensu subjectio*. Nam si natura aeque potentes et aeque liberi homines sunt, vera et ordinata potestas nonnisi electione et consensu aliorum constitui potest, sicut etiam lex a consensu constituitur"; going on to quote the phrase of S. Augustine used in the Decretum, "generale pactum societatis regibus obedire" as a proof of the contractual.

"Papa non est universalis Episcopus sed super alios primus, et sacrorum Conciliorum non in Papa sed in consensu omnium vigorem fundamus." II. 13.

" Considerari enim primo legem Christianam liberrimam, ad quam nullus nisi sponte absque coactione accedit....Coactio proprie non est in ipsa Ecclesia descensione a Christo ; sed gratia est, quae ab ipsa plenitudine fontis capitis in ipsum Corpus Christi mysticum fluit. Unitas fidelium est illa ad cujus servitium et observantiam praesidentia est super singulos. Hinc unitas fidelium sive universale concilium Catholicae ecclesiae ipsam repraesentans est supra suum ministerium et praesidem." II. 28.

(15) After the victory of the Pope over the Council it became impossible to deny that pure monarchy is the best form of government. In arguing in favour of a republic in Florence all that Savonarola is able to say is, that though the Papacy clearly proves absolutism to be the best form in general, yet circumstances alter cases, and for Florence in its then situation a republic is more fitted. He does not embrace the doctrine of the relativity of politics to the extent that Bartolus did. Cf. remarks on this subject in a paper in *Royal Hist. Soc. Transactions*, vol. XIX.

John of Torquemada, whose chief treatise is in Rocaberti, is in reality the first modern exponent of the Divine Right of Kings: his book, with that of Lainez at the Council of Trent, would give a reader who knew nothing else a very good idea of the whole controversy. Even John of Torquemada, though he allows a Pope to dispense in cases of bigamy or homicide, admits that a Pope may be a heretic, and so *ipso facto* cease to be Pope. He can err in opinion, while in judgment he remains infallible.

(16) The following form a very small selection of the passages which might be cited in illustration of the views of the Conciliar reformers. For citations from Gerson the reader is referred to Appendix B in my *Divine Right of Kings*.

Conrad of Gelnhausen (1378) in Martène, *Thesaurus* II. 1216 :

Si ergo necessitas personae privatae imminens et forsitan peccatrici solvit vincula legis, quis ambigit, quod in tali et tanta necessitate Sanctae Ecclesiae...nulla lex humana edita super congregatione concilii generalis nonnisi auctoritate papae fienda possit obsistere quominus languor curetur in capite nec morbus inficiat totum corpus.

ibid. 1225 : Convocatio concilii generalis sit summe necessaria pro bono communi, in quo etiam salus et utilitas omnium et singulorum Christi fidelium includitur et per consequens est omni privato commodo vel utilitati praeferenda.

Henry of Hesse or Langenstein. *Consilium Pacis.*

Item quam periculosae sint bono communi et quam studiose sedandae sint, potentium et praesidentium dissensiones, tanquam civitatis et totius civilis amicitiae corruptione, nos docet etiam ille gentilis Aristoteles.

Item casus novi et periculosi emergentes in Diocesi aliqua per Concilium particulare sive Provinciale emendantur. Igitur casus novi et ardui totum mundum concernentes per generale Concilium discuti debent. Quod enim omnes tangit, ab omnibus vel vice omnium tractari debet et convenit....

Quis enim nescit quod fuit impossibile regulariter Leges et Jura positiva institui, quae in nullo casu deficerent vel exceptionem paterentur....Et ergo est quaedam virtus, quam Aristoteles 5 Ethic. vocat ἐπιείκειαν, quae est directiva justi legalis. Et ea melior et nobilior, quia per eam, modo excellentiori et perfectiori, obeditur menti et intentioni Legislatoris. Dupin's Gerson II. 823, 831.

Andreas Majorensis (Hardt II. 157):

"Si Rex convocat Regnum, scilicet majores et principales regni sui, et tamen non habet ipse majorem potestatem quam totum Regnum." This is a fair example of the frequent use of the constitution of monarchy of the day, which is always *taken for granted* to create a precedent for the Church. Papa executor concilii, minister Christi.

De Modis Uniendi:

Omnes ergo constitutiones Apostolicae, sive leges factae in favorem Papae, cardinalium sive praelatorum intelliguntur et intelligi debent, ubi respublica Ecclesiastica directe vel indirecte publice vel occulte in parte vel in toto detrimento aut divisioni non videtur subesse. Et sic de legibus imperalibus et regalibus possumus intelligere.

D'Ailly, *De Jurisdictione Ecclesiastica* (Hardt VI. 44, 6):

"Communitas ipsa sola habet immediatum et verum dominium et non praelatus aliquis, aut quaevis persona singularis." Hence the Pope is not lord, but "universalis dispensator. Papa non potest ad libitum detrahere bona Ecclesiarum ita quod quidquid ordinet de ipsis teneat. Hoc enim verum appareret si esset Dominus, sed cum sit minister et dispensator bonorum communitatis, in quo requiritur bona fides, non habet sibi collatam potestatem super bonis ipsis, nisi ad necessitatem vel communem Ecclesiae utilitatem."

Zabarella definitely asserts that the sovereignty of the people is inalienable, so that it is judge, whether Pope governs well or ill. "Neque unquam ita potuit transferre potestatem in papam, ut desinerit esse penes ipsam" (708); and the same is true of the *lex regia* and the Emperor. "Major est potestas populi quam magistratus ipsius." Schardius, 709.

Zabarella:

Papa non potest immutare statum ecclesiae, vel impedire quae ad perpetuam utilitatem ordinata sunt. *Ibid.* 694.

In eo quod dixi aliud papam, aliud sedem Apostolicam, videtur intelligenda sedes Apostolica pro ecclesia Romana, quae non censetur esse solus Papa sed ipse Papa cum cardinalibus, qui sunt partes corporis Papae. 701. In defectu magistratus revertimur ad jus pristinum ante constitutos magistratus, quo tempore cuique licebat jus sibi dicere. 691.

The Pope cannot do everything, for even God can only do all things, *praeter ea* sola per quae dignitas ejus laederetur. 701.

The treatises of Zabarella and Nicolas are in Schardius' *Syntagma*.

NOTES TO LUTHER.

(1) This is of course a very rough description. All through the Middle Ages the civil power was constantly asserting its claims; but throughout society is conceived rather as a Church than a State, throughout it is recognised that "the common law of the Catholic Church" is not for princes to upset, while dreams like those of Wyclif and Marsiglio and the Conciliar adherents of Imperial and secular power must be regarded as anticipations of the tendencies, which triumphed in all states, Protestant and Catholic, in the sixteenth century.

The claim, that either the Church or the State is a *perfecta societas sibi sufficiens*, is really remarkable for its admission that these other societies are also perfect. It is not because he stated that the Church was a perfect society, that Bellarmine made a change; so much would have been admitted by any medieval papalist, indeed it was the essence of his claim. What is new is the tacit recognition that the State is also a perfect society. This was not always perceived by controversialists and they fall into inconsistencies in consequence. Barclay, *De Potestate Papae*, c. 17, Goldast III. 651 sqq., ridicules Bellarmine for arguing first that there are two societies, and then that the Pope, as head of the whole single society, can depose kings. In this he is within his rights, for Bellarmine is not quite consistent, and the conception is clearly not quite plain, as yet; for Barclay will not rise to the notion of Warburton, that there can be two quite distinct societies although composed each of the same persons, differentiated as social persons by their separate ends. Indeed Barclay in one place denies, that if the Church is a separate society, it contains anyone but the Clergy; in another, however, he seems to admit it. At any rate the argument of Barclay, of the absolute distinctness of the two powers, owing to their nature and purpose, is essentially an argument for the State being a perfect society, no less than the Church. Indeed he admits that the Church may use its own means of coercion, but that by their nature these are spiritual and not material and hence do not reach to the deposing power; this concedes to the Church its reality and independence. Further Bellarmine's argument, that the Church may act in its own interests, *i.e.* deposing a persecuting heretic, is based on the notion of the Church, as one of the persons of international law, employing what is really war to maintain its rights. This is the true significance of the *indirect* Papal power, marks the real gulf between Jesuits and Canonists, and prepares the way for the doctrine of a "free Church in a free state." As we know that Bellarmine was rather less than more of a Papalist than his writings (see Döllinger-Reusch, *Selbstbiographie*), I think it right to say that he really gave up the extremer theory of Augustinus Triumphus and Bozius; that the distinction is not merely, as Barclay tried to prove, one of words and sophistry. The whole argument as conducted by Barclay, and still mor by his son John Barclay in his *Vindicatio*, is well worthy of study, arid though it seems; a very cursory glance will shew how different is the atmosphere from that of the *Somnium Viridarii*.

For the same purpose the Venetian advocates against Paul V, and James I's defence of his oath of allegiance are important. In all these cases, there is an attempt to reconcile the existence of two distinct authorities, incarnate in two separate societies, and to maintain that allegiance to one need not impair loyalty to the other. The effort of James I was really an attempt to do for the Papists, what Newman afterwards essayed in his letter to the Duke of Norfolk in reply to Mr Gladstone's Vaticanism. It may well be, that James would never have thought of the oath of allegiance, but for the fact that he had been brought up under that system, which asserted so emphatically the doctrine of the two kingdoms.

The real crux of the question is surrendered, when it is admitted that infidel or heretic sovereigns have genuine *rights* to their crown. Barclay of course entirely denies the right of the Pope to depose a heretic like Queen Elizabeth, and also the divine right of all clerical minorities.

I quote the more important passages :

Potest et Ecclesia seu Respublica Christiana appellari Christianorum *tam clericorum, quam Laicorum* collectio qui in unum corpus adunati, Ecclesiasticis legibus sese subjiciunt, non quidem quatenus homines civilem Rempublicam componentes, sed quatenus in spiritualem coetum admissi. Eadem distinguendi ratione civilis temporalis et politica Respublica dici potest, vel quae ex infidelibus Principibus et rebus publicis constat, vel quae ex Christianis quidem, sed nullo ad Religionem respectu habito, componitur. Sed et ob charitatis sanctos nexus, et fidei communionem, dicimus Rempublicam politicam accedentem ad Christum, ita jungi spirituali et Ecclesiasticae Reipublicae ut jam utraque dici possit unam Rempublicam Christianam componere, in qua sint duo Praefecti praecipui, quorum ille omnino omnibus in spiritualibus ; hic omnino omnibus in temporalibus praesit.

Vin. c. XIII. p. 901.

Ex his patet, Bellarmine, Rempublicam Ecclesiasticam perfectam et sibi sufficientem in ordine ad finem suum esse ; *sed ad illum finem non necessarium posse uti et disponere de temporalibus rebus.* *Ibid.* c. XVII. 926.

Scribit Barclaius te iniuria potestatis Ecclesiasticam et civilem, quas antea duas unius Reipublicae potestates esse volueras, jam duas Respublicas appellare. Sed ne inutili lite certemus, sint sane duae Respublicae partiales, sint duae Potestates in una Republica utrum vis. Nihil moror. Satis quod illae duae Potestates, sive Respublicae *sunt sibi sufficientes ad suum finem,* absque quod alterutra possit de rebus disponere ad alteram spectantibus. Utriusque potestatis conditor Deus non discrevit illarum modo fines, sed etiam actus etiam dignitates. *Ibid.* 929.

Num potestas politica vim habet a Pontifice ? Certe negas. Num Pontificis potestas in eodem genere sublimior est potestate Principum ? Negas quoque. Vis enim nullam temporalem potestatem sublimiorem esse regia. *Ibid.* c. XXI. 946.

C. XXIV. p. 961 sqq. John Barclay makes great game with Bellarmine for asserting that, though the Pope had no such power of his own, kings in accepting the Christian faith gave him tacitly a pact. This argument is remarkable, as founding the original compact on the Baptismal vow and also as a means whereby authority might be claimed for Pope as head of a single state against Catholic princes, but not against infidels or heretic princes when established, *not* persecutors.

Chap. XXXV. p. 1112 he again asserts definitely, that both republics are perfect.

Non igitur subordinata est Ecclesiasticae potestas Politica, cum non propter Ecclesiasticam constituta sit, sed ad civilem concordiam et adipisci suum finem absque illius ope possit, quod ut ipse fateris in Ethnicis saepe factum ; cum Ecclesiastica jam absque illa esse queat, ut primis revera post Christum annis fuit cum denique neque ad finem, neque ad essentiam una ad aliam ordinem dicat, sed sint a sinu Dei, dignitatibus, officiis actibusque distinctae.   cap. III. 810.

It can readily be seen, how similar the admissions here made on both sides are to the position of Cartwright and other Presbyterians, so strongly condemned by Whitgift and Hooker. The Presbyterians, however, had thought out their doctrine more completely than either Royalists or Jesuits, and were under no danger of confusing the Church with the Clergy. The position claimed for the State by Barclay, the Venetians, and implied by James I, is, however, entirely different from that asserted by Luther and the English Erastians. That position really arose from the denial of the Church, as a visible society by Luther, and the belief that all law was the same. Even in his more theological treatises, where Luther discovers the difference between law and faith, there is no sign that he regards civil law as distinct from moral, or as anything but a republication of the essential parts of the Sinaitic Code. Law is for Luther, whether natural, moral, or civil, all embodied in the ten commandments, and anything else is mere administrative regulation, whether in State or Church. Melanchthon does attach more importance to *natural* law ; but the notion of two republics, essentially distinct, is foreign, both to Luther and Anglican Divines, until the eighteenth century.

Ostendi, supra, has potestates, spiritualem et temporalem ita esse distinctas ut neutra alteri quatenus talis est aut dominetur, aut pareat. W. Barclay, *De Potestate Papae*, c. XXX. 669.

It is to be noted that Barclay, while in the *De Regno* he is opposed to Gerson's views of constitutional rights, is very well able to make use of the strong assertions of lay authority and national independence, which formed another part of the Conciliar armoury.

The two powers are *liberae et sui juris* et mutuo amore coirent ; there is in fact, as Warburton said later, an alliance between Church and State, only Barclay leaves to the Church a great deal more freedom than Warburton was able to do, writing when the Whig *régime* was flourishing, although Warburton desired the revival of Convocation, and was by no means the mere Erastian he is sometimes represented. We observe further :

(*a*) The Venetian treatises are less interesting than those of Barclay and his son, but they establish some points. They are more definitely written from the standpoint of absolute territorialism ; the republic ever since 420 was omnino libera nata (299) in Fra Paolo's words. The notion of a State-paid clergy appears in the tract of the theologians, p. 338.

(*b*) The author argues much in the manner of the *Vindiciae*, that the acceptance of a Christianity involves a contract with God, so that anyone violating it may be resisted, after the example of the Maccabean princes. He then goes on to argue, that the Clergy have no right to obey the Papal interdict, because if they do they will become false to their bargain.

Dum Christiana religio recipitur, stabilitur quasi contractus per authoritatem divinam inter populum illum fidelem et Ecclesiae ministros ; ut nimirum ministri populo verbum Dei concionentur &c. *et populus vicissim iisdem victum et alia necessaria subministret.*

(*c*) It is to be noted that the writer of one answer, in order to prove the right of the republic to control the formation of colleges and societies goes right back to early Imperial law, Trajan and Ulpian, and quotes the example of Julius Caesar, as related by Suetonius. The question of right is the same as that involved in the "Associations" law in France, and the idea of a corporate body existing only by the fiat or the concession of the State is at the bottom of some recent difficulties both in England and Scotland.

(*d*) The Venetian controversialists were acute enough to see the use that might be made of the Jesuit admissions, and frequently cite Molina and Bellarmine, as on their side. (Of course the inference would not have been admitted.)

(*e*) Lastly, the constant use of *status* for republic can be discerned in these treatises. There can, I think, be little doubt that it was largely the influence of Italy and especially Machiavelli which caused the term *State* to become everywhere predominant instead of commonwealth. The use of it in these tractates, as compared for instance with those of the French or Spanish writers, is evidence, though not conclusive, of this. Like the balance of power, reason of State, both name and thing, came from Italy—whence nearly all modern politics can be derived.

(2) Cf. *Une Campagne Laïque* passim, with introduction by M. Anatole France.

(3) Weiss nun fast alle Welt, dass Niemand so herrlich vom Kaiser und Gehorsam geschrieben, als ich.

Mundt IV. 92.

Luther, Wider den Meuchler zu Dresden.

Cf. also Erlangen edition, Vol. XXXI. 83.

(4) Greift ein Kind wohl, dass christlich Recht sei, nicht, sich sträuben wider Unrecht ; nicht, zum Schwert greifen ; nicht, sich wehren ; nicht, sich rächen, sondern dahingeben Leib und Gut, dass er raube, wer da raubet ; wir haben doch genug an unserem Herrn, der uns nicht lassen wird, wie er verheissen hat. Leiden, Leiden, Kreuz, Kreuz ist der Christenrecht, das und kein anderes. Mundt II. 93.

(5) *Auf den Dritten Artikel.*

Es will dieser Artikel alle Menschen gleich machen und aus dem geistlichen Reich Christi ein weltlich äusserlich Reich machen ; welches unmöglich ist. Denn weltlich Reich kann nicht bestehen, wo nicht Ungleichheit ist in Personen, das etliche frei sind, etliche gefangen, etliche Herren, etliche Unterthanen.

Mundt II. 103.

(6) Die Bauern wussten nicht, wie köstlich Ding es sei um Frieden und Sicherheit, dass einer mag seinem Bissen und Trunk fröhlich und sicher geniessen, und dankten Gott nicht darum ; dass musste er jetzt auf diese Weise lehren, dass ihnen der Kützel verginge.

Sendbrief an Caspar Müller. Mundt II. 132.

Luther's view of the serf's position is here indicated :

Der Esel wird Schläge haben und der Pöbel mit Gewalt regieret sein ; dass wusste Gott wohl. Darum gab er der Obrigkeit nicht ein Fuchsschwanz, sondern ein Schwert in die Hand.

Mundt II. 132.

(7) See the Letter in Grisar I., Appendix.

(8) The whole question of Erastus' views is discussed by me in a paper in the *Journal of Theological Studies*, 1900. I think that the distinction there made between the views of Erastus and those of Hobbes or Machiavelli is just. But I should not now write so largely of the power of the State as in the concluding paragraphs, nor deny the need of excommunication.

(9) Cf. Luther v. Turks.

Die Welt ist aus Ende kommen, das Romisch Reich ist fast dahin und zerrissen. Erlangen edition, XXXI. 74.

It is significant that one of Luther's grounds for attacking the Turks is " sie trunken nicht Wein." What could be more cogent?

Luther knew very well that the office of the teacher is persuasion, and that all spiritual changes must first affect men's minds, and then outward institutions will tumble of themselves.

Ich habe dem Papst ohne alle Faust mehr Schaden gethan, denn ein machtiger König thun möchte.

Mundt II. 76.

(10) In Luther's reply to Henry VIII we see something of his true position :

" Consuetudo, inquit, habet vim legis. Respondeo habeat vim legis in civilibus causis, sed nos in libertatem vocati sumus, quae nec legem nec consuetudinem ferre potest aut debet cum agamus in spiritualibus causis." Jena edition, II. 339.

This should be compared with the view of a modern Lutheran, that the idea of law is unknown to the early Church, of which the organisation is purely "charismatic," and that the change to any system of law marks the beginning of Catholicism.

Sohm, *Kirchenrecht.*

Again Luther says :

" Pro libertate ergo pugno, Rex pro captivitate pugnat."

The captivity is to the dead hand of the past.

(11) Cf. I, chaps. 10 and 58, also *Discorso sulla Riforma* V., and perhaps most strongly in *Dell' Arte della Guerra*, V. 169.

(12) The same is true of the passages at the close of the *Discorsi*, and still more of that in the third book of the *Arte della Guerra* : Non abbiamo noi vinto una giornata felicissamente? Ma con maggior felicità si vincerebbe, se ni fusse concesso il metterla in atto. 191.

(13) The most important passage on this point :

Dove si delibera al tutto della salute della patria, non vi debbe cadere alcuna considerazione nè di giusto, nè d' ingiusto, nè di pietoso, nè di crudele, nè di laudabile, nè d' ignominioso, anzi posposto ogni altro rispetto seguire al tutto quel partito che gli salvi la vita e mantengale la libertà.   III. 41.

Yet in one of the few moral passages in his writings he declares in the previous chapter that territory acquired by fraud or breach of treaties can never be a source of glory.

(14) His attitude to religion is simply that of a man who regards it as a force to be reckoned with. It is not his words, but the *naïveté* of his tone that is really so remarkable—*e.g.* this is all that it occurs to him to say about Joan of Arc. He speaks of the use of the military oath.

La quale cosa, mescolata con altri modi religiosi, fece molte volte facile ai capitani antichi ogni impresa, e farebbe sempre dove la Religione si temesse ed osservasse....Ne' tempi de' padri nostri, Carlo VII re di Francia nella guerra che fece con gl' Inglesi, diceva consigliarsi con una fanciulla mandata da Iddio, la quale si chiamo per tutto la Pulzella di Francia : il che gli fu cagione della vittoria.

Dell' Arte della Guerra, V. 227.

(15) Sir Frederick Pollock, *History of the Science of Politics.* The statement is true of the way in which Machiavelli regards the facts of human life, religious, moral, and political. They are phenomena to be accounted for and made use of in his scheme. Every motive by which men are or appear to be moved is a force, and if rightly manipulated an asset, for the statesman. But the direct and practical aim of Machiavelli, breathing in all his writings, is love of Italy and her rescue from slavery, by any and every means. It is for this reason, for the sake of the community not the individual, that he prefers free government to tyranny in the *Discorsi.*

(16) Pibrac quoted by Pasquier in his *Letters,* VI. 2, p. 155.

(17) See my paper on Bartolus in *Transactions of Royal Hist. Society,* Vol. XIX. 1905.

(18) I quote the most important words :

"Cum tamen dictus Johannes Huss fidem orthodoxam pertinaciter impugnans, se ab omni conductu et privilegio reddiderit alienum, nec aliqua sibi fides aut promissio de jure naturali divino et humano fuerit in praejudicium catholicae fidei observanda."

The authenticity of this decree has been impugned, but without good reason, see Wylie, *Council of Constance.* Moreover, whether or no the decree be authentic, there is plenty of evidence that the views therein expressed represent the mind of the Council ; see some quoted by Creighton II. 30, 31. Acton's essay on " Paolo Sarpi " brings out more completely than anything else the way in which Machiavelli's doctrine was used in Italy indiscriminately by Church and State. •

(19) See in Dupin's Gerson, vol. V.

(20) The nearest approach to this statement is in the *Discorsi.*
It is to be wished that somebody would make a catena of the authorities who state the maxim definitely. Personally I have never actually found it in any Jesuit writer, though it perhaps may be inferred from the passages quoted below.

(21) Cf. *Constitutiones Societatis Jesu* VI. I. Chapter 5 goes further and admits that the vow of obedience may be allowed to induce to mortal sin in cases in which the superior commands in the name of Jesus Christ. It should, however, be stated that in Acton's opinion the real offence of the Order against ethics is not to be traced to either of these sources, but to later developments. Doubtless the passages are "patient" of an orthodox interpretation.

(22) Mr G. E. Moore declares the doctrine of ends to be far superior to that of means in *Principia Ethica* § 89 etc. From the Christian standpoint the truth in this view is that indicated below ; while for ordinary practical ethics the statement is simply made to warn the actor against the great danger of imagining exceptions to be more frequent than the rules of morality—which may not be absolute, but are certainly general.

(23) See the long account of Probabilism and Gonzalez' struggles in Döllinger-Reusch, *Geschichte der moralen Streitigkeiten.*

(24) See the matter discussed and letters quoted in *Life of Bishop Creighton*, Chapter XIII. The crucial statement is that of Creighton: "I am hopelessly tempted to admit *degrees* of criminality" (page 375). See also a Lecture by Creighton in *The Quarterly Review*, 1905, on "Historical Ethics."

NOTES TO THE POLITIQUES.

(1) The notes affixed to the vast collection known as the *Mémoires de la Ligue* in the edition published in the middle of the eighteenth century afford the strongest evidence of the complete triumph of regalist principles over ultramontane. The editor has little sympathy with the Huguenots, yet even less with the seditious spirit of the Ligueurs and the Jesuits.

(2) Tarquini in *Juris Ecclesiastici Publici Institutiones.*

(3) See a paper of mine on "Hoadly and the Bangorian Controversy" in *The Guardian*, Oct. 1905. A very cursory glance at Sherlock's pamphlets against Hoadly will shew that what the former really opposed was the idea of religious toleration. The same is not, I think, the case with Law, nor indeed could this very well be the case with a non-juror.

(4) L'intempérie de toute la Chrétienté est aujourd'hui telle qu'il n'y a Royaume ni État, qui s'y puisse maintenir en paix sans la liberté des deux Religions, voire qui ni se ruine si on s'opiniâtre contre l'une.   *Mémoires de la Ligue*, II. 133.

(5) See Dufey's *Oeuvres Complètes de Michel L'Hôpital*, vol. I. 441—458 and 468—79.

(6) See the famous pamphlet of Cecil *On the Execution of Justice in England.*

(7) See clause II of that document in Gardiner, p. 269 :

That we shall in like manner...endeavour the extirpation of Popery, prelacy, superstition, heresy...lest we partake in other men's sins, and thereby be in danger to receive of their plagues ; and that the Lord may be one and His name one in the three kingdoms.

(8) The following passage in Bodin is an illustration of the view, which can, however, be best studied *passim* in the *Letters of Pasquier* :

Si tantus fuerit principum ac populorum in nova religione consensus, ut sine Reipublicae exitio prohiberi non possit ; sapientissimi quique Rerumpublicarum moderatores in eo genere gubernatorem imitantur, qui cum eo, quo cupiat, pergere non possit, eo quo potest cursum dirigit, ac saepe velificatione mutata, procellis ac tempestatibus obtemperat ne si portum tenere velit naufragium patiatur. Ferenda igitur ea religio est quam sine Reipublicae interitu conferre non possis. Salus enim Reipublicae extrema lex esset.   III. 8.

(9) The crucial arguments are put by Brentz :

"Multo satius est et praestabilius, ut quater aut decies falsa fides tolleretur, quam quod semel vera fides insectationem patiatur."

See a discussion of these writings in my chapter on "Political Thought" in *Cambridge Modern History*.

(10) There is an interesting passage in l'Hôpital's *Traité de la Reformation de la Justice*, in which he denies that nature teaches a mere struggle for existence and asserts that it is in essence social.

He says that those who claim to rule without law assert that "Par la loy de nature les gros poissons mangent les petits, les loups et aultres bestes ravissantes, les aigles, les faulcons, les vautours, et autres oyseaux de proie mangent les oyseaux qui ont peu de force et de résistance....Mais ces beaulx diseurs ont mal étudié en la loy de nature laquelle est toute autre que celle qu'ils y se figurent, et qu'ils prennent des bestes brutes....La verité est que entre les bestes brutes, il ne se veoit jamais guères que celles d'une même espèce s'entredévorent et se fassent la guerre. *Canis caninam non est, corvus corvi oculum non eruit.* Au contraire les bestes se mettent en troupe pour se garantir contre celles qui leur sont naturellement ennemyes et qui sont d'aultre espèce... C'est donc principallement aux grands du monde à garder bien religieusement *ceste loy de nature.*"   II. 47.

(11) *Decretale* IV. 17, 13.

(12) Nunquam enim Regis alicujus tanta saevitia vel rapacitas exstitit, quae cum civilis discordiae miseriis ex rebellio natae comparata non multis partibus minor sit.

De Regno, 119.

(13) By poverty I mean serious poverty, below Mr Seebohm's border-line, not of course the mere absence of many useless luxuries.

(14) By utilitarian I mean the word in its popular sense, of placing convenience before character.

(15) The Renaissance was of course opposed to the historical spirit. The idea of development, or of the relativity of constitutions or systems, was entirely alien to it. Machiavelli uses the facts of history as so many instances on which to form an inductive science of politics ; but of the conception of politics as the result of national development or characteristics there is no trace.

The arguments of Hotman drawn from the nature of early French institutions were ridiculed by this school. Barclay scoffs at

Boucher's attempt to draw from the *Liber De Feudis* a right of deposition from the barbaric institutions of the Lombard kings. He makes however very good use of the originally insecure tenure of the feudal lord.

Quasi vero jus monarchiae, quod fere cum ipso genere humano ortum traxit, ad incertas Longobardorum feudales consuetudines a Jurisconsultis quibusdam Mediolanensibus collectas, quae apud alias gentes partim incognitae et partim aliter atque aliter observatae sunt, exigatur, contrahaturque. Quis nescit Feudorum jus et consuetudinem non valde antiquam esse et omnia primum feuda precaria concedi solita, ut ubi domino visum esset, revocarentur. Deinde usu obtinuisse, ut ea domini non intra annum ex quo concesserant rapere possent. Post vero ut beneficia ejusmodi ad totum vitae tempus clientis beneficiarii protenderentur. Mox etiam unus ex beneficiariis filius, quem dominus nominasset, fratri in beneficio succederet. Tandem denique moribus inolevit ut feuda essent perpetua.   *De Regno*, 401.

(16) *De Republica*, I. 8, p. 135: Inter Pontifices is qui jura majestatis omnium optime norat, et qui fere omnium imperatorum aut principum Christianorum potestatem sibi subjecerat, summum imperium ejus esse dixit, qui ordinario juri derogare potest.

(17) See Stubbs, *Lectures on Medieval and Modern History*, 239.

NOTES TO THE MONARCHOMACHI.

(1) I am of course using the word utilitarian with its ordinary meaning, and in no way begging any philosophical or religious question. Now from the highest point of view it is doubtless true, that in the long run the right course is the most useful. But as I pointed out in my last lecture, the moment convenience is put forward as a motive instead of character, the arguments against all forms of disturbance are conclusive, almost universally.

(2) See on this point Overton and Relton, *The English Church in the XVIIIth century*, 349—52.

(3) See Dicey's *Law and Public Opinion in England* for a description of the uniformity enforced by convention and social pressure in the days of George III.

(4) Calvin's *Institutes*, Book IV. c. 20, more especially §§ 8, 29 —32. Even in the last case it is only " Passive Resistance" that he allows, nowhere rebellion.

(5) Goodman, *How to obey*.

(6) See Filmer's *Anarchy of a Mixed Monarchy*.

(7) Leslie's most important writings on this score are various pamphlets in reply to Hoadly and *The Rehearsal*.

(8) Even Turrecremata admits, that a Pope though infallible may become a heretic ; if so, he *ipso jure* ceases to be a Pope. There is no danger of any *ex cathedra* false doctrine.

(9) Quotations from this treatise will be found in notes to my *Divine Right of Kings*. The following however may be added here :

Sequitur ergo tyrannum in populum tanquam feudi dominum, feloniam committere regni imperiique sacram majestatem laedere, rebellem esse, ac propterea in easdem leges incidere et longe graviores poenas mereri.   I. 187.

(10) The writer has a great contempt for mob rule :

An vero universam multitudinem, belluam, inquam, illam innumerorum capitum tumultuari et concurrere in eam rem, quasi agmine facto oportebit? Quis vero in ea turba ordo esse queat? Quae consilii, quae rerum gerendorum species? Cum de universo populo loquimur, intelligimus eos, qui a populo authoritatem acceperunt, magistratus nempe rege inferiores a populo delectos, aut alia ratione constitutos, quasi imperii Consortes et Regum Ephoros, qui universum populi coetum representant. Intelligamus etiam Comitia quae nil aliud sunt, quam Regni cujusque Epitome, ad quae publica omnia negotia referantur.   II. 46.

(11) Gierke's great work is really a comment on this contrast, and an illustration of the workings of the two notions—throughout history.

(12) As the book is not much read, I may cite one or two passages of Rossaeus' :

Neque enim respublicae creatae sunt propter reges, sed reges electi sunt propter respublicam. Neque populi primo in unum coetum confluxerunt, ut regum bonum procurarent ; sed multitudo consociata reges elegit, qui multitudinis bono praeessent, et commodum adjuvarent. Ergo primae sunt reipublicae partes, secundae regum.   c. I. p. 33.

(13) P. 40, c. 2.

(14) Henry III is perfidiosissima apostata, impurissimus hypo-

crita, alter Mezentius Dei contemptor, millies ipso Mahomete vel Theomacho Graeco nequior et sceleratior (p. 170).

(15) P. 159 sqq. The argument might almost be compared with Westcott or any modern writer arguing about the conception of the Atonement from the universal practice of religions.

(16) He declares *salus animarum suprema lex* to be the rule of a Christian state ; and in the same way (613), answering to the digna vox of the State, there is another : digna et necessaria est vox ut princeps Christianus legibus Ecclesiae se devinctum profiteatur.

(17) P. 129.

(18) Pp. 342, 377, 381—3.

(19) He makes very good use of Beza's argument against toleration and its consequences in Poland and Transylvania.

569. Heretici regem Catholicum optimo jure in regno praesidentem, regem suum ferre nolunt. I. 63.

(20) Einer der wesentlichsten Unterschiede der katholischen und der reformierten Monarchomachen besteht in dem grösseren Radicalismus und in dem grösseren Mangel an Klarheit und Präcision der ersteren. Landmann 11.

I think this is true about the first point ; there is all the difference between Whigs and Radicals, between Boucher and Du Plessis Mornay. But I do not think Suarez or Molina lacking in clearness or precision.

NOTES TO THE JESUITS.

(1) See especially the discussion in Reusch, *Beiträge zur Geschichte des Jesuitenordens*, also the crucial words in the two editions are compared in a note to my " Political Theories of the early Jesuits," *Royal Hist. Soc. Trans.* Vol. XI.

(2) *Die Lehre von Tyrannenmord.*

(3) Mariana *De Rege.*

(4) See Du Prat, *Le Père Coton.*

(5) *De Legibus* III. 1, 2, 3. He dismisses in § 3 of Chap. 2 the views of folk, like Filmer, who derive all power from original parental authority, asserting that Adam's power was domestic not economic, and that a "perfect community" is owing to the voluntary coalescence of several families.

De Legibus III. 9. 4 : Sequitur secundo, etiam in principe supremo esse hanc potestatem eo modo et sub ea conditione sub qua data est et translata per communitatem. Further cap. 35 he decides that princes, including the Pope, are bound by their own laws, and that not from any express or tacit contract, because that would mean a compact might release them, which is impossible. See the evils of the contrary view urged by Contarini in his Letter to Paul III.

(6) *Disputationes Tridentinae*, edited by H. Grisar. It is notable, that in arguing against the Pope having received his power from the Church, Lainez takes it for granted that a *lex regia* can never be an entire abdication on the part of the people in favour of the monarch.

(7) See Suarez' excellent chapter on the separation of powers, III. 11. His position is totally different from the medieval, that omnia jura civilia were at bottom *canonica*. The whole point of his view is, that the civil power as such is no more and no less than it was among the heathen before Christianity ; but that the Church has its own rights. An infidel prince may not be disturbed, unless he treats Christians ill, when war is of course justifiable ; but he will not say that infidels as such are without a just title, as the medievals do (*e.g. Somnium Viridarii*). Heretics are different, for the baptismal vow makes them a part of the Christian republic (III. 10. § 6). Cf. Bellarmine, *De Rom. Pon.* V. 7 : Quando Reges et Principes ad Ecclesiam veniunt, ut Christiani fiant, recipiuntur cum pacto tacito vel expresso, ut sceptra sua subjiciant Christo, et polliceantur se Christi fidem servaturos et defensuros etiam sub poena regni perdendi. Cf. *De Trans. Imp.* I. 12 (p. 1193).

(8) See Reusch, *Die Selbstbiographie des Cardinals Bellarmine*.

(9) On the other hand Molina definitely declares the civil State to be *imperfect* without the guidance of the Church. This confirms our view that the doctrine of the Church as a "societas perfecta" is only of importance when and in so far as it makes an admission, that the State is also in the same category.

(10) Suarez, *De Immunitate Ecclesiae*, written against the Venetian claims is the strongest evidence of this. What he claims is really an extra-territorial position for clergy and monasteries ; while, since the rights of property exist *jure naturae* to a private man, *à fortiori* they must to any congregation of men, and especially to the Church. What he is clearly striving for is for the

recognition of the *natural* rights of a community other than the State. What he really asks is, whether "reason of State" is always to be decisive? Or, as Molina put it, the Respublica Ecclesiae non minus sibi debet esse sufficiens, quam quaecunque Respublica secularis (547).

(11) Gosselin, *Pouvoir du Pape au Moyen Age* (2 vols., 1845), is an elaborate but unsuccessful attempt in this direction.

(12) The arguments are to be found in Palmiri, *De Romano Pontifice*, and Tarquini, *Juris Ecclesiastici Publici Institutiones*.

(13) Cf. the document printed in Denziger's *Enchiridion*, 405 sqq. It must be observed, that even Papalists like Bellarmine and Suarez admit limits to the Pope's power. Bellarmine says distinctly the enquiry is only whether the Pope has power to make just laws, nam injustae leges non sunt proprie dicendae leges (*De Rom. Pont.* in *Disputationes*, I. 1025). Suarez appears to deny that even God has power to alter natural law; and has the same view as Bellarmine about the need of justice for a true law.

(14) The following *obiter dictum* of Bellarmine illustrates the way of regarding law. The statements of Jesuits and Conciliar writers about secular government are very often the more remarkable as being purely occasional. Both Gerson and Bellarmine take for granted that in the civil State absolutism is inadmissible.

Quemadmodum in Republica civili necessarie sunt leges civiles quae sunt quaedam *quasi conclusiones deductae ex jure naturae,* vel determinationes juris naturae, sic etiam in Ecclesia praeter legem Evangelicam necessarie sunt leges Ecclesiasticae, quae sunt etiam veluti deductae ex principiis Evangelii, vel determinationes. *Ibid.* 1039.

Suarez' arguments, IV. 1, about the necessity of legislative power in the Church are based on its being a "societas perfecta," and have no special relation to the Papacy. Indeed, as one writer Vasquez saw, the power ecclesiastical was inherent in the nature of things and might have existed even were there no revelation. Cf. also Suarez, IV. 2 § 3 and c. 8, where he says, "potestates hae in suo esse plus quam genere distinguuntur."

NOTES TO THE NETHERLANDS REVOLT.

(1) Marnix, *Œuvres*, Vol. *Correspondance et Mélanges* 369, appeals to the idea of balance of power in his address to the princes of Europe to induce them to help the Netherlands.

(2) *De Imperio Summarum Potestatum circa Sacra.*

(3) See the document in Marnix, *Écrits Politiques*, App.

(4) Another early pamphlet *De Jure Belli Belgici* makes use of the ordinary feudal argument, that the same offences which justify the eviction of a vassal from his fief, give a right to exclude the lord from his ownership.

(5) The only interesting things in Daneau are his insistence on the need of free education (including crêches) for all, and of a "ladder of learning," and also on the need of provincial assemblies. He definitely denies, like others of this school, that there is a " sovereign " in the strict sense ; this is a fiction of the Bartolistae, VI. 3.

(6) Doctrinam de consociatione privata conjugum et consanguineorum, male meo judicio, quidam politici ex agro politico exterminant, et oeconomico ut propriam attribuunt. Nam hae consociationes *omnis symbioticae privatae et publicae seminarium.* Adempta igitur hac conjugum et consanguineorum doctrina, reliquarum consociationum cognitio imperfecta et manca erit, atque sine ea recte intelligi non poterit. c. III. 33.

(7) On the question of toleration Althusius wavers ; he will tolerate for the sake of peace, if the State cannot subsist otherwise, but he will not allow Papists to have Churches, or heretics to hold office. His position is somewhat similar to that of Warburton, pp. 424—430. Marnix towards the end of his life refused toleration to Anabaptists (*Œuvres*).

(8) Cf. *Apology.*

(9) An quid magis ridiculum quam quod dicunt aliqui, tamen non ridiculi interpretes juris, posse etiamnum imperatorem Romanum agere ad regnum Hispaniae, quod captum et possessum Saracenis diutissime fuit, et perdiu etiam tenetur ab Hispanis hominibus ?

Albericus Gentilis, *De Jure Belli* I. 22.

That the author should still find it necessary to write like this is a proof how slowly the Imperial and universal conception of politics vanished from men's ideals. The importance of Spain in the matter is again worth noticing.

Cf. also this passage :

Sunt vero interpretes juris, qui sic exponunt de rege Francorum, eum praescriptione saltem esse exemptum ab imperatoris subjectione. Contra quos non apte affert Alciatus, quod nulla temporis praescriptio obtineat contra imperium. *Ibid.*

(10) Cf. the argument of Albericus Gentilis that in England civilian lawyers were really the same as canonists.

Anglus ut dixi nomine civilis indigitat etiam canonicum.

Regales Disputationes I. 7.

(11) In *Public International Law.*

(12) Latet itaque jus istud. Sed et si sit omnino, revocabitur in controversiam ab aliis, qui *jus non natura sed opinione* constare omne pertinaciter contendunt, atque adeo contendunt adversus nos, quibus hoc positum, et quàm est, quaestiones bellicas jure definire gentium oportere, quod est naturae...habeo pro explorato jus aliquid naturae esse, quo et argumentum hoc tractetur bellicum.

Albericus Gentilis, *De Jure Belli* I. I.

Grotius also sharply distinguishes between rights which being unnatural have a legal character, and rights which are purely moral.

(13) As Grotius puts it *Fide sublata feris erunt similes* (III. 2, 52), the doctrine of Machiavelli accepts this, and likens men to the anti-social animals. The conception alike of Grotius and the Monarchomachi are of a law anterior to all positive laws ; and this conception was erroneously assisted by the universal acceptance of the ideal perfection of the civil law, and its concomitant the canon law. *Fidei enim non tantum respublica qualibet continetur, sed et magis illa gentium societas* (III. 25, I). For this purpose there must be two conditions, the recognition (*a*) of a natural law, (*b*) of the duty of keeping promises. Thus, alike in the civil State of Locke and the international State of Grotius, the atheist is ruled out, because he is without the belief in God which would lead him to keep his oath. The importance of this condition is very great, not in itself, but as shewing how the ground on which international law arose is exactly the same as that which reared modern theories of the rights of States as against absolutism. The enemy in both cases is the same, the " Machiavellistica ac Turcica " theory of government, which subjects all rights private and public to the ruler's conception of immediate expediency. The French pamphlets in the wars of religion form perhaps the clearest evidence of this, but it is scattered through the literature of the time.

At neque nos loquimur nunc de his qui, ferarum modo magis quam hominum viventes, sine ulla omnino religione sunt, hos enim quasi piratas, communes hostes omnium, *bello persequendos et cogendos in mores hominum arbitrarer.* Hi enim vero videntur injurii omnibus hominibus, qui in specie hominum agunt vitam brutorum brutissimorum....Juris naturae est religio. Et itaque nec patrocinabitur jus istud expertibus ipsius.

A. G., *De J. B.* I. 9. 39.

Grotius held a similar view (*De J. B.* II. 20. 46).

Moreover Grotius gives a hint, that international law arises like the State by a sort of pact. In the one case, on the popular theory, individuals surrender a portion of their liberty in order to secure peace and order ; in the other, States, as the persons of international law, surrender a portion of their "natural freedom," so as to secure the advantage of those mitigations of the struggle for existence which the rules of war and peace offer to them.

(14) Cf. Albericus Gentilis, *De Jure Belli* I. 3 :

Jus etiam, illis perscriptum libris Justiniani non civitatis est tantum, sed et gentium, et naturae. Et aptatum sic est ad naturam universam, ut imperio extincto, et ipsum jus diu sepultum surrexerit tamen, et in omnes se effuderit gentes humanas. Ergo et Principibus stat, etsi est privatis conditum a Justiniano....

Quid? non apta Principibus illa librorum Justiniani, Honeste vivere, Alterum non laedere, Suum cuique tribuere, Liberos tueri, Iniuriam propulsare, Cum omnibus hominibus cognationem agnoscere, Commercia retinere, id genus reliqua, et quae ex his quaeque in illis sunt libris fere totum? Isthaec juris gentium sunt, et juris bellici.

Grotius too treats civil law in the strict sense, as only a small part of the law of any State. Much the larger is law natural. The fact that nearly all continental States looked largely to Rome for the source of their common law is a further illustration of this view. Suarez is quite definite in his statements, that there is no common Imperial authority, and that the common law of each nation is what that nation obeys without any interference from outside ; but the notion of a Roman Law as a "source-book" undoubtedly helped to make possible the system of International Law in the form it actually took.

(15) It is of vital importance, that Grotius admits the Turkish government to share on an equality in the mass of rights and privileges.

INDEX.